Governance in Ethnically Mixed Cities

This collection of original essays breaks new ground by examining the dynamics of ethnic politics at the local level, rather than following in the footsteps of many previous studies which focus on the macropolitical level of states and nations.

Governance in Ethnically Mixed Cities is based on extensive fieldwork and local observation, providing perspectives from a range of academic disciplines including Political Science, Geography, and Anthropology. It covers a variety of geographic areas from the Middle East (Kirkuk, Haifa, and Tel Aviv-Jaffa) to Europe (Mostar, Bolzano, Toulouse, and Florence), Central Asia (Osh in Kyrgyzstan) and the United States (Durham, North Carolina). In spite of the variety of disciplinary approaches and geographic diversity of the case studies, the contributing authors uncover a number of common elements of local ethnopolitical dynamics in mixed cities: the power of informal institutions, the effect of numerical balances between groups on local politics, and the significance of local competition for material and symbolic resources. Each of these areas provides a promising avenue for foture research.

This book was previously published as a special issue of *Ethnopolitics*.

Dr. Sherrill Stroschein is a Lecturer in Politics in the Department of Political Science, University College London, and Programme Coordinator of the MSc in Democracy and Democratisation.

Governance in Ethnically Mixed Cities

Edited by Sherrill Stroschein

LONDON AND NEW YORK

First published 2007 by Routledge

2 Park Square, Milton Park, Abingdon, Oxon OX14 4RN
711 Third Avenue, New York, NY 10017, USA

Routledge is an imprint of the Taylor & Francis Group, an informa business.

First issued in paperback 2016

Copyright © 2007 Edited by Sherrill Stroschein

Typeset in Times Roman by Techset Composition, Salisbury, UK

All rights reserved. No part of this book may be reprinted or reproduced or utilised in any form or by any electronic, mechanical, or other means, now known or hereafter invented, including photocopying and recording, or in any information storage or retrieval system, without permission in writing from the publishers.

Notice:
Product or corporate names may be trademarks or registered trademarks, and are used only for identification and explanation without intent to infringe.

British Library Cataloguing in Publication Data
A catalogue record for this book is available from the British Library

Library of Congress Cataloging in Publication Data

ISBN13: 978-0-415-45126-0 (hbk)
ISBN13: 978-1-138-97535-4 (pbk)

Contents

1. Politics is Local: Ethnoreligious Dynamics under the Microscope   1
   Sherrill Stroschein

2. The Power of Administrative Categories: Emerging Notions of Citizenship in the Divided City of Mostar   15
   Larissa Vetters

3. Informal Ethnopolitics and Local Authority Figures in Osh, Kyrgyzstan   39
   Matteo Fumagalli

4. Faultline Citizenship: Ethnonational Politics, Minority Mobilisation, and Governance in the Israeli "Mixed Cities" of Haifa and Tel Aviv-Jaffa   63
   Joseph Leibovitz

5. The Future of Kirkuk   93
   David Romano

6. Living Apart in the Same Room: Analysis of the Management of Linguistic Diversity in Bolzano   113
   Andrea Carlá

7. Decentralization, Democratic Participation and Authoritarian Dogma: Local Opposition to Minority Integration in France, Italy and the United States   143
   Harlan Koff

Index   165

Politics is Local: Ethnoreligious Dynamics under the Microscope

SHERRILL STROSCHEIN

Department of Political Science, University College London, UK

Remember that we have to live here. So be careful what you do.

Such was my father's admonishment when he learned that his teenage daughter was mustering a protest against religious instruction by the local religious majority in her public school. Not long before, a rumor had spread of two families in a neighboring town who had been forced to move elsewhere after challenging a similar issue. They had allegedly taken the matter to court and won, but were never spoken to again by their fellow locals—a serious sanction given the skewed demographic balance. The informal punishment was far more powerful than the formal court victory, and the families had eventually packed up and left.[1]

Needless to say, I gave up on the protest.

However, the profound lesson remained with me: that *formal* rules set by the state to curb majorities in divisive local activities could be easily trumped by *informal* local realities, or informal institutions (Helmke & Levitsky, 2004). In mixed cities in which ethnic or religious cleavages are salient in politics, informal rules and norms serve as a powerful regulator of exchange. Moreover, at the local level, these norms can exert a greater influence over exchange than formal institutional structures. The following contributions demonstrate the local importance of informal institutions. This insight is one of several provided on the dynamics of ethnic politics at the city level, where individuals of different groups interact on a daily basis.[2]

Because informal norms of exchange are locally-generated, they can develop local particularities. A second primary insight that thus emerges is the fact that rules of interaction between individuals of different groups might differ significantly by locale, even among cities with similar ethnic or religious demographics. Third, in spite of these variations, structural factors such as demography, formal local governance institutions, and institutional relations between a city and the central state do play some role in constraining local parameters of action. A fourth insight relates to the allocation of resources. Power is not the only resource sought by different groups; material, linguistic, and symbolic resources also matter. Disputes over the distribution of resources at the local level are a common focal point of tension in any city—but in ethnically-mixed cities, these disputes often elide with ethnic cleavages.

These four insights are discussed in more detail below, with reference to evidence from the pieces in this volume and from the author's own fieldwork in mixed cities in east central Europe.[3] Much theorizing on ethnic politics has focused on macro-level entities such as states and nations. However, these pieces show that the conclusions of these theories may in fact be inappropriate for understanding local dynamics of ethnic politics. Both normative theorizing on minority rights and social science work on ethnicity would do well to pay more attention to the *de facto* dynamics of ethnic interaction in local contexts.

The contributions in this volume represent both a diverse array of cities across geographic locations, and a variety of disciplinary angles: anthropology, geography, and political science, with many insights from sociology. These theoretical perspectives combine with an impressive depth of local knowledge and extensive ethnographic fieldwork. The contributions are clear and practical examples of a growing trend to examine the infrapolitics (Scott, 1990) of ethnicity—the way in which it is actually practiced at the local level (Stroschein, 2001; Varshney, 2002; Petersen, 2001, 2002; Brubaker *et al.*, 2006), and provide a corrective to a previous trend to emphasize larger entities. A step in a new direction of research into the politics of the local, many of the themes analyzed here present promising avenues for future research.

The Power of Informal Institutions

As defined by Hemke & Levitsky, informal institutions are "socially shared rules, usually unwritten, that are created, communicated, and enforced outside of officially sanctioned channels" (2004, p. 727). Institutions structure social interactions by influencing individual behavior, whether formal or informal. However, while the presence of formal institutions is more easily visible to observers, the influences of informal institutions can go undetected, particularly in studies that overlook local-level interactions. In-depth observations of political life at the city level thus holds great promise for advancing our understanding of informal institutions. In turn, the conceptual framework of informal institutions holds great promise for understanding how ethnic politics is actually practiced at the local level.

Informal institutions may take a variety of different forms: horizontal networks, patronage networks or norms of interaction (Putnam, 1993; Stark & Bruszt, 1998; Chandra, 2004; Helmke & Levitsky, 2004; Ledeneva, 2006). Like formal institutions and bureaucracies, they provide means of allocating resources and "getting things done;" functions that are typically associated with formal institutions and bureaucracies. However, informal institutions stand in stark contrast to the structure of rational and routinized formal bureaucracies as outlined by Max Weber, which serves as the foundation of much standard work on administrative structures. In the Weberian understanding of bureaucracies, well-defined rules are applied equally and transparently to individuals regardless of their social position. A rational and routinized bureaucracy thus de-personalizes individual interactions with state or city institutions. In this way, it serves a crucial role in the modernizing project (Weber, 1946). In contrast, patronage networks and unwritten rules and norms tend to be viewed by theorists and practitioners as hindrances to the establishment of successful states or city administrations, as one's placement in a network tends to determine access to resources (Granovetter, 1985; Tilly, 1998; Petersen, 2001). While the strong importance of networks for access can indeed violate notions of equality, networks need not always work against formal institutions. As noted by Helmke & Levitsky, informal institutions may sometimes provide support for formal institutions. They outline a typology of various potential relationships between formal and informal institutions, including both positive and negative interactions (Helmke & Levitsky, 2004, p. 728).

Three of these forms are useful for the study of mixed cities in this volume. First, informal institutions may provide a foundation for positive inter-ethnic exchange that lies beyond the reach of formal institutions (Granovetter, 1985; Varshney, 2002). In terms of the Helmke & Levitsky typology, they thus may take a *complementary* or a *substitutive* relationship with formal institutions that intend to foster positive group interactions.[4] As described by Larissa Vetters and Matteo Fumagalli, informal network ties in the cities of Mostar (Bosnia) and in Osh (Kyrgyzstan) establish and preserve communication between ethnic groups. In Mostar, pre-war ties between individuals of different groups are re-forged as individuals join in a multi-ethnic protest to advocate the rebuilding of their apartment complex, destroyed during the war. In Osh, these ties are linked to patronage networks in the form of control structures that preserve inter-ethnic peace in spite of previous local violence. These strong patronage networks also allow the local Uzbek minority to make the most of the few formal offices they hold in the local government.

In a comparison of three cities across three countries, Harlan Koff observes that in Florence (Italy), local government officials often abdicate responsibilities for issues related to integrating Senegalese immigrants. In this context, non-governmental organizations (NGOs) have stepped in to provide informal services that one would tend to expect from a government. Andrea Carlá notes how in Bolzano (Italy), despite efforts of strongly divisive institutions to separate German and Italian linguistic groups, individuals tend to learn enough of the "other" language to engage in polite, informal exchanges in public life. Such linguistic politeness is also common in cities with Hungarian minorities in eastern Europe, in spite of high levels of political tensions regarding language (Brubaker *et al.*, 2006; Stroschein, 2007). Mixed communities are like ecosystems in which different components contribute to the well-being of the whole. In order for such communities to function, social norms of interaction often require at least a minimum level of politesse. This thin layer of interaction may be supported by inter-ethnic networks, but need not be—the informal norm of politesse can still permeate exchanges in which individuals have very little contact.

These linguistic examples also demonstrate a second relationship between formal and informal institutions. Formal institutions that separate groups for the purpose of preserving group identity (multiculturalism) or representation (consociationalism) may reduce the potentially integrative effects of informal institutions. As Carlá notes, in Bolzano the formation of informal networks between individuals of different groups is hindered by the formal institution of a rigid language regime, which preserves the separation of groups at the expense of city harmony. The other institutional extreme can also create trouble. Institutions structured with the opposite goal of integrating groups by not recognizing difference can also have negative effects, as Koff observes in the case of Toulouse (France). Toulouse is a city that strongly endorses the republican model in its formal institutions, and thus recognizes only individual rights claims, rather than the claims of minorities as groups.[5] He argues that the formal mis-recognition of group claims at the city level fosters resentment among the sizable immigrant community and has thus fostered local outbreaks of violence.

Third, informal institutions can contravene formal institutions in ways that encourage the *exclusion* of local minorities—the opposite of the integrative functions outlined above. They thus may engage in a *competing* relationship with formal institutions by providing counter-incentives to formal rules (Helmke & Levitsky, 2004; Deets, 2006).[6] In my hometown, the threat of a powerful informal sanction, silent treatment by the local majority, was enough to prevent those in the minority from pursuing rights claims that formal rules would have endorsed. Instruction in the local majority religion in my school thus did take place to a degree that surpassed legally recognized thresholds, but with resigned acceptance by those of us in the local religious minority. In Miercurea Ciuc, a city in Romania where demographics are reversed and Hungarians are the local majority, the Romanian state has made continuous efforts to formally enforce Romanian language use in schools and administrative offices. These efforts have been easily met by informal routines of resistance by ethnic Hungarians, who are 83% of the local population. Local Romanians, who are 16% of the local population, thus must often learn Hungarian in order to foster a meaningful local existence for themselves (Stroschein, 2007).[7] Whether or not one lauds these effects of informal institutions will likely depend on one's placement in local networks—or whether local norms tend to operate in one's favor. However, their powerful effects cannot be denied, and they are a fruitful avenue for future research.

Locally-specific Event and Discourse Trajectories

The fact that informal institutions are generated at the local level, through local events and contexts, demonstrates how cities with similar demographic structures can develop different types of interactions. In a comparative study of Indian cities, Ashutosh Varshney (2002) observes vastly different levels of Hindu–Muslim violence across cities with similar demographic configurations. He argues that the presence or absence of informal institutions such as inter-ethnic networks explains these differences. But the presence or absence of such networks can also be the symptom of deeper local histories and trajectories of either peaceful or antagonistic ethnic relations. Local histories tend to produce different types of ethnic interaction in different locales, and local discourses can become self-fulfilling prophecies of a particular city as tense or peaceful (Leibovitz, this volume, Stroschein, 2007).[8] These dynamics show that there are some limitations to the degree of generalizations we can make regarding structural influences in mixed cities. Indeed, local events may contribute to a large degree of uniqueness in each city's ethnic interactions.

The sociological perspective that perceptions and actions are embedded in social relations (Granovetter, 1985) sheds some light on how these local particularities may emerge. As individuals are socialized by local events, the actions of individuals are tied to these previous events, creating path-dependent local event trajectories. The insights from the historical and sociological institutionalist schools regarding path dependence, feedback effects, and logics of appropriateness provide a useful framework for understanding how strong differences can thus emerge even in demographically similar local contexts. Path dependence implies that interactions do not move to a generalizable efficient outcome (or equilibrium), as posited by rational choice theorists. Interactions are instead strongly channeled by local informal institutions, such as the existing networks and local norms outlined above. Local logics of appropriateness based on these networks and norms will thus constrain the possible trajectories along which events unfold, confining the potential path of local histories. (March & Olsen, 1984; Granovetter, 1985; Powell & DiMaggio, 1991; Thelen, 1999; Pierson, 2000; McAdam *et al.*, 2001).[9]

Moreover, feedback effects reinforce these local trajectories. For example, levels of support for ethnic parties can vary dramatically across cities with similar demographics and governance structures. The city of Târgu Mureş, Romania, which experienced a local riot between ethnic Hungarians and Romanians in 1990, continues to exhibit levels of support for ethnic parties of both groups that exceeds that of other Romanian cities or in cities with similar demographics in Slovakia and Ukraine (Stroschein, 2001). Local elites are thus more likely to be elected from ethnic or nationalist parties there than they are in other demographically similar locales that did not experience local violence. These reinforcing processes provide an endogenous aspect to local ethnic politics that must be incorporated into research (Beissinger, 2002).[10] Even the politics of particular neighborhoods within a city may vary according to their own local histories (Brubaker *et al.*, 2006).

In this volume, two contributions emphasize the discursive construction of local, rather than simply ethnic, identities from specific local contexts. In her study of Mostar, Vetters examines how Mostarians were able to construct a local, multi-ethnic social movement, the "Displaced," around a category constructed by international institutions. These Mostarians, who had remained in Mostar throughout the war and thus could not obtain the housing resources meted out to refugees, declared themselves "Displaced in our own town," an effective slogan for a very particular context. The identified mechanism of creating a new categorical boundary (Ron, 2000; Abbott, 2001; Tilly, 2003, 2005; Brubaker, 2004; Brubaker *et al.*, 2006; Jackson, 2006) using local discursive resources provides a valuable insight into how polarization between ethnic groups can decrease through such affiliation to a new bounded category. Similarly, Joseph Leibovitz examines how boundaries between groups are differently negotiated in two Israeli cities. Although Haifa and Tel Aviv-Jaffa are in the same country and feature somewhat similar population demographics, the local discourses that prevail in each create quite different interactions between local Jewish and Palestinian groups. As in the case of Mostar, boundary construction between groups takes shape according to local meanings, prompting a more salient mobilization cleavage between Jewish Israelis and Palestinians in Tel Aviv-Jaffa than in Haifa. Interestingly, this boundary difference is largely a discursive product rooted in particular histories, rather than a reflection of a better material situation for Palestinians in Haifa. Indeed, demographic figures do constrain possible actions for the Palestinians in both cities. As they are less than 10% in each, they will never win a majority of city offices in either. This scenario highlights the significance of structural factors, discussed below.

Structural Influences

Insights into informal institutions and locally specific event trajectories contribute greatly to an understanding of local ethnic politics. However, it cannot be denied that structural influences also play a role. Local demographics will constrain what minorities and majorities can accomplish in a local setting. Formal institutional structures for governance at the local level may also encourage some power-sharing to mitigate the dominance of a local majority in democracies. Finally, formal institutional relationships between a city and the state, which determine the extent to which the center can intervene in local affairs, will greatly affect the dynamics of local politics.

Demographics

Local demographic structure, or the "head-count" proportions of ethnic, linguistic, or religious groups, certainly enables or constricts what each group can accomplish in politics at the local level. The politics of "reversed" cities or enclave regions, in which statewide minorities comprise a local majority,[11] present a dilemma for theories of and policies relating to minority rights, because defining just who is a minority involves issues of scale. Minorities at the state level can be majorities at the local level, sometimes using their local demographic power to enact policies that harm local minorities—who may be especially resentful of this dynamic if they are majorities elsewhere in the state.

The importance of these relative group proportions is magnified in democracies, particularly those with a great deal of power devolved to local levels of government. Macro-level studies of nations and states often overlook the politics of ethnic enclaves and reversed cities. These regional demographic variations can explain why statewide majorities often favor centralized government structures, while statewide minorities often favor increased decentralization. Such is the dynamic for Hungarians in Romania, Slovakia, and the Ukraine, as devolved governance powers would give them more political control in enclave areas. For similar reasons, the titular populations (Romanians, Slovaks, and Ukrainians) are likely to oppose decentralization, and to express concern about the livelihood of their co-ethnics living in Hungarian enclave areas (Stroschein, 2006). This logic easily applies to other mixed states in which minorities hope to gain increased local control through decentralization.

It is important to keep in mind that demographic structures may undergo changes over time that strongly affect inter-ethnic dynamics and relations. In Romania, towns such as Târgu Mureş and nearby Cluj, both previously under Hungarian rule, experienced large migrations of Romanians from rural areas over the past several decades. These newly arrived, rural Romanians settled in newly-constructed neighborhoods of these cities and tend to exhibit a more strident Romanian identity than Romanians in older neighborhoods, whose families have historically lived mixed with Hungarians (Brubaker *et al.*, 2006; Stroschein, 2007).[12] When such demographic shifts are rapid, they can foster inter-group tensions and some competition for resources (Olzak, 1992; Slack & Doyon, 2001). The birthrates of a minority group may also outpace that of a majority group, allowing a minority to perceive its minority status as merely a temporary one, and fostering some resentment among majorities (MacGinty, 2003). Mixed cities may also feature an ethnic reversal of the surrounding territory, as in the cases of Osh in Kyrgyzstan, Bolzano in Italy, and Kirkuk in Iraq. Cities in this category that serve as capitals of surrounding regions may find themselves in tense engagements with surrounding smaller communities, particularly if their leaders actively engage in regional politics. These interactions serve as a promising area of further research, especially as rural areas surrounding mixed cities may be more homogeneous.

However, the examination of demographic effects also poses some potential problems for researchers, as statistics and census data on group proportions may be fraught with controversy. Groups are particularly likely to condemn official results as inaccurate when they are designated a local minority, as David Romano notes is the case for Kirkuk. In addition, attempts by the state or by researchers to classify individuals who consider themselves to be members of more than one group, or of neither, presents further complications—as groups themselves are contested categories (Anderson, 1991; Nobles, 2000; Kertzer & Arel, 2002; Brubaker, 2004).

Formal Institutions of Local Governance

The comparative study of formal local governance institutions and their potential effects in mixed cities has been a rather underdeveloped area of research. The following case studies, however, offer a number of interesting insights on these dynamics. First, in mixed cities with relatively equal demographic proportions of groups, the office of mayor will tend to be particularly contested, as it cannot be easily divided between groups.[13] Where there is a strongly skewed ethnic balance, such as an 80% majority and a 20% minority, mayoral elections tend to be associated with a sense of entitlement by the majority and resignation by the minority. Informal institutions in the form of local norms may provide a way around some of these power dilemmas. Although a formal mayoral office is not easily divisible between groups, local, unwritten local norms may dictate that a vice-mayor or a close deputy must represent the other ethnic group.[14]

Second, the distribution of other local offices for different groups in mixed cities is another commonly-contested issue. In Vetters' discussion of Mostar, there are strict institutions to ensure distributions between groups. Yet as Romano outlines in his analysis of Kirkuk, the Kurds have made explicit attempts to gain control of these offices at the expense of the Arab and Turkomen populations. Minorities have similarly small representations in the Israeli cities and in Osh. Serious asymmetries of offices at the local level in democracies can sometimes foster election boycotts by minority groups, as Arab and Turkomen populations have used in Kirkuk. However, the power of informal institutions may mean that the number of offices held by minorities does not tell the entire story. As outlined by Fumagalli, the powerful importance of patronage networks in Osh implies that the few formal offices held by Uzbeks are less indicative of the actual reach of these individuals' powers. As with the case of vice-mayors and deputies outlined above, local informal norms may also dictate how many offices should go to one group, to either the benefit or detriment of minorities. In my hometown, cross-group voting was common, with one exception. The religious majority's desire to maintain at least three of the five school board seats to influence school policy meant that if that third seat was up for election, the group would then vote along religious lines—as an apologetic friend of my father's explained to him after admitting that he had voted for his opponent.

Third, institutions may also vary in the degree to which administrative control is centralized within the city itself. The city of Mostar, as noted by Vetters, was administratively divided into Croat and Bosniak (Muslim) parts in the decade after the Bosnian war. Efforts by the international community to centralize the city administration, begun in 2004, are now bringing formerly separate institutions such as schools and local services under joint administration. Interestingly, a similar dynamic can be seen in Koff's discussion of Durham, North Carolina, where highly decentralized administrative structures create schools of very different ethnic and socioeconomic character—producing a separation of African-American and white children. Similarly, Carlá shows how separate institutional arrangements for German and Italian groups in Bolzano, established by the 1972 Statue of Autonomy, foster polarization as the population is "institutionally trained" to think of themselves as separate groups. The tension between multicultural institutional arrangements (which protect separate group identities) and integrative institutions is a common feature of institutions at the local level in mixed cities, just as it is for divided states at the macro-level.

Local Institutional Relations with the Center

A third structural area of importance is the design of formal institutional relations with the center. As noted above, the level of government decentralization, or the degree of devolved powers from the central to the local level, is of primary importance. Devolution is often presented as a positive, pro-democratic idea, as it carries an image of granting control to the people by moving more power to the local level (Watts, 1998). However, these implications become more complex in mixed cities and regions, as a glance at the local level reveals. Structural logic and empirical evidence repeatedly demonstrates local majorities may attempt to dominate local minorities as much as institutions will allow. Thus, where devolution is high, granting strong powers to local majorities, they may establish policies that are viewed as problematic by local minorities. Such domination usually relates to the allocation of material, linguistic, and social resources, but it might also go as far as to infringe upon local minority rights. These dynamics can emerge whether the local majority is a statewide majority or a statewide minority—the content of the group appears less important than the structural incentives for maximizing power in a mixed setting. Direct intervention by the central state can reduce these motivations in an effort to protect local minorities, as was the case with desegregation in the American South. Formal protections may be limited by the strength of local informal institutions, but they can improve some conditions for local minorities—here, they did so by making the conduct of practices such as segregation more difficult. This *de facto*, intervening "center" may also be the international community, as in the cases of Mostar and cities in Kosovo.

It should be noted that minority enclaves and reversed cities in strongly-divided societies can pose control issues for states. Local enclaves in which the statewide minority is a dominant majority, or "core ethnic regions," have more potential for secession than other areas of the state (Hale, 2004). The state might also express concern about the fate of statewide majorities who find themselves "stranded" as minorities in these regions or cities, due to the potential for local domination mentioned above. In addition to attempts at direct intervention in such areas the central government may also try to increase its symbolic presence there. It can be no accident that a large base for the Romanian army has been placed in Miercurea Ciuc, a city with a strong Hungarian majority—the arm of the Romanian state is thus clearly visible in the commonplace sight of uniformed soldiers walking throughout town.

Claims for Local Resources

The positive integrative effects of ethnic mixing at the local level can be reduced by local competition for resources (Olzak, 1992; Slack & Doyon, 2001). At the macro-level, competition for resources can take the form of policies that are somewhat abstract, such as legislation for or against affirmative action or to fund the activities of particular groups. However, at the local level, competition for resources usually takes more tangible forms, such as competition for ownership or access to specific land, housing, or schools. Local resource competition is identified as a strong focal point for group conflict by all of the pieces in this volume. Many local disputes emphasize property and housing, while some involve linguistic, cultural, or symbolic resources.

Land and housing are strong mobilizers (Toft, 2003). In Osh, a dispute over the allocation of land produced a local riot between Kyrgyz and Uzbeks in 1990. Protest movements emerged in both Mostar and Tel Aviv-Jaffa in relation to the development of particular residential areas. In Mostar, this movement was multi-ethnic, composed of local residents who had been displaced from their old apartment building by the war. In Tel Aviv-Jaffa, Palestinians protested a development that they feared would displace them from the neighborhood of Jaffa.

Rapid population shifts such as displacements, settlements, and resettlements can make conflicts over land and housing resources particularly charged. Government efforts to settle members of one group in a new area are often interpreted by local members of other groups as an attempt to decrease their relative demographic presence, even in the absence of efforts to force out other groups.[15] Sometimes governments use both resettlement and removal strategies simultaneously. As Romano discusses in the case of Kirkuk, Kurdish officials have made explicit attempts to encourage or force Arabs to leave the city and for Kurds to relocate to the city. He notes that this resettlement strategy is an effort to establish demographic "facts on the ground" before an official decision is made regarding the status of the city. However, settlement without removals is a more common strategy. As outlined by Carlá, the Italian government engaged in policies to encourage Italians to settle in Bolzano after it obtained control of South Tyrol in 1919, resulting in German protests. A similar strategy was followed by governments in Eastern Europe after World War II.[16] In addition, immigration patterns have also created competition over economic resources, as Koff notes in relation to the cities of Toulouse and Florence.

Non-material resources such as linguistic, cultural, or symbolic issues can also become objects of group contention in particular contexts. Carlá notes that the stated desire to preserve "pure" linguistic groups in Bolzano has fostered political polarization between groups. He argues that language itself need not be an area of division, but that it becomes particularly charged under certain conditions, to the extent that it also polarizes the political environment. Indeed, mixed linguistic communities often produce a natural bilingualism or mixing of languages, demonstrating that purity is not an inherent aspect of language.

The salience of language in particular political contexts can be understood as a product of discursive framing (Goffman, 1986; Tarrow, 1998; Jackson, 2006). Framing, or "spin" by particular officials, can construct an issue as indivisible, or non-negotiable—when it could also have the potential to be framed in more divisible, or negotiable terms (Lustick, 1995; Toft, 2003; Goddard, 2006). In the case of Bolzano, the goal of preserving linguistically pure communities has been framed by formal institutions as a non-negotiable identity issue. Similarly, Hungarian minorities in several states of Eastern Europe tend to describe the Hungarian language as an indivisible symbol, their "sweet mother tongue"[17] that must be protected from being erased due to their minority status. In both cases, language is attached to the notion of cultural survival, and with this link it becomes a non-negotiable issue. The invocation of cultural survival can frame the issue of language preservation as a crucial resource, similar to land and territory. Another symbolic effort, the "marking" of territory through the use of group-specific names for places or through statues of a particular group's heroes is also a common feature of politics in mixed cities. Local territorial marking links land, language, and culture together, and as such is often a strongly contested act between groups (Andrić, 1977; Kaplan, 1994; Csergo, 2002; Brubaker *et al.*, 2006; Stroschein, 2007).

Conclusions and Research Implications

The focus on the local in the following contributions produce a number of revelations into the actual dynamics of ethnic politics in practice. First, intensive research into mixed city dynamics illustrates the strong influence of informal institutions in local settings, an area often invisible to projects emphasizing macro-level entities such as states and nations. Second, strong variations in ethnic dynamics between cities with similar structural conditions such as demographics and formal institutions demonstrate the path-dependent nature of politics in local settings. These particularities emerge from informal institutions such as local network configurations and norms, local discourses, and the influence of past local events. Third, structural factors such as demographics, formal local governance institutions, and institutional relations between a mixed city and the central government provide background conditions to these influences that will enable or constrain the actions of groups. Finally, groups compete at the local level not simply for material resources such as land and housing, but also over linguistic, cultural, and symbolic resources. All of these areas provide promising avenues for future research.

It is worth emphasizing that the local particularities identified across city settings are one especially important insight provided by the following contributions. The specific nature of local ethnic interactions is often overlooked in research projects with a stated goal of seeking general laws of politics. A strong emphasis on generalizability may lead even those observing local politics to dismiss local particularities as undesirable "noise" in a general equation. For these reasons, a number of theorists propose the search for causal mechanisms as a preferable research goal over the search for general covering laws (see Elster, 1998; Hedström & Swedberg, 1998; Tilly, 1998). In their effort to uncover and explain these local differences, rather than bury them, the following contributions tend toward this mechanistic vein of empirically based research.

Normative theories of minority rights would also do well to pay more attention to the dynamics of politics at the local level. Whether a group is a minority depends on one's level of analysis, as minorities at the state level can be majorities in enclave areas or demographically reversed cities. In this capacity, they may infringe upon the well-being of local minorities as well. In addition, Koff's comparison of three cities across different state contexts demonstrates that strong ideological paradigms of democracy can cause problems for the *de facto* integration of groups at the local level.

The studies presented here are a reminder to theorists of all types that the dynamics of local ethnic politics are often quite different from those posited in the realms of abstract theorizing. What follows thus presents a corrective to a longstanding emphasis on macro-level entities such as states and nations in research on ethnic politics. The four areas of insight outlined here present a promising step for future locally-based research into the dynamics of ethnic politics where individuals interact directly, on a daily basis. More work in this area is sure to follow.

Acknowledgements

The author is grateful for useful comments on an earlier draft by Stephen Deets and Stefan Wolff.

Notes

1. These are rural communities in south-eastern Idaho. Although these were religious, rather than ethnic distinctions, group identification was a salient cleavage that permeated nearly all exchanges. However, in my hometown of Aberdeen (population around 1800), the demographic structure has shifted in the past few decades due to a large influx of Hispanic migrants, thus creating new cleavages.
2. Many of the author's own observations are taken from extensive fieldwork for Stroschein (2007). That project is a comparative study of local contentious politics in cities in Romania, Slovakia, and Ukraine with varying proportions of Hungarian minorities.
3. Stroschein (2007).
4. They credit Hans-Loachim Lauth with the terminology for complementary institutions.
5. It thus stands in contrast to multiculturalist models.
6. In Bosnia, for example, formal reforms in the health care sector by the center have been blocked at the local level, a scenario that Deets (2006) calls the "passive-aggressive state."
7. In addition, strong networks within one ethnic group can also facilitate stronger mobilization (Petersen, 2001).
8. On the emergence and propagation of particular discourses see Jackson (2006).
9. For a detailed examination of how politics evolves in a local context, see Brubaker *et al.*'s (2006) study of Cluj, Romania.
10. Further discussion of the importance of attention to feedback effects and their implications for the conduct of social science research can be found in Thelen (1999) and Pierson (2000).
11. A useful analyses of surveys on varied ethnic attitudes in enclave regions appears in Massey *et al.*, 1999.
12. Primary fieldwork by the author was conducted in Cluj and Târgu Mureş in 1997 and 1999.
13. These competitive dynamics were particularly visible from the author's fieldwork in Târgu Mureş and Rimavská Sobota in Slovakia.
14. Such norms may also be applied for county officials, as has been the case in some Romanian counties.
15. Governments have often intended to do just this. However, even when demographic change is not an explicit policy of governments, it is still likely to be interpreted in this way by longstanding local residents.
16. This resettlement policy has left its mark in Cluj, which experienced a large influx of Romanians from rural areas (Brubaker *et al.*, 2006).
17. "Édes anyanyelv" is a commonly used phrase.

References

Abbott, A. (2001) Things of Boundaries, in: A. Abbott (Ed.), *Time Matters: On Theory and Method*, pp. 261–279 (Chicago, IL: The University of Chicago Press).

Anderson, B. (1991) *Imagined Communities* (New York: Verso).

Andrić, I. (1977) *The Bridge on the Drina* (Chicago, IL: The University of Chicago Press).
Beissinger, M. (2002) *Nationalist Mobilization and the Collapse of the Soviet State* (New York: Cambridge University Press).
Brubaker, R. (2004) *Ethnicity without Groups* (Cambridge: Harvard University Press).
Brubaker, R., Feischmidt, M., Fox, J. & Grancea, L. (2006) *Nationalist Politics and Everyday Ethnicity in a Transylvanian Town* (Princeton, NJ: Princeton University Press).
Chandra, K. (2004) *Why Ethnic Parties Succeed: Patronage and Ethnic Head Counts in India* (New York: Cambridge University Press).
Csergo, Zs. (2002) Beyond Ethnic Divisions: Majority–Minority Debate about the Postcommunist State in Romania and Slovakia, *East European Politics and Societies*, 16(1), pp. 1–29.
Deets, S. (2006) Public Policy in the Passive-Aggressive State: Health Care Reform in Bosnia-Herzegovina 1996–2001, *Europe–Asia Studies*, 58(1), pp. 57–80.
Elster, J. (1998) A Plea for Mechanisms, in: P. Hedström & R. Swedberg (Eds), *Social Mechanisms: An Analytical Approach to Social Theory* (New York: Cambridge University Press).
Goddard, S. E. (2006) Uncommon Ground: Indivisible Territory and the Politics of Legitimacy, *International Organization*, 60, pp. 35–68.
Goffman, E. (1986) *Frame Analysis: An Essay on the Organization of Experience* (Boston, MA: Northeastern University Press).
Granovetter, M. (1985) Economic Action and Social Structure: The Problem of Embeddedness, *American Journal of Sociology*, 91(3), pp. 481–510.
Hale, H. (2004) Divided We Stand: Institutional Sources of Ethnofederal State Survival and Collapse, *World Politics*, 56, pp. 165–193.
Hedström, P. & Swedberg, R. (Eds) (1998) *Social Mechanisms: An Analytical Approach to Social Theory* (New York: Cambridge University Press).
Helmke, G. & Levitsky, S. (2004) Informal Institutions and Comparative Politics: A Research Agenda, *Perspectives on Politics*, 2(4), pp. 725–740.
Jackson, P. (2006) *Civilizing the Enemy: German Reconstruction and the Invention of the West* (Ann Arbor, MI: University of Michigan Press).
Kaplan, R. (1994) *Balkan Ghosts: A Journey through History* (New York: Vintage Books).
Kertzer, D. & Arel, D. (Eds) (2002) *Census and Identity: The Politics of Race, Ethnicity, and Language in National Censuses* (New York: Cambridge University Press).
Ledeneva, A. (2006) *How Russia Really Works: The Informal Practices that Shaped Post-Soviet Politics and Business* (Ithaca, NY: Cornell University Press).
Lustick, I. (1995) *Unsettled States, Disputed Lands: Britain and Ireland, France and Algeria, Israel and the West Bank-Gaza* (Ithaca, NY: Cornell University Press).
MacGinty, R. (2003) Constitutional Referendums and Ethnonational Conflict: The Case of Northern Ireland, *Nationalism and Ethnic Politics*, 9(2), pp. 1–22.
March, J. & Olsen, J. (1984) Organizational Factors in Political Life, *American Political Science Review*, 78, pp. 734–749.
Massey, G., Hodson, R. & Sekulić, D. (1999) Ethnic Enclaves and Intolerance: The Case of Yugoslavia, *Social Forces*, 78(2), pp. 669–693.
McAdam, D., Tarrow, S. & Tilly, C. (2001) *Dynamics of Contention* (New York: Cambridge University Press).
Nobles, M. (2000) *Shades of Citizenship: Race and the Census in Modern Politics* (Stanford, CA: Stanford University Press).
Olzak, S. (1992) *The Dynamics of Ethnic Competition and Conflict* (Stanford, CA: Stanford University Press).
Petersen, R. (2001) *Resistance and Rebellion: Lessons from Eastern Europe* (New York: Cambridge University Press).
Petersen, R. (2002) *Understanding Ethnic Violence: Fear, Hatred, and Resentment in Twentieth-century Eastern Europe* (New York: Cambridge University Press).
Pierson, P. (2000) Increasing Returns, Path Dependence, and the Study of Politics, *American Political Science Review*, 94(2), pp. 251–267.
Powell, W. & DiMaggio, P. (Eds) (1991) *The New Institutionalism in Organizational Analysis* (Chicago, IL: The University of Chicago Press).
Putnam, R. (1993) *Making Democracy Work: Civic Traditions in Modern Italy* (Princeton, NJ: Princeton University Press).

Ron, J. (2000) Boundaries and Violence: Repertoires of State Action along the Bosnia/Yugoslavia Divide, *Theory and Society*, 29, pp. 609–649.
Scott, J. (1990) *Domination and the Arts of Resistance* (New Haven, CT: Yale University Press).
Slack, J. A. & Doyon, R.R. (2001) Population Dynamics and Susceptibility for Ethnic Conflict: The Case of Bosnia and Herzegovina, *Journal of Peace Research*, 38(2), pp. 139–161.
Stark, D. & Bruszt, L. (1998) *Postsocialist Pathways: Transforming Politics and Property in East Central Europe* (New York: Cambridge University Press).
Stroschein, S. (2001) Measuring Ethnic Party Success in Romania, Slovakia, and Ukraine, *Problems of Post-Communism*, 48(4), pp. 59–69.
Stroschein, S. (2006) Territory and the Hungarian Status Law: Time for New Assumptions?, in: O. Ieda (Ed.), *The Status Law Syndrome: Post-Communist Nation Building or Post-Modern Citizenship?* (Budapest: Hungarian Academy of Sciences, Institute of Legal Studies, and the Slavic Research Centre, Hokkaido University, Sapporo, Japan). Available online at: http://src-home.slav.hokudai.ac.jp/coe21/publish/no9_ses/04_stroschein.pdf
Stroschein, S. (2007) Contention and Coexistence: Ethnic Politics and Democratic Transition in Eastern Europe. Book manuscript in progress.
Tarrow, S. (1998) *Power in Movement: Social Movements and Contentious Politics* (New York, Cambridge: Cambridge University Press).
Thelen, K. (1999) Historical Institutionalism in Comparative Politics, *Annual Review of Political Science*, pp. 369–404.
Tilly, C. (1998) *Durable Inequality* (Berkeley, CA: University of California Press).
Tilly, C. (2003) *The Politics of Collective Violence* (New York: Cambridge University Press).
Tilly, C. (2005) Identities Boundaries & Social Ties (Boulder, Co: Paradigm Publishers).
Toft, M. (2003) *The Geography of Ethnic Violence: Identity, Interests, and the Indivisibility of Territory* (Princeton, NJ: Princeton University Press).
Varshney, A. (2002) *Ethnic Conflict and Civic Life: Hindus and Muslims in India* (New Haven, CT: Yale University Press).
Watts, R. (1998) Federalism, Federal Political Systems, and Federations, *Annual Review of Political Science*, 1, pp. 117–137
Weber, M. (1946) Bureaucracy, in: H. H. Gerth & C. Wright Mills (Eds), *From Max Weber, Essays in Sociology*, pp. 198–244 (New York: Oxford University Press).

The Power of Administrative Categories: Emerging Notions of Citizenship in the Divided City of Mostar[1]

LARISSA VETTERS

German University of Administrative Sciences, Speyer, Germany

Introduction: Ethno-national Solidarity and Post-conflict Attempts to Unify the Divided City of Mostar

Twelve years ago, in December 1995, the Dayton Peace Agreement (DPA) brought an end to the war in Bosnia and Herzegovina, providing the legal framework—including a constitution—for the future development of this newly independent state with three constituent people (Bosnian Muslims/Bosniacs, Bosnian Croats and Bosnian Serbs). Bosnia and Herzegovina (BiH) was established as a state with two entities—the Federation of Bosnia and Herzegovina (FBiH) and the Republika Srpska (RS). While the RS consists of only two levels of government, the municipalities and the entity government, the

Federation being made up of ten cantons with considerable autonomy, embraces three levels of government. Resulting from the DPA's nature as a peace agreement between formerly warring parties, it prescribes not only the presence of an international military peace-keeping force in the country but also provides for the establishment of an international civilian authority, the Office of the High Representative (OHR), with far-reaching powers to oversee and actively contribute to the implementation of all civilian aspects of the peace agreement. Under the OHR's coordinating authority, a number of other international organizations (OSCE, UNHCR, UNDP) assist in the implementation of specific tasks as agreed upon in the DPA.

One of the places in BiH where the international community has been particularly involved since 1994 has been the city of Mostar. The city's special importance derives from the fact that it is the capital of a canton with a mixed Croat-Bosniac population. Only two such cantons, the Herzegovina-Neretva and the Central Bosnia Canton, exist. Mostar has traditionally been the political center of the Herzegovinian Croats, a fact that was acknowledged in the DPA by the relocation of five of the federal ministries from Sarajevo to Mostar. Both Bosniacs and Bosnian Serbs, however, have the advantage of their political centers being situated in towns (Sarajevo and Banja Luka) where they constitute a clear majority. As the Croat political leadership has frequently expressed its feeling of being disadvantaged in this regard, all matters concerning Mostar are of high importance for the political climate within the Federation.[2] From the perspective of the international community, Mostar and the Brcko District are seen as crucial factors in the overall process of post-conflict state-building, since these were contested territories during peace negotiations and special international supervision was needed in both cases. As such they function almost as a showcase on the micro-level of the overall success or failure of international approaches to governance in BiH (Bieber, 2005). Nevertheless, after over ten years of attempted politico-administrative re-unification with heavy involvement of the international community, Mostar is still what one of my interlocutors dubbed "tamo-vamo grad" (literally the city of over there and over here, but essentially meaning the city of them and us). This expression alludes not only to the spatial division of the town along the Neretva river into a western Croatian and an eastern Bosniac part, but also to a deeper-lying division along ethno-national lines which pervades all aspects of life in the city and goes back to the experience of violent conflict between ethno-nationally defined groups within the city in the years between 1992–1995.

Situated on both shores of the Neretva River, the city has long been the urban center of the Herzegovina region and was widely held to be one of the most multi-ethnic cities in the former Yugoslavia (Bose, 2002, p. 99). During the violent break-up of the Socialist Federal Republic of Yugoslavia, however, Mostar became the site of some of the heaviest violence and destruction in the region.[3] After initially defending the city jointly against Serb/JNA (Yugoslav People's Army) forces, in the spring of 1993 fighting broke out between the HVO (Croatian Defence Council) and the Army of BiH, leading to a complete division of the urban community into a Croat-dominated western part and a Bosniac-dominated eastern part. The city as a unified local community no longer existed, two separate war-time administrations were established and members of other ethnic groups either left voluntarily or were—to a greater or lesser extent—forcibly expelled or put into detention camps. The majority of Serbs left the town during the first phase of the conflict; the Serb community today is marginal in Mostar. Apart from the internal movement of inhabitants from one side of the city to the other and the exodus of Mostarians seeking refuge in foreign countries, a massive influx of displaced persons from surrounding areas into both sides of the city also drastically altered the composition of Mostar's population. Today the estimated population of the municipality of Mostar is 111 259 persons (Federalni Zavod za Statistiku, 2006), but no exact information on its composition is available—neither in ethno-national categories nor according to other criteria.

Even before Bosnia and Herzegovina was established, by force of the Dayton Peace Agreement, as a newly independent state with three constituent people, the international community sought to end fighting and reunify the city through negotiations with Croat and Bosniac leaders. As a result of the Washington Agreement, Mostar was placed under a European Administration (EUAM) from 1994–1997, headed by the Special European Representative Hans Koschnick. Under his auspices a post-war interim statute for the city was designed. In order to lessen the intensity of a bipolar division, the municipality of Mostar was established with six sub-districts (three Bosniac and three Croat), and a central zone encompassing the former frontline as well as some infrastructure objects and the central administration buildings. However, the international authorities in Mostar[4] could not prevent the growing independence of the six districts. As districts were allowed to operate their own budgets and could independently solicit credits and reconstruction aid, district councils became ever stronger and voluntary cooperation took place exclusively within the three Croat or the three Bosniac districts. Accordingly, the city-wide central administration, having its seat in the central zone, remained dysfunctional (Commission for Reforming the City of Mostar, 2003).

In January 2004 the High Representative imposed a new statute for the city of Mostar, after a lengthy process of consultation and negotiation had failed to produce a consensus among local political parties and power-holders (OHR, 2004).[5] The new statute prescribed the abolishment of the six districts as administrative units,[6] the election of one city council and the formation of one unified city administration. In order to ensure its implementation the High Representative authorized a special unit of the OHR, the Mostar Implementation Unit (MIU), as an expert advisory body with broad discretionary powers. This team closely monitored the reform process until the end of 2005 when it considered its task to be near completion and was formally disbanded.

Although the first city-wide elected city council took office towards the end of 2004 and now seems to function reasonably well, the restructuring of former district administrations into one unified city administration is still underway. The rationalization of jobs in the unified city administration is not yet complete and the reappointment of civil servants and employees following an internal assessment is still underway.[7] Another critical issue, that of the city's ownership of and control over public utility companies and other public institutions, still partitioned according to ethno-national criteria, also remains unresolved. Therefore, the inhabitants of Mostar are still facing divided institutions in the field of communal services (water, waste disposal and electricity), culture, sport and recreation, and in other sectors are facing badly performing or outright dysfunctional administrative institutions. Ultimately, the process of reunifying the politico-administrative structures of the city of Mostar has not yet been successfully accomplished. The resistance by established nationalist political parties to the reform process is still sufficiently strong enough to create serious delays and moments of political crisis.[8]

It is quite obvious that solidarity, defined in ethno-national terms, is still salient and probably remains the strongest mobilizing force.[9] At first glance, the OHR's attempt to administratively reunify the city of Mostar does not challenge this perception of

18   Governance in Ethnically Mixed Cities

ethno-national groups as bounded entities with strong in-group solidarity. The OHR concentrates its efforts on building an institutional setting (in this case on the level of local self-government) based on complex power-sharing mechanisms between the three ethno-national groups (Everly, 2005). Such power-sharing mechanisms are enshrined in the complex election regulations for the city council, the continuation of the indirect election of the mayor of Mostar,[10] and the principle that public servants have to be appointed according to ethno-national proportions from the last pre-war census dating from 1991. The creation of such an institutional setting is seen by the international community as the best guarantee for providing citizens with equal access to public services in an efficient and functional way regardless of their ethno-national background (Commission for Reforming the City of Mostar, 2003).

Theoretical Considerations: State-building and its Ramifications for Emerging Notions of Citizenship

This emphasis on institution-building as a way to overcome the consequences of violent conflicts fits well into a more general concept of state-building which has recently gained currency in post-conflict settings around the world (Fukuyama, 2004). Rather than being concerned with questions of ideology, meaning and identification processes creating an emotional attachment to the state as an imagined community of co-nationals, this state-building concept puts forward a model of rational attachment to the state. The state is envisioned as a legal and institutional setting created from above, in which citizens can realize their interests and are provided with basic services and benefits (Chandler, 2004, 2006).[11]

In this context, it is worth looking at debates on the concept of citizenship where a similar distinction can been made. A liberal line of thinkers defines citizenship as "a set of normative expectations specifying the relationship between the nation-state and its individual members which procedurally establish the rights and obligations of members and a set of practices by which these expectations are realized" (Waters cited in Peled, 1992, p. 433). Emphasizing the individual legal relationship between citizens and states it parallels the above-mentioned understanding of state-building as an exercise in creating a rational attachment to the newly evolving state institutions. But another, more communitarian line of thinking, takes membership in a community to be the hallmark of citizenship. Rights and duties related to citizenship status thus flow from this membership, giving the element of belonging to community precedence over the legal relationship between state and citizens defined in individual terms. Underlying the latter line of reasoning is an understanding of the state as an imagined community of co-nationals sharing a common sense of identity which serves to delineate membership and consequently grant citizenship (Habermas, 1999).[12]

If the political relation between state and citizens takes the shape of a democratic system—as it is supposed to do in BiH—the same difficulty presents itself in yet another dimension. Fritz Scharpf's (1999) influential distinction between input-oriented and output-oriented legitimization rests on much the same conundrum as the divergent interpretations of citizenship. Whereas the input-oriented mode of legitimization emphasizes 'government by the people', the output-oriented mode privileges 'government for the people.' In the first instance, political choices are legitimate because they can be derived from the will of the people, i.e. the preferences of the members of a community as they are expressed above all in regular elections. Nevertheless, such a model rests on the assumption that there is a clear understanding of who constitutes 'the people' and—as in the case of the nation-state—a pre-existing thick collective identity generating trust in majority decisions. In the output perspective political decisions are legitimate because they effectively advance the common welfare of the constituency affected by the decision. This form of legitimization can be achieved in constituencies where no or only thin collective identities exist—here, the state's capacity to solve problems requiring collective solutions is sufficient proof of its legitimacy. Being concerned with forms of governance in the European Union, Scharpf held that in democratic nation-states input- and output-oriented legitimacy coexist side by side creating a balance between identity-based and interest-based constituencies. On the level of European governance, however, output-oriented forms of legitimization prevail, making for a precarious balance between efficiency and democracy (Scharpf, 1999).

In a recent article on the EU's institution-building strategy in the Western Balkans, Bechev and Andreev (2005) extend this reasoning to EU support policies for the western Balkans. They argue that underlying the EU's approach to institution building in the region is a belief in output-oriented, rather than in input-oriented legitimacy, in order to elicit support for, trust in, and loyalty to newly evolving state institutions. With respect to BiH, it seems safe to advance the argument one step further and to attribute a similar understanding of the policy process to other international organizations active in the country. Most prominently, the OHR exists outside of any framework of accountability to BiH's citizens (Caplan, 2005). The High Representative's authority to use his so-called Bonn-powers undermines the direct accountability of elected representatives. Input legitimacy is further weakened by the fact that the electorate falls apart into three ethno-national groups—whose political representatives frequently deny each other the right to speak for anybody but their own ethno-national group.[13] For these reasons the provision of public services and the high performance of public institutions in terms of their problem-solving capacity become a crucial factor in legitimizing the new state (as well as the international involvement in BiH).[14] Consequently, international actors treat institution building and public administration reforms as central areas of activity, while leaving the question of a shared citizenship identity aside.[15]

The distinction drawn between identity-based and interest-based concepts of citizenship, state and legitimacy serves to clarify the normative conceptual ground of state-building efforts in contemporary BiH. Given the fact that an interest-based policy appears to dominate the scene there seems to be little room for the development of a sense of shared citizenship. However, once the analytical focus is turned towards the empirical realm of everyday practices and subjective experiences, it becomes possible to formulate a more nuanced approach to the question of citizenship identity. Among anthropologists, a renewed interest in the study of state structures has led them to postulate that it is precisely an emphasis on studying everyday practices and cultural representations of the state which might yield new insights into the state phenomenon (Sharma & Gupta, 2006). More specifically, anthropologists conducting research in post-war BiH now argue that an "anthropology of state-building" can make a contribution to "fully understand the state or state-like effects of international intervention" by "going local" and taking into account "local practices and worldviews" (Bougarel *et al.*, 2007, p. 33).

Following this lead, I argue that in the context of BiH an important unintended consequence of externally initiated institution building is often overlooked: the unifying effect of official, codified and formalized categorization practices inherent in the design of modern bureaucratic institutions. In a body of literature largely unconnected to the recent writings on external state building in post-conflict societies, such practices have often been discussed with regard to processes of official top-down nation-state formation or in the context of colonial and post-colonial settings (Anderson, 1991; Appadurai, 1993; Bourdieu, 1994; Scott, 1998). These practices are typically interpreted as techniques of state consolidation or as techniques of domination used by elites in their struggle for power. Interpretations show how top-down categorization practices shaped new processes of identification and group formation among categorized populations. One of the most thoroughly studied cases in this body of literature is the census, where categorization practices often led to the awakening of (new) ethnic groups who would later fight for their right to self-determination (Cohn, 1987; Anderson, 1991; Appadurai, 1993).

It seems to me that these practices, being indispensable for the functioning of a modern bureaucratic apparatus, also produce their effect on citizens in much more mundane contexts, even where they are not part of conscious identity politics carried out by central or peripheral elites. Furthermore, I argue that official categorization practices do not only inform processes of ethnicization but can also bring other collective identities to the forefront. Roger Brubaker's admonition to carefully distinguish between groups and categories is a point well taken in this context (Brubaker, 2004, p. 12f). Being concerned with the analysis of ethnicity in a way which does not presuppose bounded groups, he urges us to consider how various categorization practices can become the basis for a sense of ethnic "groupness". Confronting the issue from a different angle I will investigate categorization practices as the basis of a much wider variety of group-formation processes, rather than taking ethnicity as the given end point. In the spirit of anthropological approaches to studying the state outlined by Sharma & Gupta (2006), I will take a close look at categories which have been established and/or used by the city administration of Mostar in its dealings with citizens and I will argue that it is precisely these sub-categories of public service delivery that fill the abstract concept of citizenship with a concrete meaning. The following presentation of the ethnographic evidence is arranged in two parts. In the first part, I probe the divisive aspects of the emergence of the new administrative categories "refugee," "IDP," and "returnee" by analyzing popular perceptions of these terms; in the second part I turn towards more active and inclusive forms of engagement with administrative categorization practices.

Ethnographic Evidence from Mostar: The Categorization of Citizens and New Hierarchies of Provision as a Matrix for Social Division

In Bosnia-Herzegovina, as elsewhere, it was necessary to apply legal and administrative categories defining access to limited benefits and services for certain groups of persons in order to provide public services according to the needs of a differentiated population. In BiH many of the legal categories used today date back to immediate post-war requirements and have since undergone a lengthy process of (trans-)formation. Being applied in a rather improvised manner by various international agencies in the immediate post-war era, these categories were consequently standardized, and administrative procedures linked to them were handed over to local authorities. Due to this long formative period and to the amount of international donor money linked to them, some of these categories became firmly entrenched in public perceptions of all ethno-national groups. Moreover, since they were continuously backed up by international policies and funds—even when administrative procedures were handed over to local authorities—such categories tended to become effective even in divided public institutions. In this section I discuss in detail how these categories were discursively propagated, organizationally institutionalized and embedded in society through a number of policies and actors and consequently appropriated, evaded or subverted by the population in question. I conclude that, under certain circumstances, administrative categorization practices might undermine the sense of solidarity within an ethno-national group and open up grounds for new social divisions.

The Emergence of the Post-war Categories "Refugee," "IDP," and "Returnee"

Three such categories which emerged as a result of the war and received special attention from the international community are "refugee," "internally displaced person" (IDP), and "returnee."[16] These categories were first introduced in Annex 7 of the Dayton Peace Agreement (DPA). As an agreement on the status of refugees and displaced persons it states:

> All refugees and displaced persons have the right freely to return to their homes of origin. They shall have the right to have restored to them property of which they were deprived in the course of hostilities since 1991 and to be compensated for any property that cannot be restored to them. The early return of refugees and displaced persons is an important objective of the settlement of the conflict in Bosnia and Herzegovina. (Dayton Peace Agreement, 1995, Annex 7, Art. I.1.)

Hence, refugees and displaced persons were constituted as a category endowed with specific rights (restoration of property and compensation for lost property) and became the object of specific policies (early return). It is important to take note that refugee and IDP rights were, at that point, framed as human rights within the context of international human rights conventions. In BiH these categories came to be filled with meaning mainly through activities of international organizations such as OHR, OSCE, and UNHCR, as well as a variety of international NGOs in the immediate post-war environment.

From the beginning, the regulation of property repossession played an important role in general return policies. While the legal framework in this area was determined by international actors, responsibility for its implementation was consequently handed over to BiH institutions. In 1999 the major international organizations active in BiH began to develop a more standardized and comprehensive approach to this area of policy, the so-called "Property Law Implementation Plan" (PLIP), a strategy ensuring that all citizens of BiH having been dispossessed of their property in the course of conflict, could repossess it. Implementation of this legal framework fell to municipal administrations, who were supposed to create administrative structures dealing with property claims of refugees and IDPs in a standardized and professional manner. To this end, standardized forms were created and distributed and also standard procedures designed, the application of which was monitored by international teams in all municipalities of BiH (Chandler, 2004, p. 584; ICG, 2002).

By the end of 2003 PLIP was widely regarded as successfully completed in most municipalities. In the beginning of 2004 the OHR handed over the full responsibility for realization of Annex 7 to local authorities (Ministry of Human Rights and Refugees, 2005). As a first step, the State Ministry for Human Rights and Refugees (MHRR) and the responsible entity ministries agreed—in cooperation with the UNHCR—to undertake a comprehensive revision of the number and status of IDPs.[17] Public information campaigns were launched for the re-registration procedure which lasted until March 2005 (UNHCR, 2005a). Simultaneously, both entities adopted revised and harmonized IDP laws. On this basis municipal authorities started to verify each re-registration issuing either a decision on cessation or on recognition of the IDP status. As a result of stricter definitions being adopted and the existence of a unified data base, IDPs who had received reconstruction aid, had acquired property or had in some other way integrated into the community of their post-war residence lost their status and the number of persons officially recognized as IDPs has sharply dropped (UNHCR, 2005b).

Apart from this re-registration for IDP status, the State Ministry for Human Rights and Refugees called on all refugees, IDPs, and returnees to apply for registration as potential beneficiaries for reconstruction aid and return assistance. Such a call was issued in June 2004 and again in July 2005, application forms were disseminated by regional centers of the MHRR. Media as well as associations of refugees and IDPs were asked to further publicize the call. Both times the public showed an intense interest in registering as potential beneficiaries for reconstruction aid. Contrary to the revision of IDP status, the application as a potential beneficiary did not involve the verification of data given by the applicant (MHRR, 2005, p. 153). A simple declaration of the intention of return on behalf of applicants allowed the ministry to determine priority areas for reconstruction efforts, according to the number of registered potential beneficiaries. The narrow legal definition was abandoned in favor of operational requirements of the policy process. This broadening of categories is presented as follows by the MHRR in an analysis of the access to social rights for refugees, IDPs and returnees:

> (...) Applicants were supposed to indicate their belonging to one of the three following categories: Refugee, displaced person, returnee. However, the majority of the applications missed this indication and in addition the interpretations of the applicants were very often obviously improper. That is why the category in the database is entered for all applicants and the members of their families as follows:
> Refugee from BiH—for all persons whose current place of residence is outside of BiH.
> Displaced Person in BiH—for all persons whose current municipality of residence is different from the municipality of return.
> Returnee in BiH—for all persons whose municipality of current residence is the same as the municipality of pre-war residence. Thus, internally displaced persons are registered as returnees i.e. the persons who might never have left the territory of their pre-war municipality but due to damaged housing units are not capable of returning to their pre-war residence address.
> (...)
> It is necessary to make an emphasis that the "category" as defined above is being used exclusively as a technical expression and is by no means related to the legally defined status. (MHRR, 2005, p. 158)

In spite of the final explanatory remark, this procedure generated an impression in the population that once registered as a potential beneficiary reconstruction aid would sooner or later materialize. And it once again connected the prospect of reconstruction to the categories of refugee, IDP, and returnee, thus enormously increasing the attraction of these categories.

To sum up, through the legal and policy changes outlined above, the initially rather *ad hoc* and uncoordinated reference to refugees, IDPs, and returnees, originally flowing from international human rights standards became firmly entrenched in administrative practice at the local level. The attempt to refine administrative competencies in this field in order to gather better information and standardize procedures led a wider population to be increasingly aware of these categories and the provisions linked hereto. Paradoxically, this growing awareness and reference to refugees, IDPs, and returnees as a group of citizens with special entitlements went hand in hand with a rapid decrease in the number of persons officially registered and recognized as refugees and IDPs.[18] It was demonstrated that although PLIP and the various re-registration exercises turned "refugee," "IDPm," and "returnee" into administrative concepts widely applied at the local level, these policies could not establish precise and undisputed definitions of the categories in question. Consequently, public authorities could not exert much control over the uses these concepts were put to by citizens themselves, or the ways these categories were interpreted.

The Perception of IDPs, Refugees, and Returnees in Mostar

In Mostar all three categories have become highly contested among all ethno-national groups. The perceived preferential treatment of persons falling in these categories or claiming this status is constantly being commented upon: "A person from Stolac [most probably displaced Bosniac] or a person from Konjic [most probably displaced Croat] will get an apartment [allocated by the city from city owned housing stock] in two months, we [the Mostarians, whose houses have been destroyed during the war] wait for alternative accommodation for more than ten years."[19] This statement of a 50-year old Bosniac woman from Mostar refers to the common policy of international organizations as well as of local authorities to treat IDPs as a particularly vulnerable group of the population. As such, this group often was the target of specific humanitarian assistance, housing allocation or financial support.

Unequal housing reconstruction also resulted from many foreign governments funding reconstruction programs in BiH in order to repatriate "their" refugees. A 27-year-old woman of a mixed Bosniac-Croat family who fled to Switzerland at the beginning of hostilities between Croats and Bosniacs remembers about her return to Mostar: "The building we moved in when we came back is called Svicarska—the Swiss building - because the government of Switzerland reconstructed it for us returnees from Switzerland." Speculations are widespread about what persons would do once they had repossessed their original houses or apartments and these had been reconstructed: "They [displaced Serbs from Mostar] reclaimed their houses, received donations for reconstruction and then simply sold their houses to people coming from the villages and left with the profit they have made." The above and similar statements could frequently be heard from inhabitants of a now predominantly Bosniac neighborhood, where many Serbs had lived before the war.

However, complaints such as the following also stem from people living in this neighborhood:

> They [displaced Bosniacs from the territory of the Republika Srpska] have taken over the town, they have all built their nice houses here with donation money and now they run the town. They don't know how to behave in a city. They built their houses illegally and you see what the results are.

This comment came from a Bosniac man declaring himself to be a "true Mostarian" while we were walking through the neighborhood and he was pointing out where new houses had been constructed illegally on the slope of the hillside causing regular mudslides into lower parts of the city during heavy rainfalls. Croats showed a similar disdain for new settlements in the South of Mostar built in the early nineties for Croat IDPs by the wartime Herceg-Bosna leadership, with the intention of consolidating Croatian dominance in the area. While driving by such a settlement, a middle-aged Croatian woman exclaimed:

> The Croat government built these settlements and resettled them [displaced Croatians from Central Bosnia] here during the war. You see how big the houses are, they all have two floors. Who owns a house with two floors nowadays? But it is good that they have been settled outside of the city, they are people from the country and it will take them a generation or so to get used to the city. (See also ESI, 2004, pp. 42–44).

Interestingly, the categories of refugee and displaced person are integrated into a discourse on belonging which centers around the distinction between urban and rural.[20] In particular IDPs from the surrounding villages, who have continued to live in Mostar after the war, are perceived as not belonging to the community of true Mostarians: Although we stayed here the whole time during the war and endured everything, we never received any reconstruction aid. My sister's house in Donja Mahala [a neighborhood in Mostar] was completely destroyed but since she stayed in Mostar and lived with us she did not qualify as a displaced person, she is a displaced person in her own town!" insisted a Bosniac woman from Mostar. In opposition to the terms refugee and displaced person (both referring to leaving one's place of origin) a sense of belonging to a specific locality is evoked in stories about the old pre-war community of Mostarians. Even refugees who are returning to their pre-war homes in Mostar are often seen as having betrayed their city and as being wrongly privileged since they did not experience the hardships of staying in Mostar but now reap the benefits of resettlement aid.

These statements show that refugees, IDPs, and returnees are indeed perceived as distinctive groups of persons, rather than just as prescriptive terms for administrative use. Under difficult economic circumstances, there is a sharp awareness of the material benefits linked to all three categories and the division they create in the local community.[21] The division into refugees/IDPs and true Mostarians is a flexible one that can be applied either within one's ethno-national group or attributed to specific ethno-national groups. Depending on which ethno-national group one belongs to, it is easy to argue that *all* Serbs are selling their houses to newly arrived villagers and are leaving with the profits, that *all* Croats from rural areas of central Bosnia are being resettled in Mostar with financial support by the war-time Herceg-Bosna government, or that *all* Bosniacs from the surrounding villages illegally constructed houses on Mostar's eastern hillside creating infrastructural problems. Just as often, however, one can hear that it is the newcomers from rural areas in general who destroy the quality of life in the city, whereas the community of pre-war Mostarians was characterized precisely by its tolerance and multi-ethnicity. Here ethnic divisions are down-played in favor of a division along the urban-rural dichotomy. The long lasting absence of any reliable statistical data on the characteristics of recent population movements lends equal plausibility to all these claims.

The Interplay of Categories, Provisions and Lack of Statistical Information

This curious lapse in the overall state-building effort regarding the lack of statistical information deserves closer examination. The gathering of statistical data has long been understood by authors as Anderson (1991), Cohn (1987), and Scott (1998) as the first and foremost step in projects of state power consolidation. Maps and censuses figured largely in such projects and while maps showing the distribution of ethno-national groups on the territory of BiH are omnipresent (Jansen, 2005b) no post-war census has yet been undertaken (ESI, 2004, p. 4). International actors have refrained from pressuring BiH authorities to carry out a census because of the political sensitivity of such an undertaking. Not only would it seem to legitimize the results of ethnic cleansing, it might also give rise to calls for reconsidering the balance and nature of the agreement on constitutive people as established by the Dayton Accords. Local nationalist politicians in turn have profited from the absence of a census because it permits them to make irrefutable claims to territories and populations. The process of rebuilding statistical institutes at all levels of government has been slow and until recently there has been no cooperation between the Federation Statistical Institute and that of the Republika Srpska. The accuracy of their data stands no comparison with pre-war statistical data when the capacity of Yugoslavia's statistical institutes was recognized internationally.

For reasons of reliability, but also to avoid legitimizing ethnic cleansing, the census of 1991 is widely used as a point of departure in all public matters. The 2005 population of Mostar, for example, was calculated as a composite figure consisting of the following calculations: a projection of the population figure from the 1991 census, which was then corrected with the number of deaths and births registered in the municipality of Mostar during the last year, with the number of IDPs registered in Mostar and with figures on enrolment in Mostar's schools.[22] In a similar vein, attempts have been made to statistically derive the effect of recent population movements on the composition of Mostar's current population, but this effort remains at the level of estimates and speculation.[23] Currently, no official information is available on the question of whether persons dropping out of the category of IDP do so, because of their return to their pre-war residence or because they acquire property and integrate into their current place of residence. Persons returning to their pre-war residence are listed as returnees and entitled to certain benefits for a period of six months in order to make their return sustainable, but it is impossible to measure how many of them actually stay longer than this period and how many simply wait until the reconstruction of their property has been finished and then sell or exchange it against property in order to move back to their post-war residence (ICG, 2002, p. 11; Heimerl, 2006).

The difficulty of compiling exact data is further exacerbated by the complex structure of administrative competencies. Not only has there been little cooperation between the Federation and the RS until recently, but also within the Federation each canton developed its own legal framework in this area of policy and delegated competencies from this area to its municipalities to a different degree. Finally, within Mostar each of the former six districts used to have its Displaced Persons and Housing Office, granting status and benefits and collecting information according to its own criteria. In such a context it becomes almost impossible to create reliable information on recent and current population movements in BiH. This does not come as a surprise, since it is usually centralizing and centralized states that most value and apply statistical information gathering. BiH is not a centralized state; its entities (respectively the cantons in the Federation) have little interest in strengthening a central state. Even the activities of the international community are contradictory in this respect. On one hand, much energy is devoted to building-up competencies on the state level (thereby weakening the entities and cantons), on the other hand the international community is a staunch defender of decentralizing more competencies to the level of local self-government and sometimes—as in the case of registration procedures mentioned below—these two principles collide with each other and create blind spots in the administrative procedure.

The absence of reliable data, the lack of clear competencies and of channels of communication between different levels of government allow for easy manipulation of the categories of refugee, IDP and returnee by citizens as well as office holders. But rather than weakening the power of these categories, it appears to be precisely the possibility to maneuver and manipulate which secured these categories such a wide currency. Office holders recognized the power to grant refugee or IDP status and thereby housing and/or reconstruction aid as a valuable resource in politically as well as privately motivated networks of exchange.[24] Citizens on the other hand quickly learned how to use the various loop-holes in legal regulations and administrative procedures in order to gain the most benefit. Such loop-holes particularly exist in current registration procedures. While municipal bodies run the registration procedure for IDPs and check all relevant information, residence registry is done with the cantonal police and a special state agency (CIPS) issues passports and personal identification cards which carry a place of residence solely on the basis of what the applicant has declared to be his current address. There is little or no exchange of information between these different levels. It is easy indeed to manipulate one's status of current or pre-war residence according to the requirements of return and reconstruction policies.

Even if the majority of the population was not involved in wrongfully claiming benefits, suspicions of misuse and misappropriation were widespread and further contributed to the special nimbus these categories acquired. Mistrust in public institutions and in the conduct of co-citizens surprisingly enough did not lead to a rejection of administrative categories; instead they increasingly took hold of people's imagination. The same logic also applies in the case of the widely held notion the rural population might profit disproportionally from return policies. The lack of precise information provides ample grounds for speculation and facilitates an embellishment of these categories with new layers of meanings. The extent to which people from all ethno-national groups could actively and imaginatively engage with these categories, fill them with their practices and attribute meaning to them was thus much greater than it might have been under different circumstances.

In Mostar, such newly created administrative hierarchies of provision (Stubbs, 2001) could be fused with strong ideas of belonging based on locality and a specific sense of urban community and thus became new matrices of social distinction. Lines of division such as the one between IDPs (*raseljeni*) and original inhabitants (*domicilni*) which draw upon the pre-existing distinction between peasants and urbanites bridge ethno-national boundaries and might therefore work against the closure of group boundaries on purely ethno-national terms.

Ethnographic Evidence from Mostar: Reclaiming Citizenship Rights through the Use of Administrative Categories

In this second ethnographic part, I examine how a related example of administrative performance—or better non-performance—in the realm of housing reconstruction in Mostar's central zone actually provoked people, regardless of their ethnic background, to organize themselves into a protest movement in order to take collective action. Carefully tracing the protesters' course of action allows me to capture yet another dimension of the interrelationship between bureaucratic categorization practices, and group formation processes, namely the more active appropriation and utilization of administrative categories in struggles for social rights by parts of the city's population. Based on this case, I conclude that administrative categories do not solely contain the potential to create new divisions, but also the potential to serve as a unifying force across ethno-national boundaries. In the last section of this part, I elaborate on the consequences such a unifying effect has for conceptualizing citizenship on the local level.

Reconstruction and the Provision of Housing in Mostar's Central Zone

One of the major tasks facing the city of Mostar since the end of hostilities in 1994 has been the task of reconstructing housing space destroyed during fighting. Under the European Administration of Mostar a first reconstruction scheme was carried out but due to massive destruction many private homes as well as collective housing blocks in the central zone remained in ruins. As mentioned above, reconstruction programs often privileged refugees and displaced persons from rural areas,[25] or owners of private homes whose houses could be rebuilt simply by distributing building materials (Yarwood, 1999). The PLIP had provided a comprehensive strategy for property repossession as early as 1999. A unified approach to the question of reconstruction, however, was only developed after 2003 when the MHRR prepared a country-wide "Strategy for Implementation of Annex 7 of the Dayton Peace Agreement." Concerted action and planning became a necessity as funds from international donors started to drop sharply and BiH institutions had to find ways of funding reconstruction out of their own budgets.

In Mostar the various district authorities and later on the city administration apparently failed to undertake a coherent strategy regarding reconstruction in the central zone. As local authorities took over responsibility from international organizations in the areas of return and reconstruction, the division of the city into six districts and one central zone became more relevant. The central zone, which could only be administered jointly by both sides, simultaneously turned into an administrative no-man's land and a highly contested space. Practical as well as ideological reasons seem to have contributed to this. Due to the existence of the former frontline in the central zone damage to buildings was tremendous and reconstruction would require enormous financial means.[26] Pre-war inhabitants of apartment buildings in the central zone often had been of mixed ethno-national background. Neither of the two dominant nationalist political parties showed much interest in pushing for reconstruction of these buildings because benefits could not be restricted to "their" ethno-national electorate. While damaged apartment blocks were thus left to further disintegrate or were even torn down, symbolic land marks, such as a large catholic church, were erected without valid building permits and socially-owned construction land was given to individual families by administrative bodies having no competence over this area.

International donors, in turn, had their own criteria for establishing priority needs of reconstruction. Minority return often figured high on their agenda. In the context of Mostar, being divided into three Bosniac, three Croat, and one central zone, it was difficult to ascertain who—apart from the former Serb population—could be regarded as a minority in which sector. Although the reconstruction of some apartment blocks on the "Boulevard" was funded by international donors, they tended to place more emphasis on reconstructing infrastructure objects such as the Gymnasium or various bridges.

The Formation of a Collective Protest Movement

Toward the end of 2005 a multi-ethnic group of former inhabitants of apartment blocks along the "Santiceva" Street (running parallel to the more famous Boulevard but also site of the former frontline in the central zone) started to appear in public with demands for the reconstruction of their apartments. In regular intervals they staged protest meetings in front of their former apartment buildings, the city administration, or the city hall, and related their plight to the media.[27] They drew attention to their unsuccessful efforts dating back to 2001 to obtain support from the respective local authorities. Initiators of the protest were a group of persons formerly living in one of the apartment blocks on Santiceva. Their building had been heavily damaged during the conflicts and inhabitants had sought shelter in other parts of the town. When in 2001 attempts were made to tear down the ruin under unclear legal conditions, the former inhabitants rallied to defend "their" building. Subsequently, they convinced former inhabitants of the neighboring apartment blocks to jointly fight for their claims.

At the time of field work, 94 households formerly residing in eight apartment buildings in Santiceva are registered with the protest movement, expressing a wish for reconstruction and return. The number of 94 households comprises 29 Croat, 42 Bosniac and 23 Serb families. Eighty percent of these persons currently live in Mostar, either renting apartments, staying with relatives or being provided with alternative accommodation by the city in collective shelters.[28] Their former apartments along Santiceva used to belong to state companies such as the electricity board, public transport companies, or the police, and the former Yugoslav People's Army. These companies and institutions, in turn, had assigned apartments to their employees for life-long use. An employment with the police, the army or public utility companies entailed a high social status and prestige which is mirrored by the apartments' location in the center of town.[29] It can be assumed that these employees belonged to a privileged class and often were highly educated, as well as well-connected to the pre-war political establishment. Due to the altered political circumstances they lost much of their former influence and are acutely aware of the degradation in their current social situation. Yet, this group of persons is best equipped to articulate its cause and to find new ways and means to pursue it.

It is not surprising then that the protesters from Santiceva successfully formed an alliance with other former inhabitants of the central zone and persuaded the local Ombudsman office to support them. By now, the protest movement has spread all over the municipality's territory. Regardless of ethno-national background, people are willing to collectively act and insist on their right to be treated as equal citizens in their town of birth. They feel that a basic entitlement—the right to housing—is being consciously withheld from them because the city is unable or unwilling to either attract donors or invest from its own budget into the renovation of their pre-war apartments. Ideally, with the property repossession and privatization laws being carried out each household should be the owner of the apartment in which it had resided in pre-wartimes. Inhabitants of apartment blocks still in ruins cannot benefit from the administrative process of repossessing their apartments simply because these buildings have not been renovated. This feeling of being left out of administrative procedures through which they would gain access to rightful entitlements has led to the formation of the current protest movement. The externally driven reform of Mostar's municipal administration in terms of practical institution-building—although painstakingly slow and in many aspects not yet successful—has favored this development in two respects. First of all, by highlighting a local self-government accountable and responsive to the needs of its citizenry as the reform's central objective, it provided a rhetoric on which protesters could capitalize when encountering city authorities. Second, the physical unification of administrative bodies into one central administration, and the establishment of a unified city council, localized the city's government in one discernable place and thus made protests in a city-wide public space possible for the first time.

The Conflation of "Belonging" and "Displacement" in the Protesters' Slogans

Two of the slogans to be seen most frequently on the banners during demonstrations in the central zone were "Podstanari u svom gradu" (Tenants in our own town), or "Raseljeni u svom gradu" (Displaced in our own town).[30] Being a tenant and paying rent is a strange situation for persons having been provided with social housing in Yugoslav times and now seeing how others around them profit from the property repossession and privatization procedure.[31] To rent a flat is commonly attributed to strangers having no roots in town. Protesters, in contrast, emphasize their belonging to the urban community of Mostar and use this background as a justification in their engagement with the city administration and their struggle for their social rights. This insistence on belonging to the urban community and the continued will to engage with local authorities, holding them accountable for the state of reconstruction in the central zone, points to an interesting development. Social rights, which had been firmly tied to the status of refugee, IDP, or returnee through the application of international human rights norms in the immediate post-war situation, are here brought back into the realm of domestic citizenship rights.[32] The slogan "Displaced in our own town" is an apt expression of this balancing act between a universal, international human rights legitimation and a claim to notions of citizenship anchored in a sense of belonging to a specific locality.

Protesters recognized, though, that insisting on their urban citizenship did not yet constitute a powerful category in a legal or administrative sense. To the contrary, the location of their pre-war homes in the central zone was a disadvantage since this area remained for a long time an administrative no-man's land and a highly ambivalent space. The protesters' slogan—"Displaced in our own town"—can therefore also be seen as an attempt to align themselves to the powerful administrative category of displaced person by elegantly combining the element of displacement with the element of belonging to the urban community. The adoption of the IDP category and the construction of the aforementioned slogan were enforced among members of the protest movement during their regular meetings. In last year's October meeting, a representative of the BiH-wide "Council of refugees and IDPs" repeatedly requested participants to register as IDPs, or if previously done so to verify their status. Participants' reactions clearly indicated that so far many of them had not considered themselves to be displaced. The representative had to spell out once more the correlation between IDP status and eligibility for reconstruction aid. Being in the municipal Office for Social and Housing Affairs on the next morning, I witnessed a participant of this meeting entering and asking for verification of her IDP status. Apparently, the members of the protest group had now understood the importance of supporting the metaphorical use of "displacement" with concrete administrative actions. By consistently using the language of displacement in their own town the protesters were able to elucidate financial and organizational support from the "Council of refugees and displaced persons in BiH"—the main interest organization for this category of people— while at the same time pressuring the mayor of Mostar into announcing new forms of support for these fellow citizens. In the meantime, a first donor conference for the reconstruction of houses in Mostar has been organized. In the new city budget a special fund for reconstruction has been set up and within the city administration a commission for the distribution of these funds has been installed. Three members of the protest movement were appointed by the City Council as representatives to this commission.

The future will show whether this collective and multi-ethnic protest movement can survive, or whether it will fall apart once some of its members have achieved reconstruction of their buildings. Many outside observers doubt the intention of protesters to live in the apartments they are claiming, assuming that they will soon sell and move to mono-ethnic environments of their choice. Yet a more positive vision of future co-residence can be gleaned from conversations with members of the protest group. A former inhabitant of one of the Santiceva buildings, a woman of Croat background actively engaged in the movement, related how she had spent hours on the phone trying to convince an elderly immobile lady—a former Serb neighbor—to hand over her passport in order to register her for return. Fondly smiling she recalled having to converse on the whereabouts of all neighbors formerly living in their building before she could proceed to the reason of her call. When she jokingly complained about the time and costs consumed by this endeavor, relatives of the elderly lady showed up on her door with a big supply of home-made preserves. The same woman also invited her former neighbors to her home in order to collectively prepare an application for a reconstruction program.

In the cause of collectively pursuing the reconstruction of their former apartments (from which each household would individually benefit) former neighbors necessarily interact and cooperate. During these encounters older forms of good neighborliness slowly revived. Typically, this behavior includes reciprocal offers of food, visits to each other's houses and the exchange of gossip (Sorabji, 2003, cited in Hann 2003; Pickering, 2006). These re-established relationships of neighborliness at the level of everyday life (not to be confused with an idealized concept of multi-ethnic harmony) might be a basis for consciously choosing to invest in a common future. A shared sense of community—in this case arising from common identification with a specific locality and leading to joint actions—does not entail a guarantee for peaceful and harmonious co-existence but rather establishes a common ground on which conflicting individual and collective interests can be negotiated. As Turner (1993, p. 12) rightly points out, it lies in the character of citizenship to simultaneously function as a form of social incorporation, and as a set of conditions for social struggle.

The case of the protest movement is theoretically relevant because it illustrates how citizenship is imagined and enacted not as an abstract concept but as the concrete experience of a process which contains both elements of social integration and the pursuit of particularistic goals. Members' participation in the protest group was motivated by a struggle for an increasingly scarce resource—reconstruction aid granted to a legally and administratively defined sub-group of the population, e.g. IDPs, refugees, and returnees. By fusing the power of the administrative category of IDPs with an appeal to the notion of belonging to a local community, the protest movement developed an integrative power superseding particularistic as well as ethno-national divisions; based on this inner cohesion it was then able to successfully confront the city administration with its demands for reconstruction. Such a prolonged engagement and close contact with city authorities, as well as an increased level of interaction and cooperation within the protest group, opens up new ground for the members' self-construction as citizens of Mostar with legitimate political claims. Citizenship is thus not a matter of either identity- or interest-based notions of community; it evolves out of a dialectical relationship between both poles. In communities deeply divided along ethno-national lines, administrative categories linked to the provision of services can serve as a rallying point outside the frame of reference of ethno-national belonging and can thereby provide new avenues for imagining and enacting citizenship.

Conclusions

By presenting ethnographic evidence on the uses of the categories IDP, refugee, and returnee in the local context of Mostar, my intention was to explore the consequences of administrative categorization practices for constructions of citizenship. In the course of this exploration, it became evident that such newly created legal and administrative terms take hold in people's lives and imaginations to a considerable degree, but not necessarily in the way envisioned by international and national policy makers. Difficult economic circumstances among most of Mostar's inhabitants lead to a sharp awareness of the material benefits linked to IDP-, refugee-, and returnee-status and of the manner in which such benefits are distributed.

On the one hand, newly created administrative hierarchies of provision can discursively be articulated as an opposition between original inhabitants and displaced newcomers. Such an articulation, which draws upon the pre-existing distinction between peasants and urbanites, points to divisive forces within ethno-national groups, and to the possibility of downplaying ethnic divisions in favor of social divisions along the rural-urban dichotomy. On the other hand, the same administrative category, when fused with a sense of belonging to the urban community as in the case of the protest movement, can also become a powerful incentive for collective action, and an avenue for imagining and enacting local forms of citizenship that transcend ethno-national boundaries.

It is by no means predictable whether and when inhabitants will take up such bureaucratic categorizations and will transform them either into new stereotypes of a divisive nature or into meaningful self-descriptions thus forming the basis for further collective action. Categories such as IDP, refugee and returnee—because they denote a sense of up-rootedness and displacement—might be an especially suitable site for the negotiation of belonging. In the material presented here, belonging was thus defined in relation to a specific locality, e.g. the city of Mostar—it remains to be further investigated how important the element of urbanity is in constructions of citizenship. Can one conceptualize a model of BiH-wide citizenship along the path outlined here, or will such constructions necessarily be limited to the local context? Should there be—or more to the point, can there be—an intentional effort to engineer a sense of belonging to a BiH-wide community through building up public institutions and services in a way which is attentive to the power of administrative categories? Or could a new form of urban citizenship, as it has been proposed by Rainer Bauböck (2003) in the context of transnational migration, be the adequate solution—at least in order to overcome divisions on the local level?[33] These are questions which can only be answered after a considerable amount of further research has been undertaken.

Nevertheless, what can be concluded from this contribution is that such research would indeed be helpful in a number of ways. Investigating bureaucratic categorization processes in different administrative subfields or on higher levels of government (canton, federation, state) might bring other forms of engagement with state institutions to the forefront. It might shed light on the question whether the element of urban belonging is a necessary ingredient in the construction of citizenship or whether categorizations practices employed, for example, in the public health sector or in the pension system constitute a source of shared experience setting in motion similar processes of social integration through the pursuit of common interests. Comparative research would also pay attention to the level of international involvement in these different sectors and the effect this has on the power of specific categorization practices. To explore such processes in more detail will thus contribute to gaining a fuller understanding of the complexities of state-building in post-conflict societies.

Ideally, such an anthropological approach which includes people's everyday practices and representations of their interactions with state institutions into an analysis of the current institution-building processes in BiH will contribute to debates on externally initiated state-building projects in two ways. By documenting that newly formed administrative institutions and categorizations practices can take hold in the population in ways not imagined nor intended by international policy makers, it can caution against an overly optimistic assessment of the prospects for such undertakings. On the other hand, it can also demonstrate that people engage with state institutions - even under conditions where such institutions have been established by external force—and that in the course of such engagements new forms of imagining belonging might indeed emerge.

Notes

1. An earlier version of this paper was presented at the ASN Conference on Globalization, Nationalism and Ethnic Conflict in the Balkans and its Regional Context (ASN Conference, Belgrade 2006). I owe special thanks to my co-panelist Monika Palmberger and the panel's discussant, Stef Jansen, for their helpful comments. I also benefited from the anonymous reviewers' valuable suggestions.
2. An articulation of this sentiment of disadvantage is Žepić (2003). The author originally presented this arguments in a roundtable organized at an early stage of the debates about a new statute for the city of Mostar.
3. It was no coincidence, that the term "urbicide" was coined by a group of authors from Mostar, documenting the destruction of their town in the early phase of the conflict (cf. Vucina, 1992). Unlike to other regions, where fighting was less heavy because of minority populations having been expelled by majority forces without much resistance, the loss of property and housing in Mostar was not solely a problem of refugees and IDPs but afflicted the city's population in general.
4. The EUAM lasted until early 1997. From then on, the regional office of the OHR took over its mandate.

5. The two main nationalist parties, the Croatian Democratic Union (HDZ) and the Bosniac Party of Democratic Action (SDA), could not agree on two crucial questions: the distribution of seats in the city council and the control over territory, e.g. the future status of the six districts. Both questions are directly related to the power of SDA and HDZ to exert influence on "their" ethno-nationally defined electorates and the territories linked to them (cf. Commission for Reforming the City of Mostar, 2003).
6. Districts are retained, though, as electoral units with each district electing three councillors on a separate list, whereas the other 18 councillors in a city council with 36 seats are elected on a city-wide list.
7. Partly, this delay is due to the constitutional principle of proportional ethno-national representation in all public bodies according to the last pre-war census from 1991. When this principle is applied simultaneously with an internal re-appointment procedure, as it was agreed upon in the case of Mostar, it clearly leads to problematic if not paradoxical outcomes.
8. In September 2006 the High Representative felt the need—after a series of unmet deadlines—to once again nominate a special envoy for the City of Mostar, whose task it has been to arbitrate solutions for the aforementioned still unresolved issues in the reform process by the end of the year (cf. OHR, 2006a).
9. The mobilizing force of ethno-national appeals became especially evident in the months preceding the general elections which were held on 1 October 2006. In Mostar, as elsewhere, nationalist parties and organizations drew on ethno-national sentiments and the number of violent incidents attributed to inter-ethnic tensions rose.
10. The direct election of mayors has been one of the focal points of reform in the area of local self government. Mostar today is one of the rare exceptions where the mayor is still elected indirectly by the city council.
11. In the case of post-conflict situations, the process of state-building is usually not entrusted to local elites (despite wide-spread rhetoric of local empowerment and capacity building) and the intervention of outside experts is seen as a necessity. For critical evaluations of this phenomenon see Chandler (2004, 2006) and Bliesemann de Guevara (2003).
12. Even supporters of a more republican interpretation of citizenship who highlight active participation in community affairs as the distinguishing feature of citizenship in many cases fail to adequately address the underlying assumption that the nation state is the community in question. See Habermas (1999, p. 5f).
13. The outcry of Croat parties at the election of Želko Komšić as the Croat member of the presidency in recent elections is symptomatic. According to them the legitimacy of Komšićs success is questionable because he was elected to the position with Bosniac votes (cf. OHR, 2006b).
14. The relative ease with which such a strategy took hold in BiH might partly be explained by the peculiar similarity it has with older forms of legitimization in the region. The former system of socialist self-management relied heavily on extensive public services and social provisions as a means to achieve legitimacy. In the case of the GDR, implications of the relation between a high level of social provisions and a low level of participation in political decision-making are now being discussed under the term "welfare dictatorship" (cf. Jarausch, 1999). In BiH the influx of humanitarian aid which accompanied the international presence and often functioned as a substitute for social services provided by the state (Stubbs, 2001) aided the perpetuation of such a functional logic.
15. Attempts are often made to create a common identity by the mere use of symbolic means. A good example of such an approach was the elaborate opening ceremony for the reconstructed Old Bridge in Mostar in 2004, which was widely celebrated by the international community as a symbol for re-uniting East and West, Bosniacs and Croats, who would once again live together in a multi-ethnic city. For the city's inhabitants the bridge represents a shared meaning only in so far as its attraction for tourists can be converted into economic benefits. The bridge's symbolic meaning and economic potential continue to be contested. What is more problematic, however, is the tendency of such symbolic identity politics to paint a significantly different picture of community relations, than the ones which are actually created through concrete measures. During the bridge's opening ceremony a community of Mostarians, who would once again freely mix and mingle, was evoked. As pointed out above, the model of conviviality enshrined in the city's statute is one based on interest-representation of relatively closed ethno-national groups, not one of mixing and mingling.

16. Contrary to the long-recognized term refugee, IDPs only recently became the object of specific international human rights policies (Weiss, 1999). The use of the term returnee evolved as a consequence of administrative and statistical needs, only later was it legally defined.
17. The first official and comprehensive registration exercise had taken place in 2000.
18. In 1994 an estimated number of up to 40 000 displaced persons lived in Mostar (Yarwood, 1999, p. 4), according to the first standardized registration of IDPs in the year 2000 Mostar still was home to 7176 households with IDP status. Multiplied with an average household size of 2.8, this would constitute a population of roughly 20 000 IDPs (Information provided by the Herzegovina-Neretva Cantonal Ministry for Human Rights and Refugees). At the moment, there are 1274 persons in Mostar with recognized and confirmed IDP status; this is only about one-third of all households which applied for re-registration in the period from January 2005 until today. 498 households received a negative decision and for another 393 households no decision has been passed yet. These figures were provided by the Office for Social and Housing Affairs of the city administration of Mostar.
19. All quotations are translated by the author. They are part of interviews conducted in Mostar between 2005 and 2006.
20. This discourse on urban-rural distinctions is widespread throughout the region and has been analyzed by a number of scholars. See for example Jansen (2005a) and Bougarel (1999). For earlier remarks on the urban-rural phenomenon see Spangler (1983) and Simić (1983).
21. For the current economic situation in BiH see Bieber (2006, pp. 33–6), for a catalogue of benefits IDPs and returnees are entitled to, see the FBiH law on displaced persons and returnees, especially art. 11. (Zakon FBiH o raseljenim osobama i povratnicima, 2005).
22. Information provided by Mr Dedović, Office of the Federal Institute for Statistics in Mostar. Since 2001, the Statistical Institute no longer publishes estimates for the population according to ethno-national groups.
23. This can be done by looking at the ethno-national composition of the municipalities where population displacements were forcibly carried out (for Mostar the neighboring municipalities of Trebinje, Nevesinje, Gačko, Lubinje, Bileca, and some municipalities in Central Bosnia whose Croat populations fled to the HVO controlled Herzegovina). By adding an estimated percentage of the afflicted ethno-national groups (Bosniacs from the Serb-controlled areas and Croats from Central Bosnia) from these municipalities to the population of Mostar and subtracting an estimated figure of Mostarians who left the country as refugees as well as approximately 20 000 Serbs formerly living in the city, it is possible to have at least an impression of the current composition of Mostar's population. Most of these municipalities had their own urban centers, tough, and the majority of displaced persons lived in settlements classified as urban in the census of 1991. This would refute the thesis of a peasantization of Mostar.
24. A similar tendency was observed in the management of socially owned housing funds before the war. The ability to decide on the distribution of apartments functioned as a means to gain power and influence (cf. Verlič-Dekleva, 1991, p. 111).
25. The assumption being that overcrowded living space in the city first had to be freed by sending rural IDPs back to their pre-war homes before reconstruction and repossession could be undertaken on greater scale within the city.
26. A number of less damaged apartment blocks had indeed been restored soon after the war with the help of European Commission assistance programs.
27. Both are highly significant localities. Protesting in front of the ruins of their former homes added visual and moral weight to their claims. The demonstrations in front of the city hall when sessions of the city council took place were staged as a highly visible way of calling for accountability. Just a year earlier no such possibility to air discontent and to demand accountability was given, as no unified city council did then exist and responsibility for the central zone was avoided by all parties. For the importance of urban space in protest movements see Jansen (2001).
28. Information provided by the protest group on 19 September 2006.
29. For the system of socialist housing provision in Former Yugoslavia and the inequalities it produced see Gantar & Mandič (1991), Mandič (1990) and Caldarović (1991).
30. Starting in the winter of 2005/6 demonstrations were held every second Monday with their location alternating between the protesters' apartment blocks, the seat of the city administration and the city hall. As the protest movement consolidated itself, they gave up demonstrations in favour of regular public meetings, either with various officials or in order to discuss further steps to be undertaken.

31. Private sub-letting was a marginal phenomenon in socialist times since ownership was legally limited to two housing units. Thus, a market for rented housing did not develop (cf. Mandič, 1990, p. 263).
32. See Marshall's classical definition of citizenship consisting of legal, political and social rights (cf. Marshall & Bottomore, 1992; Turner (1993).
33. Whether a model of urban citizenship developed in the context of transnational migration could be applied to the situation in post-conflict BiH would indeed require very careful consideration. In an article which appeared while this contribution was under review Robert Hayden (2007) rightly cautions anthropologists as well as international administrators active in BiH against relying on a naïve cosmopolitanism/multiculturalism. The possibility, that our insights might be impaired by our underlying moral visions, is, however, one that must be risked "if social scientists are to be involved in the process of helping the people of Bosnia establish new social and political solutions that are acceptable to them" (Hayden, 2007, p. 115). It can at least partially be countered by combining macro-level socio-economic data with detailed, ethnographically grounded, research into the complex and often contradictory realities which emerge in post-war BiH. In the case of urban citizenship such an approach, taking into account the situation in other (rural and urban) parts of the country, might lead to the rejection of this model without, however, disqualifying the insights into constructions of belonging in urban settings gained from ethnographic research.

References

Anderson, B. (1991) *Imagined Communities. Reflections on the Origins and Spread of Nationalism*, rev. ed. (London: Verso).

Appadurai, A. (1993) Number in the colonial imagination, in: C.A. Beckenridge & P. van der Veer (Eds), *Orientalism and the Postcolonial Predicament*, pp. 314–339 (Philadelphia, PA: University of Pennsylvania Press).

Bauböck, R. (2003) Reinventing Urban Citizenship, *Citizenship Studies*, 7(2), pp. 139–160.

Bechev, D. & Andreev, S. (2005) Top-down vs Bottom-up Aspects of the EU Institution Building Strategies in the Western Balkans, *SEESOX Occasional Papers* 3, available online at: http://www.sant.ox.ac.uk/esc/esc-lectures/bechev_andreev.pdf

Bieber, F. (2005) Local Institutional Engineering: A Tale of Two Cities, Mostar and Brcko, *International Peacekeeping*, 12(3), pp. 420–433.

Bieber, F. (2006) *Post-War Bosnia. Ethnicity, Inequality and Public Sector Governance* (New York: Palgrave Macmillian).

Bliesemann de Guevara, B. (2003) *External State-building in Bosnia and Herzegovina: A Boost for the (Re-)institutionalization of the State or a Catalyst for the Establishment of Parallel Structures*, available online at: http://www.kakanien.ac.at/beitr/theorie/BbliesemandeGuevara1.pdf

Bose, S. (2002) *Bosnia after Dayton. Nationalist Partition and International Intervention* (London: C. Hurst & Co.).

Bougarel, X. (1999) Yugoslav Wars: "The Revenge of the Countryside." Between Sociological Reality and Nationalist Myth, *East European Quarterly*, 32(2), pp. 157–175.

Bougarel, X; Helms, E. & Duijzings, G. (2007) Introduction, in: X. Bougarel, E. Helms & G. Duijzings (Eds), *The New Bosnian Mosaic. Identities, Memories and Moral Claims in a Post-War Society*, pp. 1–36 (Aldershot: Ashgate).

Bourdieu, P. (1994) Rethinking the State. Genesis and Structure of the Bureaucratic Field, *Sociological Theory*, 12(2), pp. 1–18.

Brubaker, R. (2004) *Ethnicity without Groups* (Cambridge, MA: Harvard University Press).

Caldarović, O. (1991) Socialist Urbanisation and Social Segregation, in: J. Simmie & J. Dekleva (Eds), *Yugoslavia in Turmoil: After Self-management*, pp. 131–142 (New York: Pinter Publishers).

Caplan, R. (2005) *International Governance of War-torn Territories. Rule and Reconstruction* (Oxford: Oxford University Press).

Chandler, D. (2004) The Problems of Nation-Building from Above: Imposing Bureaucratic "Rule from Above", *Cambridge Review of International Affairs*, 17(3), pp. 576–591.

Chandler, D. (Ed.) (2006) *Peace without Politics? Ten Years of International State-building in Bosnia* (New York: Routledge).

Cohn, B. (1987) The Census, Social Structure and Objectification in South Asia, in: B. Cohn, *An Anthropologist Among the Historians and Other Essays*, pp. 224–254 (Oxford: Oxford University Press).

Commission for Reforming the City of Mostar (2003) *Recommendation of the Commission—Report of the Chairman*, available online at: http://www.ohr.int/archive/report-mostar/pdf/Reforming%20Mostar-Report%20(EN).pdf

Dayton Peace Agreement (DPA) (1995) available online at: http://www.ohr.int/dpa/default.asp?content_id=380

European Stability Initiative (ESI) (2004) *Governance and Democracy in BiH: Post-industrial Society and the Authoritarian Temptation*, available online at: www.esiweb.org/index.php?lang=en&id=156&document_ID=63

Everly, R. (2005) Complex Public Power Regulation in Bosnia and Herzegovina after the Dayton Peace Agreement, *Ethnopolitics*, 5(1), pp. 33–38.

Federalni Zavod za Statistiku (2006) *Hercegovačko-Neretvanski Kanton u Brojkama* (Sarajevo: Federalni Zavod za Statistiku).

Fukuyama, F. (2004) *State Building: Governance and World Order in the 21st. Century* (Ithaca, NY: Cornell University Press).

Gantar, P. & Mandič, S. (1991) Social Consequences of Housing Provision: Problems and Perspectives, in: J. Simmie & J. Dekleva (Eds), *Yugoslavia in Turmoil: After Self-management*, pp. 119–130 (New York: Pinter Publishers).

Habermas, J. (1999) Citizenship and National Identity: Some Reflections on the Future of Europe, *Praxis International*, 12, pp. 1–19.

Hann, C. (2003) Is Balkan Civil Society an Oxymoron? From Königsberg to Sarajevo, via Przemsyl, *Ethnologia Balkanica*, 7, pp. 63–78.

Hayden, R. (2007) Moral Vision and Impaired Insight, *Current Anthropology*, 48(1), pp. 105–131.

Heimerl, D. (2006) The Return of Refugees and Internally Displaced Persons: From Coercion to Sustainability?, in: D. Chandler (Ed.), *Peace Without Politics? Ten Years of International State-Building in Bosnia*, pp. 71–84 (New York: Routledge).

International Crisis Group (ICG) (2002) *The Continuing Challenge of Refugee Return in Bosnia & Herzegovina*, Balkans Report No. 137 (Brussels/Sarajevo: ICG).

Jansen, S. (2001) The Streets of Beograd. Urban Space and Protest Identities in Serbia, *Political Geography*, 20, pp. 33–55.

Jansen, S. (2005a) Who's Afraid of White Socks? Towards a Critical Understanding of Post-Yugoslav Urban Self-perceptions, *Ethnologia Balkanica*, 9, pp. 151–167.

Jansen, S. (2005b) National Numbers in Context: Maps and Stats in Representations of the Post-Yugoslav Wars, Identities, *Global Studies in Culture and Power*, 12, pp. 45–68.

Jarausch, K. (1999) Care and Coercion. The GDR as a Welfare Dictatorship, in: K. Jarausch (Ed.), *Dictatorship as Experience. Towards a Socio-cultural History of the GDR*, pp. 45–68 (New York: Berghahn Books).

Mandič, S. (1990) Housing Provision in Yugoslavia: Changing Role of the State, Market, and Informal Sectors, in: W. van Vliet & J. van Weesep (Eds), *Government and Housing: Developments in Seven Countries*, pp. 259–272 (London: Sage Publications).

Marshall, T. H. & Bottomore, T. (1992) *Citizenship and Social Class* (London: Pluto Press).

Ministry for Human Rights and Refugees BiH (MHRR) (2005) *Comparative Analysis of Access to Rights of Refugees and Internally Displaced Persons* (Sarajevo: Ministry of Human Rights and Refugees).

Office of the High Representative (OHR) (2004) Decision on Enacting the Statute of the City of Mostar, Wednesday 28 January, available online at: http://www.ohr.int/decisions/mo-hncantdec/default.asp?content_id=31707

OHR (2006a) Statement by Christian Schwarz-Schilling, the High Representative for BiH at the Press Conference in Mostar, Friday 15 September, available online at: http://www.ohr.int/ohr-dept/presso/pressb/default.asp?content_id=38075

OHR (2006b) All for One an One for All, available online at: http://www.ohr.int/ohr-dept/presso/pressr/default.asp?content_id=38425

Peled, Y. (1992) Ethnic Democracy and the Legal Construction of Citizenship. Arab Citizens of the Jewish State, *American Political Science Review*, 86(2), pp. 432–442.

Pickering, P. M. (2006) Generating Social Capital for Bridging Ethnic Division in the Western Balkans: Case Studies of two Bosniak Cities, *Ethnic and Racial Studies*, 29(1), pp. 79–103.

Scharpf, F. (1999) *Governing in Europe. Effective and Democratic?* (Oxford: Oxford University Press).

Scott, J. (1998) *Seeing Like a State. How Certain Schemes to Improve the Human Condition Have Failed* (New Haven, CT: Yale University Press).

Sharma, A. & Gupta, A. (2006) Introduction, in: A. Sharma & A. Gupta (Eds), *The Anthropology of the State. A Reader*, pp. 1–41 (Oxford: Blackwell Publishing).
Simić, A. (1983) Urbanization and Modernization in Yugoslavia: Adaptive and Maladaptive Aspects of Traditional Culture, in: M. Kenny & D.I. Kertzer (Eds), *Urban Life in Mediterranean Europe: Anthropological Perspectives*, pp. 202–224 (Chicago, IL: University of Illinois Press).
Spangler, M. (1983) Urban Research in Yugoslavia: Regional Variation in Urbanization, in: M. Kenny & D.I. Kertzer (Eds), *Urban Life in Mediterranean Europe: Anthropological Perspectives*, pp. 76–108 (Chicago, IL: University of Illinois Press).
Stubbs, P. (2001) *International Support Policies to South-Eastern European Countries—Lessons (Not) Learned in BH, "Social Sector" or the Diminution of Social Policy?—Regulating Welfare Regimes in Contemporary BH*, available online at: http://www.esiweb.org/pdf/bridges/bosnia/Stubbs_ChVIII.pdf
Turner, B. S. (1993) Contemporary Problems in the Theory of Citizenship, in B.S. Turner (Ed.), *Citizenship and Social Theory*, pp. 1–18 (London: Sage Publications).
United Nations High Commissioner for Refugees (UNHCR) (2005a) Press statement, Re-registration of Displaced Persons in Bosnia and Herzegovina, available online at: http://www.unhcr.ba/press/2005pr/150405.htm
UNHCR (2005b) Preliminary Report on the Number of Applications Filed for Re-registration of Displaced Persons in BiH, available online at: http://www.unhcr.ba/press/2005pr/150405Tab.htm
Verlič-Dekleva, B. (1991) Implications of Economic Change to Social Policy, in J. Simmie & J. Dekleva (Eds), *Yugoslavia in Turmoil: After Self-Management*, pp.107–117 (New York: Pinter Publishers).
Vucina, S. (Ed.) (1992) *Urbicid* (Mostar: Hrvatsko Vijeće Obrane Općine).
Weiss, T. G. (1999) Whither International Efforts for Internally Displaced Persons?, *Journal of Peace Research*, 36(3), pp. 363–373.
Yarwood, J. (1999) Rebuilding Mostar: Urban Reconstruction in a War Zone, *Town Planning Review*, Special Studies 3 (Liverpool: University of Liverpool Press).
Žepić, B. (2003) Problemi, teškoće i perspektive organizacije, funkcioniranja i razvitka Mostara kao jedinice lokalne samouprave, in: Fakultet političkih nauka Univerziteta Sarajevu/Centar za razvoj lokalne i regionalne samouprave (Eds), *Okrugli stol: Položaj i ustrojstvo gradova u Federaciji BiH sa posebnim osvrtom na razvoj lokalne samouprave u gradu Mostaru*, Mostar, 24. maj, pp. 41–56 (Sarajevo: Štamparija FOJNICA).
Zakon FBiH o raseljenim osobama i povratnicima u Federaciji Bosne i Hercegovine i izbjeglicama iz Bosne i Hercegovine (2005), *Službene Novine*, 15(5), 16.03.2005, (Sarajevo).

Informal Ethnopolitics and Local Authority Figures in Osh, Kyrgyzstan

MATTEO FUMAGALLI

University College Dublin, Ireland

This paper seeks to address one of the central puzzles in the study of ethnic conflict: what prevents ethnic violence from (re-)occurring in places with recent history of violent conflict? The absence of violence—although not necessarily conflict—in the city of Osh, site of the largest and bloodiest inter-communal conflicts in post-Soviet Central Asia, is indeed empirically as well as theoretically puzzling. As a result, understanding what happened in post-Soviet Osh constitutes a particularly useful starting point for examining the more general question of identifying the factors that helped maintain inter-ethnic peace.

In June 1990 tensions originating from perceptions of unfairly distributed land and housing erupted in a sudden and short-lived, but particularly bloody, series of riots[1] in the south of the Soviet republic of Kyrgyzstan, then called Kirghizia.[2] Concentrated in the multi-ethnic city of Osh and the nearby town of Uzgen,[3] the Kyrgyz and Uzbek population clashed leaving about 200 people dead, and many more injured in what seemed to herald an era of ethnic conflict in the region (Naumkin, 1994; Rumer & Rumer, 1992). The conflict was not an isolated episode in Central Asia, and the clashes can be located in a broader trend of inter-communal violence and riots which marked the dusk of the Soviet era. Among similar types of events taking place in the USSR at the time, the Osh conflict was one of the largest and most violent (Tishkov, 1995, p. 134).

Kyrgyzstan was among the most ethnically heterogenous republics when the Soviet Union collapsed in 1991. The "titular" community,[4] the Kyrgyz, constituted a bare majority (see Table 1). More than 100 small ethnic groups live in the country. The two largest minority groups, Russians and Uzbeks, represented about 21% and 12.9% of the country's overall population respectively. They were spatially concentrated; the former in the northern regions bordering Kazakhstan, the latter in the southern regions (Osh, Jalalabad and Batken established in 1999), all neighbouring Uzbekistan. The Osh region was home to the largest Uzbek settlement. Various other cleavages were present within the Kyrgyz population, most notably a regional divide northern (Talas, Naryn, Chuy, Ysyk-kol) and southern (Osh, Jalalabad, Batken) regions, as well as clan groupings.[5] The southern city of Osh is a mirror of such complexity and of the challenges and opportunities that ethnically mixed environments present. At about 300 000 inhabitants, Osh is home to Kyrgyz and Uzbeks, as well as to Tajiks, Roma, Russians and other nationalities.

The aim of this paper to understand why this was the case: what prevented violence from re-occurring? Because of space constraints, attention is given primarily to the Uzbek population of Osh.[6] Building on Kalyvas's (2003) research on the interaction between centre and periphery, the study of a particular community and one specific locale and the implications of local issues for national politics constitutes a particularly useful vantage point from which to examine centre-periphery relations in post-Soviet Central Asia. The contribution also examines the interplay between formal and informal institutions in a context (Kyrgyzstan) where initial democratic reforms gradually gave way to a consolidation of authoritarian practices (Huskey, 2002). Formal institutions progressively became more ceremonial, thus making an analysis of the role of informal ones all the more pressing for understanding how politics was conducted outside formal channels. It is the paper's main contention that a full account of Uzbek political behaviour in post-Soviet Osh should pay attention to how formal and informal institutions contributed to prevent the conflict from escalating to violence.

Before proceeding further, it is now important to define the key concepts discussed in the following pages. I have already drawn attention to the distinction operated between

Table 1. Ethnic composition of Kyrgyzstan

	1989 (no.)	1989 (%)	1999 (no.)	1999 (%)
Kyrgyz	2 229 663	52.4	3 128 144	64.9
Russians	916 558	21.5	603 198	12.5
Uzbeks	550 096	12.9	664 953	13.8
Ukrainians	108 027	2.5	50 441	1.0
Germans	101 309	2.4	21 472	0.4
Tatars	70 068	1.6	45 439	0.9
Uighurs	37 318	0.9	46 733	1.0
Kazakhs	36 928	0.9	42 657	0.9
Dungans	36 779	0.9	51 766	1.1
Tajiks	33 518	0.8	42 636	0.9
Other	137 491	3.2	125 499	2.6
Total	4 257 755	100.0	4 822 938	100.0

Source: *Narodnoe khoziaistvo Kirgizskoi SSR* (1982); *Naselenie Kirgizskoi Respubliki* 1999 (Komitet po Statistikoi, 2000).

ethnic conflict and ethnic violence. Following Varshney, the former refers to the condition of ethnically plural societies, democratic and authoritarian, whereby the voicing of various—and potentially clashing—political demands is "more or less inevitable" (2002, p. 24). Conflicts are likely to exist 'over resources, identity, patronage, and policies' (*ibid.*, p. 25). The real issue, Varshney continues (*ibid.*), is whether conflict is "waged in the institutionalised channels [...] of non-violent mobilisation", or instead takes the form of riots or pogroms. Thus, I refer to the 1990 Osh conflict as an episode (or better a series of episodes) of ethnic violence, whereas the subsequent developments, occasionally characterixed by tensions are referred to as "conflict". I accept the fact that because the 1990 riots are now commonly known as "the Osh conflict" there may be some terminological confusion in the text. Second, what is meant by institutions, formal and informal, needs clarification. Institutions are understood as "rules and procedures [...] that structure social interaction by constraining and enabling actors' behaviour" (Helmke & Levitsky, 2004, p. 727). Formal institutions comprise "rules and procedures that are created, communicated, and enforced through channels widely accepted as official" (*ibid.*), whereas informal institutions could be defined as "socially shared rules, usually unwritten, that are created, communicated, and enforced outside of officially sanctioned channels" (*ibid.*)

The paper shows that an analysis of how multi-ethnicity is managed in ethnically plural societies should pay attention to both types of institutions. While an analytical distinction is important, one should be wary to assume that empirically the difference may also be clear-cut. The two are in fact practically intertwined, as the way informal institutions permeate formal channels in the case study of Osh well illustrates. Local authority figures have drawn on their formal role as leaders of official cultural organizations to act as brokers between the local and the national, between their clients and local (Osh) demands and politics at the centre, where they acted as intermediaries between the state authorities and local demands. Patronage politics has "dressed up" as a formal process of group participation to the local and national life of post-Soviet Kyrgyzstan.

The contribution that this paper intends to make is therefore two-fold. First it provides an empirical discussion of a particularly puzzling case study: that of dogs (of nationalism) that did not bark, namely of a setting, the city of Osh, where previous conflict and unresolved ethnic issues seemed to provide fertile ground for a repetition of the conflict. Second, it aims to contribute to the theoretical discussion on management of multi-ethnicity at a local (city) level by emphasizing the salience of informal politics, patronage and leadership, where avenues for participation and/or routinized instrument for conflict management or resolution are absent (Hughes & Sasse, 2001; Melvin, 2001). In so doing, the paper draws from and speaks to both the political science literature, particularly that adopting an institutionalist approach (Helmke & Levitsky, 2004; Hughes & Sasse, 2001; Koopmans, 2000; North, 1990) as well as to scholarly work conducted in post-colonial contexts on patronage politics (Berman, 1997; Brass, 2003; Collins, 2006; Lemarchand, 1972; Powell, 1970; Radnitz, 2006; Scott, 1972; Varshney, 2002; Weingrod, 1968). Here I am less interested in showing how informal institutions inhibit democratization (a subject increasingly discussed in the literature: O'Donnell, 1996; Collins 2003, 2006), and more—following Helmke & Levitsky (2004, p. 728)—in illustrating how, by performing a function that is complementary and at times substitutive (of formal ones), informal and formal institutions interact.

The paper is structured as follows. First I briefly introduce some of the tools used to accommodate ethnic diversity in plural societies. This necessarily entails discussing the question of both territorial and non-territorial autonomy, as a mechanism of conflict prevention, management, and/or resolution and more generally "state-construction" (Weller & Wolff, 2005, p. 1). This is especially relevant because of the role that territorialized ethnicity played in the formation and demise of the Soviet state (Roeder, 1991; Gorenburg, 2003; Beissinger, 2002). Next I examine the formal politics of Kyrgyzstan by discussing how the question of territorial autonomy was progressively sidelined from the public debate, and the extent to which the party system and local governance reforms have provided outlets for ethnic minority institutional representation and participation. The views of the Uzbek minority about perceptions of efficacy of both state and local institutions are then presented. The second part of the paper deals with one particular type of informal institutions relevant to the case study, clientelism,[7] and particularly a sub-type thereof: patron-client relations, which James C. Scott defines as "an informal cluster consisting of a power figure who is in a position to give security, inducements, or both, and his personal followers who, in return for such benefits, contribute their loyalty and personal assistance to the patron's designs" (1972, p. 92). The section focuses on three main examples of patronage politics within the Uzbek community of Osh by discussing how local authority figures have acted as patrons of the local population and have mediated between weak or ineffective formal institutions and group demands.

Methods and Approaches

The contribution concentrates on the city of Osh for two main reasons. First, Osh constitutes a typical case of how ethnopolitics unfolded in post-communist Central Eurasia in the aftermath of the Soviet collapse. Osh closely resembles other Central Asian cities where several ethnic groups have lived intermingled for centuries, and where different identities overlapped and co-existed. The decision to focus here on ethnicity should not be read as an attempt to essentialize or reify one particular form of allegiance of one specific community, but rather as an illustrative example of how local politics plays out in post-Soviet Kyrgyzstan and arguably in analogous settings elsewhere in the region. Second, the case study is relevant because of the precedent of a violent, although short-lived communal conflict, the largest of its kind in the former Soviet space. In many ways the case of Osh seemed to provide a conflict in waiting. The case of the Uzbek community in Kyrgyzstan was indicated by many as being a potential hotbed for conflict and was then warranted often unwelcome and excessive attention.[8] Fortunately this was not the case and though grievances exist among all communities, the situation remained remarkably calm in the post-Soviet period.

I do not make any claim to generalizability or representativeness of the findings generated from a study of ethnopolitics in a single town, but nevertheless I believe that an in-depth study of Uzbek ethnopolitics in Osh sheds important insights on the way ethnic issues are addressed (or not) at a local level and how informal politics balances the shortcomings of formal institutions, thereby contributing to preserve ethnic stability. Data were collected in Osh during two periods of research in 2003 and 2005 (for a total of five months). Methods used include a small-scale survey across the Uzbek population of Osh (61 respondents, comprising elite and ordinary citizens). Survey data were used to measure the general perceptions of efficacy of the main formal institutions, including the national, provincial and city administration, the national parliament, and the Uzbek cultural organizations. It is impossible to establish how widespread perceptions of inefficacy need to be to lead up to outbreaks of violence.[9] Rather, data are used here to highlight how formal institutions are viewed as having little impact on the conditions of the Uzbek community. Semi-structured interviews with members of the local Uzbek elite (46 overall, 34 in 2003 and 12 in 2005) were held after the completion of the survey. A semi-structured format was preferred because it allowed to cover a number of issues listed in a topic guide and at the same time it enabled the respondent to elaborate on a question that he or she deemed relevant. In addition, because of the long-lasting scars that the 1990 conflict left on the local population, I avoided addressing the causes and implications thereof directly. The issue eventually emerged naturally during the interview but came out of the respondent's desire to locate current issues in a historical context.

Because ethnic issues are politically sensitive in the country and because of the difficulty (practical, but also in terms of resources) of achieving a statistically representative sample, I relied on snowballing as a main technique to contact potential informants. While I acknowledge the risk of having a skewed sample (with groups of like-minded people recommending each other) data seem to point to a reasonably varied range of opinions. Finally, it is important to note that ethnic issues have not been object of open debate in Kyrgyzstan, and therefore publicly available data on the topic are scarce. This makes media content analysis a supplementary rather than primary source of information. Interviews and surveys were primarily conducted in Russian language. This was due to two reasons. First the study was part of a larger research involving also non-Uzbek respondents in Kyrgyzstan as well as in neighbouring Tajikistan. Russian continues to be not only the language of inter-ethnic communication, but an idiom that is used on an everyday basis on a number of occasions. While I am not disputing the extent to which state authorities have sought to promote the use of other languages, during my fieldwork I found that speaking Russian would not raise any question by respondents (or request to switch to another language). Second, because the survey was submitted to non-Uzbek respondents and interviews were held with members of other ethnic communities, having comparable data (in the same language) allowed consistency in the research. A final point has to be made with reference to elite interviews: elite groups in the region are culturally Russified, which means that the respondent who would frequently identify himself/herself as Uzbek would not be fluent in Uzbek language. In order to cover all possibilities, I was usually accompanied by an Uzbek speaker who would help fill the many gaps in my stumbling Uzbek.

Soviet and Post-Soviet Territorial Autonomy

Territorial forms of autonomy are but one of the "variety of mechanisms designed to help minorities survive and prosper" (Brunner & Küpper, 2002, pp. 17–32), that is to preserve and/or promote their cultural and political rights. As Weller & Wolff note (2005, p. 1), autonomy, after being long perceived as a "first step onto a slippery slope that inevitably leads towards irredentist or secessionist claims", has gone through a rebirth since the end of the cold war. A "breakdown of mechanisms of external (through the Warsaw Pact Organization) or internal (through dictatorial forms of government) control has led to the re-emergence of the national minority question" (*ibid.*). Hence, autonomy has been rediscovered as a "potential remedy to self-determination claims" and in fact a powerful "tool of state construction [...] addressing the needs of diverse communities" (*ibid.*).

The issue of territorial autonomy appears relevant here because of the particular role that this has played in the construction of the Soviet state, as a pillar in the Soviet ethnofederal structure, and indeed in its demise as well (Hughes & Sasse, 2001; Roeder, 1991). Soviet ethnofederalism, according to which the territory was divided into hierarchically organized units each associated with one particular ethnic group (of which it was supposed to be the historical homeland) defined the institutional design of the Soviet state. [10] Scholars working on the former Soviet Union have paid increasing attention to the importance that ethnic institutions have played in allowing local political entrepreneurs to accumulate economic, cultural and political resources to mobilize the masses along ethnonationalist lines (Beissinger, 2002; Gorenburg, 2003; Roeder, 1991; Slezkine, 1994). In a volume on ethnicity, regions, and territory in the Former Soviet Union, Hughes & Sasse have insightfully examined the importance of the Soviet institutional legacy ("institutionalised multinationality") in the process of post-Sovet state-building (2001, p. 3). In fact, Hughes & Sasse argue, "the Soviet institutional legacy [...] is a crucial factor in the causation of post-Soviet conflicts" (*ibid.*).

Ethnofederalism certainly constitutes an important explanatory factor as to why and how certain conflicts occurred, but others did not. It is important to recall here that according to the "Soviet nationality policies" national groups were supposed to have one and one only homeland (*rodina*). This inevitably meant that "Soviet internal diasporas", or members of ethnic communities to whom Soviet authorities had already granted the state of titular or indigenous (*korennaya*) nation within a given territory (e.g. Uzbekistan for Uzbeks, Kyrgyzstan for Kyrgyz and so forth), were *not* awarded any form of autonomy outside such territories. As a result, Uzbeks living in Osh, which lies in Kyrgyzstan's territory, but a few minutes away form the Uzbekistan–Kyrgyzstan border, were never considered "eligible" for territorial autonomy. In Soviet times Uzbeks used to have the possibility to perform what Marianne Kamp, paraphrasing Benedict Anderson's work, has referred to as "pilgrimages to Tashkent" (2002, p. 273). Uzbeks could "embark" on a visit to the Uzbek capital, receive education there and opt for employment in Soviet Uzbekistan. Such option was hardly hampered from the tightening of the border regime from the Uzbekistani side during the past decade or so. With opportunities to rely on Uzbekistan's institutions dramatically reduced and no explicit conceptualization, let alone implementation of an ethnic policy within Kyrgyzstan, how did Osh Uzbeks cope with transformation? And, more generally, would the Uzbek population of Kyrgyzstan adjust to living in Kyrgyzstan at a time when previous cross-border links had been severed? The lack of territorial autonomy certainly contributed to diminish the resources available for group mobilization. Resource mobilization theory and studies on the Soviet institutional legacy have correctly emphasized the importance that institutional resources (e.g. the presence of local assemblies and governments, the availability of material resources, the official status of language in a particular territory and the status of an ethnic group) have played in the process of late Soviet and early post-Soviet mobilization across the former USSR. This alone does not tell us why the 1990 conflict was more a product of local grievance and local organization than a consequence of cross-border meddling (through Uzbekistani institutions).

It was when coercion and control declined in the dusk of the Soviet era as a result of Gorbachev's perestroika that many ethnic and regional conflicts surfaced. Such was the case of the city of Osh in southern Kyrgyzstan, where a relaxation of Soviet-induced balance between ethnic groups and ethnic stratification of labour (e.g. with Kyrgyz occupied in the administration and Uzbeks in the trade sector) led a breakdown of social order out of increasing economic hardship. After a brief historical background to Soviet Osh, I turn to a discussion of Kyrgyzstan's formal politics since independence.

From Soviet Times to Independence

Osh is one of the largest cities in the Ferghana Valley, a region spanning the borders of Uzbekistan, Kyrgyzstan and Tajikistan, in what is Central Asia's most densely populated area, and one of the more ethnically mixed. The city has been home to several ethnic groups for centuries. Situated at the east-most edge of the Kokand khanate before the Soviet annexation thereof in 1876 (Soucek, 2000), Osh later became the object of a long dispute between the Uzbek and Kyrgyz Soviet Republics[11] which clashed over the right to exercise sovereignty over the city and its population[12]. The importance of Osh at the time lay in its being one of the few industrial centres in the region, and depriving Soviet Kirghizia of the city would have left the republic without any industrial infrastructure, thereby contradicting the Soviet logic of modernization which instead required every Union republic to be nominally viable economically[13]. Economy was but one of the logic driving the Soviet process of national delimitation in Central Asia, the other, often competing, being nationality (Haugen, 2003). Deciding whether Osh would be an Uzbek or Kyrgyz (the two larger ethnic groups at the time) was far from straightforward. In fact, these communities had not developed a clear national consciousness at the time, and religion (Islam) and locality (and lineage for Kyrgyz) were much stronger identity markers for the local population than ethnicity. During the Soviet period claims made in the name of nationality eventually ended up in Moscow and central authorities had to settle, not without difficulty, local disputes[14] by leaving Osh and the eastern part of the Ferghana Valley within Kyrgyz territory (Koichiev, 2003; Haugen, 2003). Although Kyrgyz now constitute the overall majority in post-Soviet Kyrgyzstan (about 65%, Table 1), the southern part of the country is ethnically more heterogeneous (Table 2). This is because the ca. 700 000 Uzbeks living in the country are mostly concentrated in the southern provinces of Osh, Jalalabad and, to a lesser extent, Batken. According to the latest 1999 census data Uzbeks constituted at least one third of the population in the province of Osh (Table 2).

Uzbeks occupied a privileged position in Soviet Uzbekistan, whereas they played a secondary role in the life of the neighbouring republics. As Kamp notes, Uzbeks "could expect access to positions and opportunities within Uzbekistan but did not find doors opened wide within the larger boundaries of the Soviet Union" (2002, p. 273). While Uzbeks could enjoy

Table 2. Ferghana Valley provinces—composition by nationality (1989 census)

	Uzbeks (%)	Tajiks (%)	Kyrgyz (%)	Russians (%)	Total (mln)
Kyrgyzstan	14.2	0.8	60.3	15.7	4.7
Ferghana Valley region	26.7	1.6	73.5	2.7	2.4
Osh province	28.0	2.1	63.8	2.4	1.5
Osh city	40.9	0.4	67.3	3.3	0.9
Jalalabad province	24.5	0.6	29.1	n.a.	0.2

Source: Lubin & Rubin (1999, p. 37).

cultural rights as individuals, no Uzbek autonomous region was established because Uzbeks already enjoyed titular status in the Uzbek SSR. An informal agreement lay at the core of an ethnic stratification of labour and a precarious balance of power which allowed the Kyrgyz to retain their privileged status while not alienating members of the Uzbek community. This meant that, in Soviet times, Uzbeks maintained their niche in the trade and media sectors; at a political level Uzbeks occupied key places in the agriculture and water ministries (Jones Luong, 2002). What changed with independence was that the establishment of five independent states in Central Asia progressively cut off Uzbek co-ethnics from the opportunity of receiving education or finding employment in Uzbekistan.

Cultural commonalities between Uzbeks and southern Kyrgyz did not prevent the outbreak of riots between Uzbeks and Kyrgyz in the southern Kyrgyzstani towns of Osh and Uzgen in June 1990. There was no single cause to the violence. Towards the end of the 1980s, a conjuncture of socio-economic crisis, decreasing living standards, and political destabilization, led to the eruption of inter-communal tensions over the competition for increasingly scarce resources (Tishkov, 1995, p. 135). The triggering factors included disputes over the allocation of land lots and housing. Mass riots broke out on 4 June and were "extinguished" on 10 June 1990 only after armed forces intervened and a state of emergency was declared in the republic (*ibid.*). Perceptions of losses in both socio-economic status, and in political influences resulting from the political changes (related to the distribution of political positions between regionally-based kin networks[15]) constituted the background factors leading to the outbreak of violence (*ibid.*). The unfolding of events was marked by the striking absence of organized groupings. Loose and informal organizations were indeed agitating and inflaming spirits (most notably "Osh Aimagy"—Osh region—among Kyrgyz, and "Adolat"—Justice—among Uzbeks). The conflict had essentially socio-economic causes, but it manifested itself along ethnic lines, and demands started to take on ethnic tones, including requests for recognizing Uzbek as official language or even a request for annexation of parts of territory to Uzbekistan (Spector, 2004, p. 6).

The Osh conflict brought to the attention of the political elites the centrality of interethnic relations for the viability of the country. In fact, Askar Akaev, elected president in October that year, emerged as a candidate who would make inter-ethnic stability a cornerstone of his campaign first and administration later. For large part of the post-independence period, and certainly in the early years of his presidency, Akaev managed to build a broad coalition, attentive not to alienate ethnic minorities, who would otherwise feel under threat from nationalist organizations, on which Akaev himself also depended for support in an uneasy balance between concessions to Kyrgyz nationalists and attempts to integrate ethnic minorities.[16]

The Kyrgyzstani leadership and particularly former President Akaev made an effort to implement his vision of Kyrgyzstan as a "common home" for all ethnic groups. As the following section shows, some progress was made to make formal institutions receptive of the country's multi-ethnic composition. However, goodwill and gestures were not sufficient to settle disputes which became increasingly politicized, such as the issue of language status, outlined below.

The Controversy over Language Status

The controversy over the status of the Uzbek language well illustrates how issues related to ethnicity are extremely politicized and potentially explosive in Kyrgyzstan (Dave,

2004). Following the elevation of Kyrgyz to the status of the republic's sole official language in 1989, a transitional period was initially set in place until 31 December 1998, when the actual replacement of Russian with Kyrgyz would become effective. The transitional period passed without leading to a diminished use of Russian. With one in a hundred Slavs being fluent in Kyrgyz and with an elite still predominantly Russian-speaking (Dave, 2004. pp. 138, 142), the debate over the use and status of Russian remains central in Kyrgyzstani politics. In 2000, Russian was finally given official language status. This measure was meant to reassure ethnic minorities and emphasize the multi-ethnic and harmonious nature of the country. On the other hand, it represented the acknowledgement from the state leadership that measures aimed at enhancing the position of Kyrgyz had simply failed. The majority of the population remained comfortable with the use of Russian. The debate on language(s) in Kyrgyzstan clearly shows that it has always been an "affaire à deux", between the Kyrgyz and Russian languages, and that the state has failed to address the situation of the Uzbek language (*ibid.*, p. 122).

The demographic composition of the country has significantly changed over the past decade or so, and while the Russian population has decreased dramatically, demographic growth and the relative balance shift between groups has made the Uzbek population the second largest community in the republic.[17] This created expectations among the Uzbek population that the Uzbek language might also be elevated to official status. However, as Dave (2004) notes, not only this has never been the case, but the very idea of elevating the status of Uzbek has never made it onto the negotiating agenda, leaving the hopes of the Uzbek community dashed. The reason for this was the widespread concern among Kyrgyz that an initial concession to the large Uzbek community may usher in a series of further demands, possibly leading to calls for Uzbek cultural autonomy or the establishment of an Uzbek region (*ibid.*, p. 144).

Formal Politics in Kyrgyzstan

It is not the aim of the paper to examine the complexity of state–group relations in Kyrgyzstan and I will limit myself here to cover three main issues that appear relevant to a debate on the management of multi-ethnicity at a local level:

- the party system and institutional representation;
- the question of territorial autonomy;
- local governance reforms and other institutional arrangements.

The Party System in Kyrgyzstan and Institutional Representation

The party system is still in its embryonic form in Kyrgyzstan. In fact it is not possible to speak of political parties in terms of formal organizations, with relatively well-defined ideological platforms, programmes, membership, internal structure and institutionalization, and a capillary presence across the country.[18] On the contrary, political parties appear to be ideologically vaguely defined, personalized, and inactive in the periphery except for during the electoral campaigns (Abazov, 2003, p. 559). The current political formations are now inter-ethnic in terms of membership or that they put forward an agenda which favours a civic notion of Kyrgyzstani identity. Quite the contrary, political parties and organizations are now *de facto* overwhelmingly Kyrgyz. Ordinary members are predominantly ethnic Kyrgyz and so are party officials occupying senior positions, sidelining minority groups from political and party life, which contributes to fuel Uzbek frustration.

The fact that no Uzbek party exists should not suggest that representation of Uzbek interests is non-existent, however. Eight Uzbek deputies, six Slavs and six belonging to other minority groups were elected to the national parliament—alongside 85 Kyrgyz—in the first 1995 elections. In other terms, about 41% of the population (non-Kyrgyz) won as little as 19% of seats (Dave, 2004, p. 137). The following legislature (2000–2005) included five Uzbek deputies, pointing to a decline from the previous parliamentary elections. One should note that in 2000 all deputies were elected in Osh electoral districts, leaving Jalalabad Uzbeks without representation.[19] The latest elections (2005) saw an increase in the number of Uzbek deputies elected to the parliament (seven, up from the previous five, out of a total of 75 deputies). In Kyrgyzstan there are Uzbek deputies in the city and provincial assemblies, but none in senior positions (deputy) could be found in the southern provinces as of Summer 2003. By the mid-1990s, Uzbeks occupied less than 5% of key posts in provincial administrations (*ibid.*, 2004, p. 145). The situation does not appear different in the local judiciary where only a handful of Uzbeks could be identified, as reported by an Uzbek lawyer who was working there in 2003.[20] Uzbek representation appeared to improve in the early aftermath of the so-called "Tulip revolution", as the convoluted process that lead to the ousting of then President Akaev was later referred to. Anvar Artykov, an ethnic Uzbek, became governor of the Osh province; ethnic Uzbeks now serve as deputies in the offices of the mayor and governor. Artykov's remotion in December 2005 was a major blow to the most active Uzbek political figure during the March events and raised an alarm bell with regard to the place Uzbeks might occupy in post-Akaev Kyrgyzstan. At a national level the situation was no better, with Bakhodir Fattakhov alone occupying a senior position (deputy) in the ministry of transport and Alisher Sabirov sitting in a number of committees (but mostly dealing with religious issues).

Territorial Autonomy: Solution or Stigma?

It is worth recalling that the Kyrgyzstani Uzbek population resided almost entirely in the southern part of the country, and in some border districts constitutes the majority. In 1990, requests for land swaps with Uzbekistan, or even autonomy, if not outright secession, were voiced before and in the immediate aftermath of the June riots.[21] Particularly active in mobilizing the more radical elements of the Uzbek community and in voicing such demands was "Adolat", the informal organization created by Uzbek nationalist intellectuals in the late 1980s. If at the time requests for territorial autonomy or even outright secession did not appear totally unrealistic, they progressively waned from the Uzbek agenda. Lack of support from Uzbekistan[22] and pragmatism eventually prevailed and Uzbeks—willingly or reluctantly—adjusted to the idea of being citizens of independent Kyrgyzstan. During the various research trips conducted over a number of years in the region (in Kyrgyzstan, but also in neighbouring Uzbekistan) it emerged that the number of Uzbeks who openly support the idea of institutionalizing Uzbek autonomy is marginal at best. The following are commonly held views on the topic from members of the Uzbek community in Osh:

"We do not need autonomy."
"Acknowledging our cultural demands is enough."

"Autonomy is dangerous."
"Autonomy leads to secession."[23]

Uzbeks have been traditionally wary of making any move that might be interpreted from the Kyrgyz authorities as 'disloyal'. Rather than developing a critical stance towards state authorities, local Uzbek leaders have openly supported the Akaev adimistration. It is important to emphasise the shadow cast by experiences of ethnofederalism elsewhere in the former Soviet territory, where institutionalized autonomy provided local political entrepreneurs with critical political and cultural resources to mobilize the population. This Soviet legacy did not pass un-noticed, but rather shaped the way territorial autonomy has been perceived by the local population. It is worth mentioning, however, that although Osh never became separate from the rest of the country, geographic separation *within* Osh was in fact achieved after the 1990 events. As one of the causes behind the conflict lay in perceptions of unfair allocation of land and housing, Kyrgyz authorities gave new land to the Kyrgyz (in the Ak-Tilek district of town) and Uzbeks (in Turon) in the hopes of avoiding future clashes.[24] Although these were avoided, the move should not be taken in isolation, but rather placed in the broader context of the local and national authorities' efforts to prevent tensions from escalating. Whether imposing physical separation between communities is an effective measure to manage conflicts in the long term is, of course, debatable.

Local Governance and Other Institutional Arrangements

Since independence, Kyrgyzstani authorities have spent considerable time and resources on conceiving and implementing reforms aimed at enhancing local governance. Timid reforms introduced in the 1990s brought some re-thinking to the state of centre-regions relations. The 1991 law transferred local government powers to local councils; these, however, appeared incapable to mediate between local and national interests (Alymkulov & Kulatov, 2002, p. 525). Omuraliev notes that local government reforms have failed to provide innovative solutions as they maintained the existence of a Soviet-style "power vertical" (2002), leaving the mechanisms for dealing with centre-regions conflicts as well as local issues, including ethnic ones, undeveloped.

The establishment of the Assembly of the People of Kyrgyzstan (APK) in 1994 constituted a first opening to ethnic minorities by the then president Akaev. The institution was set up as an advisory body to the president on ethnic issues and included a series of public organizations (national-cultural centres), each representing an ethnic group. Uzbeks were represented by the Uzbek National-Cultural Centre (*O'zbek Milliy Madaniyat Markazi*, UNCC hereafter). The APK was based in the capital Bishkek, and local branches were opened in Osh and Jalalabad. While interviews held with various member of the Uzbek population show that they are aware of the APK, data from a survey conducted by the author in the summer 2003 (Table 3)[25] suggest that similarly to other formal institutions, the APK as a whole and the Uzbek cultural organizations were not viewed as actors capable to effectively respond to the demands of minority groups, with just about one-third of the respondents considering them as either effective or very effective. The quandary here is obviously that perceptions of effectiveness may not reflect the actual effectiveness of an institution or an organization.[26] I do not dispute that this may be the case even here, but the

Table 3. How effective are the following institutions/organizations in dealing with Uzbek-related issues?

Institution	Effective/very effective	Not effective	Don't know
State administration	35.6	57.8	6.7
Parliament	29.5	59.1	11.4
Provincial administration	36.6	53.7	9.8
Assembly of the People of Kyrgyzstan	28.9	71.1	–
Uzbek national-cultural centre	26.1	59.5	14.3
Society of Uzbeks	35.7	42.9	21.4

Table 4. Are Uzbeks adequately represented in state organs (*gos-struktura*)?

Yes	No	Don't know
6.7%	80.0%	13.3%

Table 5. Do Uzbeks enjoy fewer rights than Kyrgyz?

Yes	No	Don't know
62.1%	24.1%	13.8%

data presented appear to be in line with a constant feeling of marginalization by the Uzbek community in Osh and in Kyrgyzstan more generally (Fumagalli, 2005).[27]

Data presented in Tables 4 and 5 confirm the impression that Uzbeks are far from satisfied with the current level of representation in state organs and that overall they appreciate that equal rights may be formally extended to all citizens, reality on the ground may be less balanced towards members of the Uzbek community. This does not mean that Uzbeks, or even other minority groups, view the situation in the country as one of formal discrimination; in fact, according to Omuraliev (2002), only a small percentage (33%) of the respondents in a poll conducted by the Bishkek-based Institute of Regional Studies openly support this view.

Summary

A survey of formal politics in Kyrgyzstan shows that state authorities were aware of the challenges posed by the presence of disenfranchized ethnic communities to the country's stability. Formal institutions that aimed at addressing the issue have been introduced. Formal politics should not therefore be dismissed as irrelevant even as the country backtracked from initial democratic reforms to authoritarian practices during the middle of the past decade. Irrelevant or not, field research highlights a clear sense of ineffectiveness of formal institutions among the Osh Uzbek community, which raises an obvious question: if grievances persisted throughout the post-independence period and formal institutions were either absent or viewed as ineffective, why did tensions not erupt? An analysis of formal institutions in authoritarian systems only tells us part of the story. What remains un-accounted for at the moment is an understanding of how the Uzbek community responded to institutional weakness or ineffectiveness, and it is only by shifting the attention to informal politics and specifically to local authority figures that a fuller picture of Uzbek ethnopolitics in post-Soviet Kyrgyzstan becomes evident.

Informal Politics and Local Authority Figures: Uzbek Leaders and Patron–Client Relations

This section brings patronage politics into the analysis of Uzbek ethnopolitics in Osh. Relations between patrons (political leaders, businesspeople, members of the intellectual community) and clients (ordinary Uzbeks) have created an additional channel for influence on state authorities beyond formal institutions. Local authority figures in Osh have mediated between a weakening state and the demands of the local Uzbek community. The mechanisms through which informal institutions impact on formal ones and shape Uzbek ethnopolitics, as well as their implications for are illustrated by reference to three main figures who have played a significant role within the local Uzbek community and in Kyrgyzstani politics as a whole: Mukhammadjan Mamasaidov, Alisher Sabirov and Davron Sabirov (no relation between the two).

Among Uzbek leaders, Mukhammadjan Mamasaidov has certainly been the one most closely associated with the Akaev regime. Mamasaidov has chaired the UNCC from the late 1990s until he resigned in 2005 following the electoral frauds in the parliamentary electoral round in February and March that year—which ultimately led to Akaev's ousting. Mamasaidov has contributed to shape the strategy of the main Uzbek organization in Osh and elsewhere in Kyrgyzstan. Mamasaidov's emphasis has been on the higher education sector, where his contribution has been more evident. The Kyrgyz-Uzbek University (KUU), a joint project of the governments of Uzbekistan and Kyrgyzstan, was established in 1997, for which he lobbied the authorities. The KUU provides tuition in secondary and higher education and is host to more than 14 000 students in 47 subjects (Mamasaidov & Khudayberdiev, 2003). Linked to the UNCC are also the particularly active Uzbek theatre "Babur" and the Centre for Textbook Production (a printing house established in 1998), based at the KUU, which seeks to address one of the most pressing concerns of the Uzbek population: the lack of textbooks in the Uzbek language. Mamasaidov has not been leading figure in the Uzbek cultural elite, but due to his status as the national chair of the UNCC he has benefited from large access to the state leadership and particularly Askar Akaev has been able to act (or be perceived as) the intermediary between the ordinary population and the "state".

Mamasaidov's alter ego is Davron Sabirov. While the former has taken a more conciliatory stance towards the authorities, the latter has occasionally resorted to the use of nationalist frames to mobilize the Uzbek community and raise his profile and that of the organization he leads, the Society of Uzbeks. Previously a leading figure in the local youth communist organization (*Komsomol*), D. Sabirov was appointed deputy mayor of Osh in 1989 (Radnitz, 2006, p. 10). He was later elected at the Kyrgyz Supreme Soviet and then regularly at the national parliament. At the same time he developed links that he had forged in the late Soviet era while working for a gas company and became involved in gas imports from Russia and Kazakhstan (*ibid.*). He also maintained close relations with partners in the gas sector in Andijan on the Uzbekistani side of the border, Sabirov recalls.[28] It was in fact thanks to these links that he managed to circumvent the frequent Uzbekistan-imposed energy cuts to Kyrgyzstan's supplies during the mid-1990s. While most of the city's homes were left without gas, Sabirov, then head of the Osh branch of KyrgyzGas, negotiated with his Uzbekistani counterpart and succeeding in having gas supplies restart. However, apparently only Uzbek-populated districts received gas supplies, some local analysts report.[29] Unlike Mamasaidov, who retained a primarily cultural focus, Davron Sabirov embarked on a whole range of activities, including the construction of a mosque and a school in the Amir Temur district. A combination of inflammatory rhetoric (at least until 2000[30]) and philanthropic activities earned him a reputation as a local Uzbek hero. The findings of a survey conducted by the local newspaper, *Demos Times*, seem to confirm D. Sabirov's status as the most popular figure among the Uzbek population (Table 6).[31]

Another important figure among Osh Uzbeks is that of Alisher Sabirov. After a past in the security services of the Ministry of Internal Affairs (Radnitz, 2006, p. 11), A. Sabirov added a series of business activities (most notably, restaurants) to his political career. Since 1995, A. Sabirov has been a deputy at the national parliament. His mother chairs the Bishkek branch of the UNCC and more recently his wife Hulkar entered the Osh city council. The Sabirovs have embarked in a wide range of philantropic activities in the city of Osh which have benefited several areas of the city, including their own mahalla (neighbourhood) and Alisher Sabirov's own constituency (more recently, the deeply impoverished Amir Temur, at the southern outskirts of the city). These included the establishment of a charity (*Elim Uchun*, "For my people"), payment of welfare benefits to the more economically deprived households of their constituency, the concession of micro-credit, and the opening of a sewing workshop where about 75 people were employed (*ibid.*). It comes with no surprise, then, that Hulkar Sabirova was elected virtually unopposed to the city council, and her husband Alisher also won his seat in the controversial 2005 elections.[32] At a national level Alisher Sabirov has advised a number of NGOs and international organizations on the inter-ethnic relations in Kyrgyzstan and has led the committee on religious affairs for a number of years[33].

Mamasaidov, Davron and Alisher Sabirov constitute a clear example of how informal and formal institutions are practically intertwined. All three occupy a formal role in Kyrgyzstan's local as well as national politics; they are leading members of the official organizations, they sit in the parliament and occupy formal positions in local universities. However, findings presented earlier in these pages suggest that formal institutions are seen as either weak or ineffective by the local population. What is noteworthy here is that Mamasaidov and the Sabirovs have not resigned and left such posts. Instead, they have used their official status in three key ways. First, they have acted as patrons of the local Uzbek population by providing key benefits and *de facto* complementing if not

Table 6. Trust in local Uzbek leaders

Name/no. of respondents	Who should be the leader of the UNCC?	Who should be re-elected in the national parliament?	Who deserves to be member of the parliament?
M. Mamasaidov	87	178	104
B. Juraev	39	139	78
D. Sabirov	181	362	174
A. Sabirov	83	234	60
I. Abdurasulov	29	–	189

openly substituting a weak or absent state. Second, they have made themselves of critical importance to their own patrons, namely the president and the ruling elites because they are viewed as being "in control" of the Uzbek community. An ethnic minority under their "supervision" was a "safe" or trouble-free community. Third, patrons have turned themselves into brokers between local and national demands and politics.

Informal institutions have permeated formal ones. This finding sits well with research conducted on the salience of regional groups in Central Asia before and after the Soviet collapse (Jones Luong, 2002). Pauline Jones Luong has very insightfully shown how pacts between the national elites and the president in particular on the one hand, and regional leaders on the other, have defined post-Soviet transformation in Kyrgyzstan. Regional leaders have made themselves seemingly indispensable for maintaining power and control. Analogous relations, between the three patrons considered and their respective clients operate at a lower level too.

This section has shown that patronage politics in Kyrgyzstan works *all the way down from the national centre to the periphery*. Let there be no misunderstanding here: patron–client relations are structurally unequal. Benefits are exchanged with loyalty, which makes patrons and clients mutually dependent. At the same time, by building on local support, patrons enhance their visibility, their status and their bargaining power *vis-à-vis* the authorities at the centre. Self-aggrandisement rather than generosity is their driving motive. Control of a potentially unstable periphery is an invaluable prize in a multi-ethnic polity such as Kyrgyzstan and being perceived by the state authorities as a "bulwark" against instability is a valuable asset.

What are the implications of patronage politics for the stability of the country and of the larger Central Asian region? In a recent analysis of the process of state deconstruction in Kyrgyzstan and Uzbekistan, Scott Radnitz shows how Central Asian states are likely to be increasingly "governed by patron–client relations outside of the state apparatus" (2006, p. 2). Autonomous elites can use their income and ties to other political figures to "develop an independent base among the populace". The argument resonates well with the case of Uzbek ethnopolitics in Osh. As Radnitz remarks, [Uzbek elites] "have an incentive to provide public good and private assistance that the state can no longer provide to its citizens. Elites earn the loyalty of the communities they patronise, which they can 'cash in' through votes" (*ibid.*). Radnitz well captures the consolidation of local patron–client networks that have emerged in post-Soviet Kyrgyzstan and notes how they may be a response to a breakdown of state power and indeed suggests that they contribute to further state withdrawal (*ibid.*, p. 4). State implosion in the late 1980s and early 1990s was among the key factors leading to the breakdown of social order in Soviet Osh. At the time, however, no ethnic cultural organizations were present (the UNCC was established just a few months after the events, in September 1990). In addition, local figures contributed to foment nationalist frames among the more radical elements of the Uzbek population.

Establishing formal institutions has allowed local authority figures access to the system (and the resources thereof). This has not translated in democratic participation or in the open airing of demands and grievances. It has, however, enabled local patrons to act (to their own benefit, of course) as "social safety nets" in societies where Soviet rigid mechanisms of control and coercion had imploded and no routinized instruments of conflict resolution had been established. Put simply, they have contributed to make the fall-out from the Soviet collapse somehow less painful and less uncertain for the local population. In so doing they have performed a crucial stabilizing function in the country. At the same time, as Radnitz notes, by filling the gap left by state withdrawal local patrons have performed a function which at the same time complements and substitutes formal institutions, *de facto* blurring the lines in Helmke & Levitsky's quadripartite typology (2004).

The section concludes by addressing a question that has been made particularly actual by the elite re-alignment that has followed the March 2005 events,[34] but that research conducted in 2003 had already identified: to what extent do the local patrons considered do really represent the Uzbek community? Table 6 seems to suggest that they do, particularly Davron Sabirov. Follow-up interviews, however, seem to qualify this statement and actually point to a wider diversity of views:

Davron Sabirov does not represent anyone. He is a populist.[35]

Mamasaidov is not an Uzbek: He is a Kyrgyz![36]

Look at what [Davron] Sabirov does: he goes to Amir Temur [a completely Uzbek district at the periphery of Osh, arguably the poorest area in town], he brings a bus there and takes people to vote]. Who do you think they vote for?" "He only cares about his personal interest: he founded his own TV and newspaper [Mezon TV and Mezon] and after being elected he shut his own newspaper because he did not need it anymore.[37]

What the comments above illustrate is first of all the variety of opinions within the Uzbek community—which should not be understood as a cohesive whole or a unitary actor simply because of common ethnic bonds, but also that patrons should not take their status for granted. Although they have performed two critical functions in the post-independence period (distributing services and goods in return for political loyalty shown during elections) and acting as brokers between their clients and state authorities at the centre, research conducted in 2003 and 2005 points to a progressive uncoupling between leaders and lead. There is no space here to examine this disjuncture in detail,[38] but suffices it here to say that there are Uzbeks, particularly women, who are increasingly active in civil society organizations which are unrelated to the state or to the local Uzbek organizations. There are also elements, mostly academics, intellectuals and students who gravitate around the Uzbek philology department at Osh State University who appear increasingly disaffected with the Uzbek leadership, perceived as ineffective and too complacent towards the state authorities.

Did anything change in the aftermath of the 2005 events that lead to the ousting of former President Akaev? The extent to which the Uzbek population played an active role in the events is highly disputed.[39] The initial involvement of southern political elites (including Kurmanbek Bakiev, then elected president in July 2005, who is originally from Suzak, an area of compact Uzbek settlement) and of Uzbek leaders (Anvar Artykov was briefly named governor of the Osh region from March to December 2005) seemed to suggest a new era in state–community relations. More recently, instead, the situation seems to have taken a turn for the worse. Artykov was forced to leave his post and in January 2006 the Jalalabad Uzbek Cultural Centre (headed by the local businessman, philanthropist and patron Kadyrjan Batyrov) sent a petition to the state authorities pointing to the rise in anti-Uzbek discrimination following the so-called revolution (Rotar, 2006). It is of course too soon to evaluate the impact of the ousting of the Akaev regime on interethnic relations and to speculate whether this points to a new rift in Kyrgyz–Uzbek relations.

Although the situation is still in flux, a re-alignment of political actors has indeed followed, with older authority figures discredited by their association with the previous regime (Mamasaidov and Alisher Sabirov) and challenged by new competitors for leadership. The fate of yet another Uzbek authority figure epitomises the contradictions that followed the so-called "Tulip revolution" as well as the Uzbek population's unease and ambivalence towards it. Despite depicting himself as a "revolutionary" and heading to Moscow to receive the resignation letter from Askar Akaev,[40] the Jalalabad-based businessman and deputy at the national parliament Kadyrjan Batyrov soon "retreated" to safer patron–client relations with his loyal constituency in the southern city of Jalalabad, where he chairs the local Uzbek organization, funds the local private Batyrov University, and owns a private airline (Batyr-Avia); similarly to Osh patrons, Batyrov exchanges favours and services with political loyalty (he was elected deputy in the March 2005 elections).

Competing Explanations

Before heading towards a conclusion, it is necessary to consider, briefly given space constraints, possible alternative explanations. What difference did informal institutions actually make in terms of preventing ethnic violence from re-occurring? Opportunities to "perform pilgrimages to Tashkent" were curtailed by Uzbekistan's increasingly tight border regime, making it difficult for Osh Uzbeks to benefit of Uzbekistan's resources in the same way as they did in Soviet times. Cross-border links continued to some extent, but Uzbekistan's increasingly authoritarian system (compared to Kyrgyzstan's softer one) and Tashkent's neglect of Uzbek co-ethnics abroad made any separatist scenario in the post-independence period totally unrealistic. If anything, by abstaining from intervening, Uzbekistan played a stabilizing role in the issue.

Exhaustion could be seen as a factor helping to preserve ethnic peace. Data suggest that grievances continued in the post-independence period and political conflict, although not violence, occasionally resurfaced. Given persisting grievances what changed was an opportunity to have some demands met, even if outside the formal channels of political participation. In the months preceding the Soviet collapse, political order was breaking down. Akaev engaged in a complex process of reconstruction of order and consolidation of a fragile republic. With all his shortcomings and contradictions, the Akaev regime managed to preserve a balance between groups by never allowing grievances to spill out of control. More than exhaustion it is the memory of and the pain for the past conflict that are worth mentioning here. Could it then be that leaders of the various ethnic communities actually went through a process of learning? Perhaps, but Davron Sabirov's acknowledgement that he did consciously use nationalist frames strategically in the 2000 electoral campaign to mobilize the Uzbek vote in his favour does not suggest reflexivity.[41] Quite the contrary, the persistence of patron–client relations combined with the leader's strategic calculation suggests that patrons may be able to mobilize clients *ad hoc*, whenever needed. This is also improbable as clients would be little more than pawns. Clients, as well as patrons, are conscious political agents, not passive recipients of the actions of the leader.

Conclusion

The contribution has sought to build on the requests that institutional analysis incorporate the study of both formal and informal institutions (Helmke & Levitsky, 2004; Lauth, 2000). Insights from the literature on patron–client relations in post-colonial societies (Berman, 1998; Lemarchand, 1972; Scott, 1972; Weingrod, 1968) and more recently in post-Soviet Central Asia (Collins, 2003, 2006; Radnitz, 2006) have been particularly useful in designing a study that focuses on one empirical case only (Osh), and at the same time aims to answer a more general question of interest to scholars of ethnic conflict: why do episodes of violence occur in some circumstances and not others, and what prevents them from re-occurring?

The findings presented in this contribution lead to the following conclusive remarks. First, the case of local authority figures in the Osh Uzbek community has shown not only that informal institutions matter, but how they do so. In particular attention has been given to the way in which formal and informal politics are closely intertwined. There is no disjuncture between formal and informal,[42] but informal institutions permeate formal ones. Informal leaders in the periphery occupy a formal role and it is this formal role that grants them access to power, status, resources, and links to their own patrons at the centre. Formal institutions, as a result, appear of critical importance. Their absence in 1990 and more generally the collapse of Soviet institutions helps making sense of why the 1990 events took place. Although no panacea, the establishment of a number of institutions by the Akaev regime has helped preserve the peace. Equally, informal institutions matter because, in light of persisting grievances and state weakness, patronage politics has created spaces for political action and for achieving goals even where little formal space actually exists. This is in line with the findings of Hughes & Sasse's comparative analysis of the presence and absence of conflict in the post-Soviet space (2001, pp. 24–25). The case of Osh confirms that it is not just formal institutions that structure incentives for political behaviour, but a "combination of formal and informal institutionalised autonomy that constitute a device for managing regional and ethnic challenges" (*ibid.*).

Second, this type of politics in the periphery is built on profoundly unequal relationships between the authority figures and ordinary members of the community. With this regard this study of Uzbek ethnopolitics in Osh highlights how local patrons and clients (the wider Uzbek community) have developed a relationship which benefits both, albeit in unequal measure. Local authority figures have been able to develop their own power base thanks to their links to the system, which allow them access to resources, as well as to the local otherwise disempowered minority. The favours this receives contribute to alleviate grievances and provide a temporary, although thus far relatively effective way of managing multi-ethnicity. In addition, this paper has shown that informal authority figures perform a role which is often substitutive of the one that formal institutions are normally expected to do. This is not without consequences for the country's stability, capacity or even democratization prospects. Surely both benefit to some extent. Ordinary Uzbeks benefit from the establishment of schools, provision of textbooks, access to university, media in Uzbek language. Patrons benefit from political loyalty which is "presented" to them during electoral campaigns.

Third, what emerges very clearly from a study of local authority figures and patron–client relations is that referring to an "Uzbek community" actually reifies it. Uzbeks in Osh, and arguably elsewhere in the republic, constitute a highly heterogeneous group. It is not a unitary actor; competing voices struggle to be heard. Some of them (those of the patrons) are successful, whereas others are almost silenced by the lack of resources. This calls for further research to be conducted on the diversity of ethnic groups and the mechanisms through which political elites establish and consolidate control over the community and marginalize competing voices and actors. Illustrating the variety of communities traditionally perceived as cohesive has critical implications for understanding the many strategies of participation, engagement or resistance, often at play at the same time.

Fourth, and in conclusion, the study of local authority figures in post-Soviet Osh has shown the importance of local-level ethnopolitics to understand, and address, larger issues of state and regional stability in Central Asia. The periphery (the "local") constitutes a useful prism through which to look at the specific dynamics at play on the ground, but also an oft-neglected departure point for observing larger processes at the centre as well as the interaction between the centre and the local itself.

Acknowledgements

The author wishes to acknowledge the support from the Economic and Social Research Council, the British Academy, the British Association for Slavonic and East European Studies and the British International Studies Association for their generous support to this research. The author is also grateful to Scott Radnitz, Indraneel Sircar, the editors and the anonymous reviewers of *Ethnopolitics* for their valuable comments to earlier drafts of this paper.

Notes

1. By riot is meant here a kind of conflict involving 'no structured armed forces and organized long-term fighting' (Tishkov, 1995, p. 148, fn. 1).
2. Kirghizia was better suited to Russian pronunciation. Since independence the country has been known as either Kyrgyzstan or Kyrgyz Republic (used interchangeably).
3. The conflict spread to other villages in the surroundings of Osh and Uzgen (Tishkov, 1999, p. 581).
4. In Soviet parlance this indicates the community after which the country was named.
5. There are three main clusters of clans in the country: Ong (concentrated in the south), Sol (north and west), and Ichkilik (south) (Dukenbayev & Hansen, 2003, pp. 25–26).
6. Studies discussing the perspectives of Kyrgyz, Russians and other groups include Faranda & Nolle (2003), Alisheva *et al.* (1999) and Elebayeva *et al.* (2000).
7. Clientelism can be defined as a form of social interaction that derives from "a specific, personally stratified relationship, [...] bound to fixed roles and dominance structures" (Lauth, 2000, p. 27).
8. See Megoran (2000a) for a critique of this "Ferghana Valley conflictology".
9. I am grateful to one of the reviewers of the journal for raising this point.
10. Units at the higher end of the hierarchy (the 15 union republics) enjoyed greater cultural and political autonomy than those subject to them (e.g. autonomous republics, autonomous provinces, etc.).
11. Originally Soviet Kirghizia enjoyed the status of autonomous province (oblast') within the Russian Soviet Republic, being two degrees lower in terms of autonomy compared to Uzbekistan along the Soviet hierarchy of territorial autonomy. Kirghizia was finally upgraded to full Union status (SSR) in 1936.
12. Koichiev (2003) and Haugen (2003) extensively cover the territorial disputes over Osh in 1926–1927.
13. Of course this was not the case in practice where all the republics were tied in an economic specialization.
14. In her insightful research on border-making in Soviet Central Asia, Francine Hirsch (2005) shows how claim-making was made in the name of nationality, contributing to embedding national consciousness in the minds of populations that until then had hardly viewed themselves as members of clearly distinct communities.

15. There is a considerable debate as to the appropriate term to be used in this circumstance: Collins seems to prefer the more popular "clan" (2002 and 2003) whereas Radnitz opts for "strategic groups" (2005) and Olivier Roy for regionally-based kin networks (1997).
16. This paradox is illustrated by the emphasis given by Kyrgyzstani authorities to both Manas as historical figure and hero of the Kyrgyz people and the inclusive concept of "Kyrgyzstan our common home", which implies a non- ethnic substratum in state ideology (Megoran, 2002).
17. The balance shift is evident when one compares the ethnic composition of the country in 1989 (Uzbeks: 12.9%; Russians: 21.5%) with that of 1999 (1999 Census).
18. Not that this is anymore valid in Western context any way.
19. Declaration of the Uzbek Kurultai in Jalalabad 2002 (Khamidov, 2002).
20. About four, as of summer 2003 (interviews held with lawyers working at the Osh judiciary, 16 July 2003).
21. Pravda (1990) and Sovetskaya Kirghizia (1990) quoted in Asankanov (1996).
22. This is also examined elsewhere in Fumagalli (2007b, forthcoming).
23. Interviews held with members of the Uzbek community in southern Kyrgyzstan (June–July 2003 and August 2005).
24. I am grateful to Scott Radnitz for pointing out this aspect to me.
25. As outlined earlier in the text the survey was conducted in the city of Osh from June to August 2003. Respondents included 61 members of the Uzbek community. Again, the sample was not representative of the community itself, and thus generalizable inferences are not possible. Data seem, nevertheless, to suggest a clear trend which was also confirmed in follow-up interviews.
26. Although "informal rules may be embedded within [these] organizations", the two should not be conflated (North, 1990, p.4; Helmke & Levitsky, 2004, p. 727). Informal institutions are defined as "socially shared rules, usually unwritten, that are created, communicated, and enforced outside of officially sanctioned channels" (*ibid.*).
27. Fumagalli (2005).
28. Interview held with Davron Sabirov (Osh, 17 July 2003).
29. Interviews with Alisher Toksonbaev (Osh, 19 July 2003) and with Almaz Kalet (Osh, 17 July, 2003).
30. Following his election in 2000, Sabirov's tones softened and visibly became less interested in confronting the authorities (he was threatened of being stripped of his control of KyrgyzGas, which did eventually occur) and more interested in the construction sector (among the other things he owns a series of complexes on the right bank of the city, including the well-known hotel "Stary Gorod".
31. The sample included 540 Uzbeks from the Osh region. Thanks go to Makhmud Kazakhbaev for sharing these data with me.
32. Sabirov's campaign was marked with accusations of frauds and bribes. Essentially Sabirov was accused of "buying" his victory, not just thanks to their philanthropic activities, but also because they handed out 200 soms (about 5 US dollars) to interested voters (interview with a local journalist in Osh, 22 July 2005).
33. Interviews held with Alisher Sabirov (Bishkek, 14 June 2003) and Sabirov's aide in Osh Ergeshbaev (Osh, on repeated occasions in June and July 2003).
34. Here I am simply using a term ("revolution") which has entered the popular and scholarly parlance and I am not referring to the proper meaning of the term.
35. Interview with the editor of *Jalalobod Tongi* (Dawn of Jalalabad), (Jalalabad, 11 July 2003).
36. Interviews held with local academics and students at an Osh University (Osh, June 2003).
37. Interview with a local Uzbek journalist (Osh, July 2003).
38. This is done elsewhere (Fumagalli, 2005, particularly Ch. 7).
39. For contrasting views see Saipjanov (2005) and Saipov (2005).
40. Interview with local journalist (Osh, 25 July 2005).
41. Interview with Davron Sabirov (Osh, 17 July 2003).
42. I am grateful to one of the reviewers for emphasising this point.

References

Alysheva, A., Shukurov, E. & Tabyshalieva, A. (1999) *Kyrgyzstan: Some Aspects of the Social Situation* (Bishkek: Institute for Regional Studies).
Alymkulov, E. & Kulatov, M. (2002) Local Government in the Kyrgyz Republic, in: I. Munteanu & V. Popa (Eds), *Developing New Rules in the New Environment*, pp. 521–600 (Budapest: OSI/LGI).

Asankanov A. (1996) Ethnic Conflict in the Osh Region in Summer 1990: Reasons and Lessons, in: K. Rupesinghe & V. A. Tishkov (Eds), *Ethnicity and Power in the Contemporary World*, pp. 116–125 (New York: United Nations University Press).
Axelrod, R. (1986) An Evolutionary Approach to Norms, *American Political Science Review*, 80, pp. 1095–1111.
Beissinger, M. R. (2002) *Nationalist Mobilization and the Collapse of the Soviet State* (Cambridge: Cambridge University Press).
Berman, B. J. (1998) Ethicity, Patronage and the African State: The Politics of Uncivil Nationalism, *African Affairs*, 97, pp. 305–341.
Brass, P.R. (2003) *The Production of Hindu-Muslim Violence in Contemporary India* (Oxford: Oxford University Press).
Brunner, G. & Küpper, H. (2002) European Options of Autonomy: A Typology of Autonomy Models of Minority Self-Governance, in: K. Gál (Ed.), *Minority Governance in Europe*, pp. 13–54 (Budapest: OSI/LGI).
Collins, K. (2003) The Political Role of Clans in Central Asia, *Comparative Politics*, 35(2), pp. 171–190.
Collins, K. (2006) *Clan Politics and Regime Transition in Central Asia* (Cambridge: Cambridge University Press).
Dave, B. (2004) A Shrinking Reach of the State? Language Policy and Implementation in Kazakhstan and Kyrgyzstan, in: P. Jones Luong (Ed.), *The Transformation of Central Asia. States and Societies from Soviet Rule to Independence*, pp. 120–155 (Ithaca, NY: Cornell University Press).
Dukenbayev, A. & Hansen, W. W. (2003) *Understanding Politics in Kyrgyzstan* (Aarhus: Demstar Research Report No. 16).
Elebayeva, A., Omuraliev N. & Abazov, R. (2000) The Shifting Identities and Loyalties in Kyrgyzstan: the Evidence from the Field, *Nationalities Papers*, 28(2), pp. 343–349.
Ellickson, R. (1986) Of Coase and Cattle: Dispute Resolution among Neighbours in Shasta County, *Stanford Law Review*, 38, pp. 623–687.
Faranda, R. & Nolle, D. B. (2003) Ethnic Social Distance in Kyrgyzstan: Evidence from a Nationwide Opinion Survey, *Nationalities Papers*, 31(2), pp. 177–210.
Fumagalli, M. (2005) *The Dynamics of Uzbek Ethno-Political Mobilization in Kyrgyzstan and Tajikistan (1991–2003)* (PhD diss., University of Edinburgh).
Fumagalli, M. (2007a, forthcoming) Framing Ethnic Minority Mobilisation in Central Asia: The Case of Uzbeks in Kyrgyzstan and Tajikistan, *Europe-Asia Studies*, 59(4).
Fumagalli, M. (2007b, forthcoming) Ethnicity, state formation, and foreign policy in post-Soviet Central Asia: Uzbekistan and Uzbeks abroad, *Central Asian Survey*, 26.
Gorenburg, D. P. (2003) *Minority Ethnic Mobilization in the Russian Federation* (Cambridge, MA: Cambridge University Press).
Haugen, A. (2003) *The Establishment of National Republics in Soviet Central Asia* (Basingstoke: Palgrave).
Helmke, G. & Levitsky, S. (2004) Informal Institutions and Comparative Politics: A Research Agenda, *Perspectives on Politics*, 2(4), pp. 725–740.
Hirsch, F. (2005) *Empire of Nations. Ethnographic Knowledge and the Making of the Soviet Union* (Ithaca, NY: Cornell University Press).
Hughes, J. & Sasse, G. (2001) Comparing Regional and Ethnic Conflicts in Post-Soviet Transition States, *Regional and Federal Studies*, 11(3), pp. 1–35.
Huskey, E. (2002) An Economy of Authoritarianism? Askar Akaev and Presidential Leadership in Kyrgyzstan, in: S. N. Cummings (Ed.) *Power and Change in Central Asia*, pp. 74–96 (London: Routledge).
Jones Luong, P. (2002) *Institutional Change and Political Continuity in Post-Soviet Central Asia* (Cambridge: Cambridge University Press).
Kalyvas, S. N. (2003) The Ontology of "Political Violence": Action and Identity in Civil Wars, *Perspectives on Politics*, 1(3), pp. 475–494.
Kamp, M. (2002) Pilgrimage and Performance: Uzbek Women and the Imagining of Uzbekistan in the 1920s, *International Journal of Middle Eastern Studies*, 34(2), pp. 263–278.
Khamidov, A. (2002) Ethnic Uzbeks store unrest in southern Kyrgyzstan, *Eurasianet*, 26 June.
Khamidov, A. (2004) Critics see Political Games in Kyrgyz Language Law, *Eurasianet*, 23 January.
Kietschelt, H. (1986) Political Opportunity Structures and Political Protest: Anti-nuclear Movements in Four Democracies, *British Journal of Political Science*, 16, pp. 57–85.
Koichiev, A. (2003) Ethno-territorial Claims in the Ferghana Valley during the Process of National-delimitation, 1924–27, in: T. Everett-Heath (Ed.), *Central Asia. Aspects of Transition*, pp. 45–56 (London: RoutledgeCurzon).

Koopmans, R. (2000) Migration and Ethnic Relations as a Field of Contention: A Political Opportunity Structure Approach, in: R. Koopmans & P. Statham (Eds), *Challenging Immigration and Ethnic Relations Politics. Comparative European Perspectives*, pp. 13–54 (Oxford: Oxford University Press).

Kriesi, H. (2004) Political Context and Opportunity, in: D.A. Snow, S.H. Soule & H. Kriesi (Eds), *The Blackwell Companion to Social Movements*, pp. 67–90 (Oxford: Blackwell Publishing).

Lauth, H. J. (2000) Informal Institutions and Democracy, *Democratization*, 7(4), pp. 21–50.

Lemarchand, R. (1972) Political Clientelism and Ethnicity in Tropical Africa: Competing Solidarities in Nation-building, *American Political Science Review*, 66(1), pp. 68–90.

Lubin, N. & Rubin, B. R. (1999) *Calming the Ferghana Valley. Development and Dialogue in the Heart of Central Asia* (Washington, DC: The Twentieth Century Fund).

Mamasaidov, M. and Khudayberdiev, O. (2003) Edinyi Obrazovatel'nyi Standart—Stimul dlya mezhetnicheskoi integratsii, in: *Multilingual Education and Mother Tongue Education for National Minorities in Kyrgyzstan* (Geneva: Cimera).

Marat, E. (2006) *The Tulip Revolution: Kyrgyzstan One Year After* (Washington, DC: Jamestown Foundation). Available online at http://www.jamestown.org/images/pdf/Jamestown-TulipRevolution.pdf

Martin, T. (2001) *The Affirmative Action Empire. Nations and Nationalism in the Soviet Union 1923–1939* (Ithaca, NY: Cornell University Press).

Megoran, N. (2000a) Calming the Ferghana Valley Experts, *Central Asian Monitor*, 5, pp. 20–25.

Megoran, N. S. (2000b) Elections and Ethnicity in the South of Kyrgyzstan, *Eurasianet*, 29 March.

Megoran, N. (2002) *The Borders of Eternal Friendship? The Politics and Pain of Nationalism and Identity along the Uzbekistan–Kyrgyzstan Ferghana Valley Boundary, 1999–2000* (PhD diss., University of Cambridge).

Melvin, N. J. (2001) Patterns of Centre-Regional Relations in Central Asia: The Cases of Kazakhstan, the Kyrgyz Republic and Uzbekistan, *Regional and Federal Studies*, 11(3), pp. 165–193.

Narodnoe khoziaistvo Kirgizskoi SSR (1982) (Frunze, Komitet po Statistiki).

Naselenie Kirgizskoi Respubliki 1999 (1999) (Bishkek, Komitet po Statistiki).

Naumkin, V. V. (Ed.) (1994) *Central Asia and Transcaucasia: Ethnicity and Conflict* (Westport, CT: Greenwood Publishing Group).

North, D. G. (1990) *Institutions, Institutional Change and Economic Performance* (Cambridge: Cambridge University Press).

O'Donnell, G. (1996) Illusions about Consolidation, *Journal of Democracy*, 7(2), pp. 34–51.

Omuraliev, N. (2002) Kyrgyzstan's Innovative Solutions to Ethnic Relations are Insufficient, in: V. Tishkov & E. Filippova (Eds), *Local Governance and Minority Empowerment in the CIS*, pp. 297–322 (Budapest: OSI/LGI).

Özkırımlı, U. (2000) *Theories of Nationalism: A Critical Introduction* (Basingstoke: Palgrave).

Powell, J.D. (1970) Peasant Society and Clientelist Politics, *American Political Science Review*, 64(2), pp. 411–425.

Radnitz, S. (2005) Networks, Localism and Mobilization in Aksy, Kyrgyzstan, *Central Asian Survey*, 24(4), pp. 405–424.

Radnitz, S. (2006) State Deconstruction, Patronage, and Mobilization in Kyrgyzstan and Uzbekistan. Paper presented at the 11th Annual Convention of the Association for the Study of Nationalities, Columbia University, New York, 23–25 March.

Roeder, P. (1991) Soviet Federalism and Ethnic Mobilization, *World Politics*, 43(2), pp. 196–232.

Ro'i, Y. (1991) Central Asian Riots and Disturbances 1989–1990: Causes and Context, *Central Asian Survey*, 10(3), pp. 21–54.

Rotar, I. (2006) Uzbeks Appeal to Bakiyev, Claiming Ethnic Discrimination, *Eurasia Daily Monitor*, 10 February.

Roy, O. (1997) *La nouvelle Asie centrale ou la fabrication des nations* (Paris, Le Seuil).

Rumer, B. & Rumer, E. (1992) The Next Yugoslavia?, *World Monitor*, 37 November.

Saipjanov, A. (2005) Uzbeks in Kyrgyzstan View the Revolution with Caution, *Eurasianet*, 31 March.

Saipov, A. (2005) Myth of Pro-Akaev Uzbeks Shattered, *IWPR*, 364, 30 March.

Schöpflin, G. (2001) Minorities and Democracy, in: A.-M. Bíró & P. Kovács (Eds), *Diversity in Action. Local Public Management of Multi-Ethnic Communities in Central and Eastern Europe*, pp. 3–18 (Budapest: OSI/LGI).

Scott, J. C. (1972) Patron–Client Politics and Political Change in Southeast Asia, *American Political Science Review*, 66(1), pp. 91–113.

Slezkine, Y. (1994) The USSR as a Communal Apartment, or How a Socialist State Promoted Ethnic Particularism, *Slavic Review*, 53(2), pp. 414–452.

Soucek, S. (2000) *A History of Inner Asia* (Cambridge: Cambridge University Press).
Spector, R. A. (2004) *The Transformation of Askar Akaev, President of Kyrgyzstan* (Berkeley, CA: Post-Soviet Program).
Tabyshalieva, A. et al. (1998) *South Kyrgyzstan: Ethnic Situation* (Bishkek: Institute for Regional Studies).
Tishkov, V. (1995) "Don't Kill Me, I'm a Kyrgyz!": An Anthropological Analysis of Violence in the Osh Ethnic Conflict, *Journal of Peace Research*, 32(2), pp. 133–149.
Tishkov, V. (1999) Ethnic Conflicts in the Former USSR: The Use and Misuse of Typologies and Data, *Journal of Peace Research*, 36, pp. 571–592.
Varshney, A. (2002) *Ethnic Conflict and Civic Life. Hindus and Muslims in India* (London: Yale University Press).
Weingrod, A. (1968) Patrons, Patronage, and Political Parties, *Comparative Studies in Society and History*, 10(4), pp. 377–400.
Weller, M. & Wolff, S. (2005) Self-determination and Autonomy: A Conceptual Introduction, in: M. Weller and S. Wolff (Eds), *Autonomy, Self-Governance and Conflict Resolution. Innovative Approaches to Institutional Design in Divided Societies*, pp. 1–25 (London: Routledge).

Faultline Citizenship: Ethnonational Politics, Minority Mobilisation, and Governance in the Israeli "Mixed Cities" of Haifa and Tel Aviv-Jaffa

JOSEPH LEIBOVITZ

Institute of Geography, The University of Edinburgh, UK

Divided, "mixed", or ethnically fractured cities are cities which are torn by ethnic and nationalist conflict.[1] The planning and management of such cities is typically characterized by conflicting aspirations presented by different ethnonational groups. This is all the more so in more extreme, or explicit, case where such fractured cities are embedded within a broader framework of ethnonational and territorial conflict (Hepburn, 2004). This paper examines the interaction between urban governance, citizenship and ethnonational politics among Israeli-Palestinian citizens[2] in two Israeli ethnically fractured cities: Haifa and Tel Aviv-Jaffa.

This paper aims to highlight how contested cities can be viewed potentially as platforms for political projects through which aspects of citizenship evolve beyond the national political system. While I do not argue that urban politics is situated within an autonomous, or isolated, political field, it does argue that urban governance and politics should be taken more seriously in debates about social and ethnic movement politics, claim making and minority rights. The paper contributes to the further exploration of two particular dimensions that have been relatively neglected in the literature on ethnic politics and movements: first, the construction of urban political opportunity structures as a dynamic process, which is played out through the context and logic of urban politics; and, second, the various intricacies and internal, as well as external, complexities of marginalized minority mobilization, that do not merely respond to opportunity structures in a straightforward manner, or in ways that suggest that they are simply "dependent variables" (see Vermeersch, 2003). Taken together, the emphasis on the constant altercations of opportunity structures (and their interpretation by minority elites and activists) and mobilizing agendas paves the way for a relational view of the way citizenship politics is played out. Furthermore, a focus on the politics of place—the struggles and political relations that revolve around the material and symbolic aspects of particular communities and neighbourhoods—might help to crystallize the notion of urban governance and citizenship in practice. It is often within the politics of place that the various meanings of citizenship claims are articulated by activists and elites. Conversely, it is the struggle around particular city spaces that enables us to highlight the state's role in the construction and allocation of rights. Focusing on the politics of place has rarely been undertaken by political studies of ethnic mobilization and contentious politics, and yet it might provide a powerful prism through which both state strategies and the choices of minority activists can be viewed and understood (Boudreau & Keil, 2001; Harney, 2006; Martin, 2003).

The empirical discussion in this paper does not intend to be exhaustive. Rather, my emphasis is on pointing to missing links in current approaches to studies of urban political mobilization, minority ethnic politics and the territoriality of citizenship. The empirical material aims to illustrate the potential benefits of such an approach, as a means of encouraging scholars of ethnonational politics to engage more explicitly with comparative and multi-scalar research.

In this context, the urban political arena is recognized as a platform through which the relationship between ethnic groups is established. For ethnic minorities, especially ones that are economically marginalized and numerically too small to have a significant impact on the national political system or on the direction of policy (through, for instance, the formation of national voting blocks), the local level is potentially an important scale within which they can make political claims such as the promotion of equality, the protection of distinctive cultural institutions, or the eradication of social exclusion and discrimination. At the same time, it is all too easy to fall into the trap of conceiving the city as either an autonomous level, or as a utopian political alternative, more inclusive and accommodating than the national political system. Cities can be just as, if not more, exclusionary in their political, social and economic dynamics as are nation states (Bollens, 2000). In developing a nuanced framework for an institutionalist analysis of ethnic politics and of the territorialization of political struggles around citizenship, the paper contributes to a relational sense of citizenship construction in the context of conflicting nationalist discourses and aspirations, especially in divided societies. It is relational in that the substances of and claims to citizenship are considered in the context of how the urban political field develops in relation to the national political framework, and how forms of making claims (through mobilization) and of political opportunities develop are contextualised in and through the politics of place.

Citizenship, Scale and the City

In its broadest sense, citizenship is understood to confer rights, responsibilities and membership in a political community. While the "political community" has been traditionally associated with the nation-state, there are increasing challenges to the monopoly of the nation-state on civic rights and membership in society (Smith, 1995; Staeheli, 2003). Rather than treating citizenship in the abstract, this paper offers a concrete and empirical window on the substance of claims to various meanings of citizenship made by minority activists in ethnically diverse cities. Immigration, globalization, and cultural and economic change have brought about new dynamics so that political communities are said to be increasingly defined by members' identities such as gender, ethnicity, sexuality and a range of political dispositions, rather than on the basis of the nation-states alone (Archibugi *et al.*, 1998; Balibar, 1995; Baubock, 1994; Krause, 2003; Urry, 2000; Phalet & Swyngedouw, 2002; Yuval-Davis, 1999). It is also commonly argued that sub-national territories and supranational institutions have become increasingly important scales through which power, political decisions and struggles take place. Consequently, citizenship is said to be shaped, experienced and claimed through a complex intersection of local, national and international political spheres (Ball & Piper, 2002; Ehrkamp & Leitner, 2003; Ghosh & Wang, 2003; Soysal, 1994; Staeheli, 2003; Staeheli & Thompson, 1997; Urry, 2000). For instance, Purcell (2003) has recently talked of "a new territorial openness" in which urban institutions can help to shape alternative sense of political membership and belonging, and to even challenge current citizenship regimes. Similarly, others have identified the city as the most meaningful level through which multicultural politics can be realized (van den Berghe, 2002; Bell & Keil, 1996).

Yet some of the discussions that have tended to "glorify" the role of the city in the construction of citizenship regimes have remained largely abstract. While generalizations have been made about the potential of new understandings and practices of citizenship to emerge at the urban level, and in doing so to challenge established national orders of citizenship regimes, evidence to demonstrate the extent and significance of such developments remains limited.

The conceptual framework guiding this paper therefore seeks to highlight a missing link in contemporary studies of ethnic mobilization: the intersection of institutional features— drawing primarily on the contentious politics literature—with "place making" approaches in political geography that highlight how collective action is deeply embedded in the politics of specific places. While the contentious politics literature has provided immense contribution on the role of political opportunity structures, resource mobilization, and symbolic politics in understanding patterns and forms of collective action (related to social movement in particular; McAdam *et al.*, 1996 and McAdam *et al.*, 2001), it has lacked an adequate "capturing" of the role of specific places and spaces in animating ethnic movement mobilisation (Jacobs, 2000). On the other hand, studies in political geography have often lacked a careful assessment of how institutional features (for instance, organizational capacity, political opportunities and so on) enable or constrain the strategic options available to those engaged in collective action (see Boudreau & Keil, 2001; Martin, 2003). This paper should therefore be seen as taking some of the first steps necessary for such an incorporation. As much of the dynamics and contentious of ethnic mobilization takes place in an urban context, we run the risk on missing out on a very important dimension in explaining ethnic politics should our research continue to be driven by either institutionalist approaches or by space-based perspectives alone, without attempting an inter-disciplinary perspective on this topic. I therefore share Hooghe's (2005) and Bousetta's (2000) attempts to understand better the possibilities and limitations of political opportunity structures in explaining ethnic mobilization, but go a step further by calling for taking the city seriously in such studies.

In what follows, then, I first draw attention to the potential contribution of the contentious politics literature to studies of ethnic politics and patterns of claim-making, and then turn the attention to how city spaces and their governance are themselves important subjects (and at times objects) of collective action in the context of ethnic politics and territorial contestations. By incorporating the two perspectives, a richer picture of minority collective action, citizenship aspirations and claims can emerge, but one that defies straightforward assumptions about correlations between variables.

Conceptualizing Contentious Politics

Contentious politics largely refers to a field of inquiry which examines the role of protest, civic mobilization, social movements and other forms of ex-parliamentary politics in giving rise to a variety of public agendas, including civic equality, women rights, minority incorporation, anti-war protests, environmental campaigns, trade union politics and so on. Within studies of contentious politics, three particular analytical perspectives have traditionally occupied the centre stage (although these are not the only ones, cf. McAdam *et a.*, 1996 and Della Porta & Diani, 1999). First, the political opportunity structure approach has largely stressed the role of the political system—broadly defined—in enabling or constraining the possibilities for collective action (Tilly, 1978; McAdam, 1982; Tarrow, 1983). The political system has largely been referred to in institutional terms, providing important insights as to the role of electoral systems, parliamentary and constitutional structures, party politics, elites, and so on in providing or constraining access for social movements. The point of reference has often been to national political systems, and has enabled illuminating cross-national comparative studies of protest and mobilization (McAdam *et al.*, 2001).

A second perspective is that of resource mobilization, referring to the various mechanisms through which collective action is made possible: from formal financial and organizational resources to less formal features such as inter-personal ties, coalitional arrangements, community acquaintances, the workplace and the family (McCarthy & Zald, 1977; Tilly, 1978). Again, this has facilitated research on the various degrees of success or failure of movement politics to make an imprint on public agendas and policies, mostly at the national scale of politics.

A third perspective, as conceptualized by McAdam *et al.* (1996), has highlighted the role of symbolic politics, or framing more specifically, in consolidating political contestation. This perspective has largely surfaced as a result of scholars' dissatisfaction with either the opportunity structure approach or resources mobilization perspectives (or their combination) in providing a comprehensively incisive account of collective action. The argument is that what links people together into a social movement and engagement in contentious politics—beyond opportunities and resources—is the development of shared understandings and meanings of particular problems, challenges and possible solutions. Without such shared conventions it would be hard to imagine engagement in collective action (Snow *et al.*, 1986). As McAdam *et al.* (1996) define it, framing refers to "the conscious strategic efforts by groups of people to fashion shared understandings of the world and of themselves that legitimate and motivate collective action" (p. 6). Furthermore, I concur with them that framing and the symbolic dimensions of contentious politics remain the relatively underdeveloped and under-studied facet of collective action and social movements.

In particular, I wish to stress in this article the ways through which urban ethnic politics can highlight the intimate interaction between the institutional, symbolic and place-making properties of mobilization and mobilizing agendas. To do so, we need to take account of the material and symbolic role that city political spaces play in the consolidation of identity politics. Put in other words, the urban dimension of movement politics is not simply an add-on to already existing patterns of collective action, but in fact a politically constitutive facet in the territorialized nature of contemporary citizenship (Jacobs, 2000). Furthermore, symbolic politics operates both within and beyond the formal politics of rights. For some ethnic minorities and marginalized indigenous groups, electoral and formal politics offer very limited opportunity structures because their numbers are simply too small to affect party structures through bloc voting, or elites through linkages and patronage (Hooghe, 2005). Here, symbolic politics, both internal (and at times hidden) and external, can play the most important role in underlying patterns of collective action and mobilization. For instance, minority elites can engage in the politics of memory, identity and belonging almost regardless of opportunity structures. Remembering that nation's or ethnic group's history and culture may become one of the most important "internal" priorities for collective action. In other words, in the absence of clear-cut opportunity structures, existing research has tended to neglect latent, and at times "sub-surface", forms of mobilizing agendas. Focusing on these forms of mobilizing agendas in their urban, localized and relational contexts can reveal the richness and territorially differentiated forms of ethnic movement politics. This article therefore contributes an important dimension to existing ethnic and contentious politics studies: the intersection of ethnic mobilization dynamics with the territorialized nature of citizenship, expressed in the politics of places.

It is in this context that it may be useful to recall the potential fruitfulness of stressing the dynamic nature of the state. In calling for greater attention to "dyanmic statism", Tarrow (1996, p. 44) essentially criticizses the tendency in many opportunity structure-inspired studies to treat the state and its institutions as static. Instead, he has argued for the need to highlight the enormous elasticity of the state. States, their policies, elite structures and institutional dynamics are in fact constantly being remade by a complex constellation of political, economic and social process, among them the dynamics of contentious politics. More specifically, Tarrow (1996) has suggested that we pay more careful attention to the dynamic environments in which social movements operate, including the importance of subnational and subgroup variations in movement opportunities. Yet, even Tarrow is not sufficiently specific about this. In particular, I would like to suggest that by introducing the sub-national and intra-group dynamics to the contentious politics of ethnic movements, we can begin to attain a more richly nuanced understanding of the strategic choices and political agendas that underpin mobilization, contention, protest and resistance.

Taking the City Seriously: Urban Ethnic Mobilization and Infra-politics as Political Arenas

An important missing element in studies of ethnic mobilization and movement politics is that of "taking the city seriously". In analyses performed at the national and international scales, the political science and political sociology literatures have identified a number of institutional structures through which tensions between ethnic groups might be mediated (Banton, 2000; Bulmer, 1998; Schöpflin, 2000). The Israeli case has been sometimes associated with the "ethnic democracy model" (Smooha, 2002), or even more pronounsly an "ethnocracty" (Yiftachel, 2001), stressing the ethnic ascendancy of the dominant (Jewish) group, while extending to the minority individual and collective rights only inasmuch that they are deemed non-threatening to the majority. The model is often considered a "second-rate" type of democracy because it lacks features of civic equality and grants explicit privilege to the ethnic majority group, leading to what Jamal (2002) terms "differentiated citizenship".

Since such models have developed with reference to the national level, they tend to neglect the possibility of local variances and dynamics in the management of minority–majority relations. While nation-states remain, of course, crucial in underwriting the legal, formal and constitutional framework for the politics of ethnicity and national identity, local contexts provide much of the substances and everyday practices—what Amin (2002) calls "prosaic negotiations"—that underpin inter-ethnic and inter-community relations. As Bousetta (2000, p. 230) has argued, "the quest for theoretical and political tools suitable for refining our understanding of the socio-political behaviour of immigrant ethnic communities is also driven by a changing political context, characterised by the empirical transformation occurring on the field and especially in European cities". Yet, the conceptual specifities of cities, whether in Europe or elsewhere, as political arenas remain underdeveloped in this context. It is not to suggest that cities should be viewed independently from the national, and where relevant supra-national, context in which they are situated. Rather, the contention is that a theoretical understanding of cities needs to be developed in tandem with developments in the conceptualization of political contention at higher levels.

I would therefore suggest that taking the city seriously means that features of urban governance and their relation to the citizenship experience and struggles of minority groups should be accorded a more central position than previously attempted. Struggles over particular places—be it through an urban development programme or resistance to the erection of disruptive of urban projects—often crystalize the combined effect of opportunities, constraints, mobilization and symbolism. The emergence of the notion of "urban governance" in the past 20 years, firstly in North American and, later on, European urban studies, can foster a much needed sense of dynamism into research of urban minority politics. The literature on urban governance emphasizes power in urban politics as an outcome of regime politics embedding a diverse range of institutional features such as coalition-building, leadership, and a combination of formal and informal arrangements (Stone, 1993). It seeks to capture the institutional nuances of urban politics against a background of economic change and the restructuring of inter-governmental relations.

While certain sectors, such as business interests, may be privileged because of their access to resources, local communities can become influential partners in governing coalitions (Smith & Beazley, 2000). Although recent studies have sought to expend the application of urban regime analysis beyond its American origins (Harding, 1994; Savitch & Kantor, 2002), examples of urban political analyses in non-core nations remain scarce. Since governance perspectives can be sensitized to capture national and local variations in institutional contexts, economic circumstances, and historical legacies (see Dowding, 2001; Mossberger & Stoker, 2001), it has the potential to highlight important institutional and political features within which the governance of Palestinian–Jewish relations is performed in Israel's contested cities.

Two issues are worth mentioning in that regard. First, the crucial role of elected mayors in the regime politics of the European city, especially those belonging to the southern group in which elected mayors have long been regarded as embodying community identity and as bearers of political legitimacy due to their directly elected status (Page & Goldsmith, 1987). This is largely the situation in Israel. In many ways, in Israel and possibly in other Mediterranean urban political cultures, mayors are the key "institution" of an urban regime.

Second, a particular emphasis should be put on the balance between the material and the symbolic role of governance politics. While material refers to the "hard" allocation of resources, the symbolic role of regime governance relates to a host of methods and "technologies" which construct discourses and symbolic gestures designed to co-opt minority leaders and other actors into either cooperation or, at least, lack of effective resistance to urban policy and development programmes. The role of discourse in building a common frame of references around political institutions and policies is particularly deserved of theoretical attention, as it is through discourses that conceptions and interpretations of political opportunity structures are built (Benford & Snow, 2000; Koopmans & Olzak, 2004).

Finally, the localized dimension of ethnic movement politics draws attention to the internal organization of minority movements and mobilization, and is another important dimension which should be considered in tandem with the "supply side" opportunity structures for claim-making. Fragmentation versus solidarity, the availability or lack of leadership, the ability and willingness to engage in broader coalition-building politics, minority movement resources and so on are important elements shaping the strategic choices and the forms through which identity is politicised. Bousetta's (2000) theoretical contribution on the hidden, or what he has termed "infra-political", dimension of political mobilization, offers a particularly powerful capturing of the subtleties of minority political organization. Its promise is in addressing one of the more crucial weaknesses in conventional political opportunity structure analyses, namely their tendency to reduce the complexities and nuances of minority political strategies to a unified independent variable.

While keeping sight of the role of the state and its policy environment, as well as explicit forms of political organization among diverse groups, the introduction of infra-politics draws attention to political process, struggles and actions that take place in the back-rooms of visible politics. This is often the locus of informal and hidden arenas of power struggles and even personality politics, which in turn help to shape the forms of minority mobilization. As Bousetta argues, the distinguishing element of infra-politics "is the more opaque mode of political operation it requires. At this level, the strategic actions of the actors involved are oriented towards the control of community agenda"

(2000, p. 237). I would add that infra-politics is also potentially about the control of resources, both internal and the ones that can be extracted externally through coalition-building and alliances with elites of other groups or the state. The analysis of the politics of urban governance in relation to majority–minority relations can thus be enriched through a theoretical emphasis on the interconnected nature of macro-level contentious politics, the institutional infrastructure of urban governance, and the micro-level subtleties of local infra-politics. The constellation of these forces is perhaps rarely more significant than in the process of place-making, where particular city spaces become the subject of potentially conflicting aspirations.

Israeli Local Power Structure

Potential forms of local infra-politics may revolve around symbolism as well as around material issues. In the Israeli context, where local government authority is constricted by centralization of formal power (owing to the British mandatory legacy), the dynamics of urban governance, and with them the contours of local political contention and mobilization, are likely to gravitate towards the symbolic elements of politics. In the absence of formal political power and resources, politics is likely to be shaped by the symbolic gestures and by struggles over the discursive terrain of politics. It is not that material issues would not be of importance. But, on balance, such a context may draw greater energies into symbolism, the distribution of benefits and spoils, and the use of public gestures and symbolic constructions around the relations between the (Palestinian) minority and the (Jewish) majority.

More specifically, Israeli city councils ("municipalities") are among three forms of local government in the country, the other two being a "local authority" generally for small and mid-sized towns, and "regional councils" usually in rural areas. Formally, the Israeli system of central-local government relations is highly centralized due to its origin in the British Mandate in Palestine (in fact, elements of this 1930s local government law are still in place; (Blank, 2004). The Ministry of Interior is responsible for overseeing local government, and local government areas of responsibilities are limited to the ones set out by the Ministry. In practice, Israeli local government plays a double role, that of service delivery administration at the local level, especially in education and social welfare, and in representation of local interests, vis-à-vis the central state (Blank, 2004). In that regard, Israeli local politics has much in common with the southern European group of local government, with its traditionally weak formal powers and reliance on the informal ties of elected mayors with high level officials and different interest groups.

In Israel, the direct election of mayors with policy-leading powers since 1975 has strengthened the legitimacy of local leadership,[3] and has brought to the scene a series of charismatic mayors in the big cities, notably Teddy Kolak in Jerusalem, and Shlomo Lahat in Tel Aviv. In practice, the group known as the "big 15 municipalities" (in which Tel Aviv-Jaffa and Haifa are the first and third ranked, respectively) raise most of their income from local revenue sources and use much of their informal and formal capacity to initiate policies over which the Ministry of Interior does not always have much say. The most significant area tends to be in the realm of urban development policy, where informal ties between mayors, planners and property development actors often lead to the local initiation of urban projects. While legally every local plan must be approved by the regional and national planning institutions, in practice the power to initiative and implement development projects varies greatly according to various constellations of relationships between actors. Likewise, in urban social policies and in educational issues, while formal powers lie with central government, informal arrangements and political clout count for much variation in the policy emphasis and performance of different cities, with Tel Aviv taking a leading example in the initiation of a range of social initiatives since the mid-1990s in response to the presence of foreign migrant workers (Schnell & Alexander, 2002).

The conclusion of the above discussion is that while formal opportunity structures for the deployment of distinctive urban political terrains of identity politics might seem limited in Israel, it is the combination of formal powers with informal arrangements—both external and intrinsic to ethnic organizations and groups—that has the potential to result in distinctive forms of ethnic mobilization and claim-making politics. Nowhere is this more evident in instances where particular city sites become the subject of conflict. In these crucial moments of place-making, the substance of citizenship and political mobilisation is re-enacted.

Between State, City and Movement: Israeli-Palestinian Mobilization and Fault-line Citizenship in Haifa and Tel Aviv-Jaffa

The Empirical Context: Historical Legacies, Demography and Geography

The position of Israel's Palestinian citizens (within the country's "Green Line", which demark its borders prior to the 1967 war) is particularly complex. Israeli-Palestinians account for about 20% of the total population of Israel,[4] they have been formal citizens of Israel since 1966, and are a "trapped minority": they are a segment of a larger group spread across at least two states, and their identity transcend the geographic boundaries of existing nation-states (Rabinowitz, 2001). Strong linkages and a shared sense of identity between Israel's Palestinian citizens and the Palestinian population in the Occupied Territories of the West Bank[5] give rise to a complex geography of identity and national allegiance (Bulmer, 1998; Jamal, 2002; Ghanem, 1998; Smooha, 2002; Yiftachel, 1997, 2001, 2002).

Most Palestinian and Jewish Israelis live in separate settlements and towns (Falah, 1997; Falah *et al.*, 2000). Only seven Israeli cities are considered "mixed cities", or fractured communities, where both groups live: Haifa, Tel-Aviv-Jaffa, Lydda, Ramla, Acre, Upper Nazzareth and Jerusalem (which should probably be treated as a category in its own right). These communities account for some 9% of the total Arab population in Israel and represent the only meaningful examples of shared Arab-Jewish spaces in Israel/Palestine (Falah, 1996, 1997; Falah *et al.*, 2000; Menahem, 2000; Mesch & Manor, 2001). For some, the political realities of Palestinian citizenship in these cities represent a "double discrimination syndrome": suffering already from differentiated and inferior citizenship experience at the behest of national institutions, the Palestinian residents of these cities concurrently have to contend with another layer of unfavourable citizenship regimes (Yaacobi & Tzfadia, 2004) . While it would be tempting to derive this somewhat general assertion, my contention is that the intricacies and complexities of mobilization, shaped simultaneously by external and internal factors, portray a richly varied and complex picture of "fault-line citizenship": a territorialized form of claim-making and collective action that is constantly shaped and re-shaped by state—ethnic movement interaction at different scales of politics (Tzfadia & Yiftachel, 2004).

In Haifa, Israeli-Palestinians number, according to recent estimates, 30 000 people, constituting just under 10% of the city's total population (the rest being mostly Jewish). About 55% of this group are Christian Arabs, and the remaining 45% are mostly Moslems (City of Haifa, 2006). In Tel Aviv-Jaffa, the size of the Israeli-Palestinian community is much smaller. It is estimated to number some 15 400 people, which is 4.5% of the city's total population. Within the district of Jaffa, one the oldest Mediterranean port cities, where the vast majority of the city's Israeli-Palestinians live, this community constitutes about a third of the population, with the other two-thirds being Israeli-Jews. Moslems are the overwhelming majority among Jaffa's Israeli-Palestians, numbering 12 000 people (City of Tel Aviv-Jaffa, 2005). Politically, Jaffa was incorporated to the Tel-Aviv municipality in 1950, thus losing its municipal "independence".[6]

In both Haifa and Tel Aviv-Jaffa, arriving at precise demographic data is hampered by the fact that the last Israeli census of population dates to 1995, and later data is based on municipal estimates on the basis of a 20% sample. In spite of this, long-term trends reveal the shifts in the demographic balance between the Israeli-Jewish majority and the Israeli-Palestinian minority. In the late 1930s, Haifa and Jaffa saw significant growth as Palestine's two major coastal cities. As Kimmerling & Migdal (2003, p. 46) have put it, these two cities "had come to represent the new face of Palestinian Arab society, taking second place to Jerusalem only in the realms of politics and religion". Between the two of them, they comprised more than 10% of Mandatory Palestine's Arab population. Haifa's port and railroad connections supported its development as a centre of regional innovation and culture, while Jaffa's location and traditional role as Palestine's *entreport* encouraged its rise to a cultural, commercial and service centre (Kimmerling & Migdal, 2003; LeVine, 2005).

Both places were deeply affected by the process of Zionist nation-building since the early years of the twentieth century. They were subject to significant waves of Jewish in-migration and settlement. Thus, during the 1920s and 1930s, these cities became de-facto bi-national communities. On the eve of Israel's independence in 1948, the Palestinian population of Haifa constituted 48% of the city's total (Goren, 2004). In Jaffa, the demographic history was even more complicated, as Jews settled both in Jaffa and in its modern off-spring, the city of Tel Aviv. Nevertheless, it is estimated that just before the 1948 war, which followed Israel's declaration of independence, Jaffa's thriving city contained about 80 000 Palestinians. This community was practically decimated, with only 4100 people not fleeing. Haifa's Palestinian community faired little better, falling from 70 000 people to between 3000 and 4000 in 1948 (Morris, 2002). In both cities, the breakdown of Jewish–Arab relations took place through a series of cross-community hostilities during the 1930s, culminating in a combination of the conflict in 1947–1948 (Morris, 2002).

Segregation has also become an important feature in inter-community dynamics in the two cities. From the outset, Jewish migrants to Haifa chose to settle in the city's higher latitudes on the Carmel Mountain, while the Palestinian community dominated the areas of Lower Haifa. This demographic and topographic pattern also reflected increasing social and economic differences, with the Jewish community, in general, occupying the higher income brackets (Goren, 2004). In Jaffa, following the establishment of Israel, the Arab community found itself increasingly spatially confined to the centre of Jaffa, especially in and around the deprived neighbourhood of Ajami (see Figure 2; Fabian, 2001; LeVine, 2005). In both cities, these patterns of segregation remain salient features (Falah *at al.*, 2000; see Figures 1 and 2, where the designation of "non-Jewish population" in the Israeli Census largely refers to Israeli-Palestinians). The publication of the last Israeli census dates back to 1996, and thus prevents the display of reliable current socio-economic data. However, given the broader trend of neo-liberal policies and growing inequality in Israel in the past 20 years (Svirsky & Connor-Attias, 2006), Table 1 captures effectively the relative aspects of the lower socio-economic status of the Palestinian citizens residing in Haifa and Tel Aviv-Jaffa, along a range of indicators.

In what follows, a particular focus on the politics of urban development policy – in its broad sense—will be used as a prism through which to address questions of citizenship and ethnonational politics. As the public policy process which affects the type, location, scale, design and timing of development in the built environment, urban development policy is a crucial element shaping the well-being, opportunities and quality of life of groups and communities (Healey, 1997). In societies where identity politics and territorial conflict complicate the picture further, urban development planning is highly politicized: it has the potential to contribute to the expansion of citizenship rights and social inclusion through democratized planning processes, or it can exacerbate inter-community tension through divisive planning strategies (Beall *et al.*, 2002; Bollens, 2000; Mabin & Smit, 1997; Ellis, 2001; Yiftachel, 2001).

Governance and Minority Mobilization in Tel Aviv-Jaffa

> Yaffa (Jaffa) was once an independent city. Since its annexation by Tel Aviv in 1950 it has become an undesirable entity in the big city, and it looks that way. Many Jews have fled it to the nearby towns, but for us—its Arab residents—there's nowhere else to run. (local political activist, Jaffa)

Tel Aviv-Jaffa functions as Israel's major financial and business centre. Its Arab-Palestinian community is a small minority largely concentrated in the Jaffa district, and constitutes one of the city's poorest groups. Within the district of Jaffa itself, the *Ajami* neighbourhood represents the largest concentration of Israeli-Palestinians residents in Tel Aviv-Jaffa with some 6000 residents, 80% of which are Arabs (see Figure 2). The Jaffa district of Tel-Aviv, an independent and vibrant commercial centre before the creation of the state of Israel, is still suffering the traumatic legacy of mass evacuation and fleeing of the its Arab community, which numbered some 80 000 people before 1948 and was reduced to merely 4000 of the city's poorest in 1948. This population grew rapidly subsequently through in-migration of poor villagers and through natural increase. Since Tel Aviv-Jaffa as a whole functions as the country's main economic core, housing most of Israel's corporate headquarters and highest concentration of financial, insurance, legal and business service activities, the relative poverty of Jaffa makes its social exclusionary nature even more accentuated. This situation affects both Jewish and Palestinian Israelis, and is more generally a part of a prominent division between the relatively wealthy northern parts of Tel Aviv and the lower income nature of the city's southern parts. The shared destiny between the Arab and Jewish residents of Jaffa has not led, however, to the formation of either significant electoral and municipal party-based

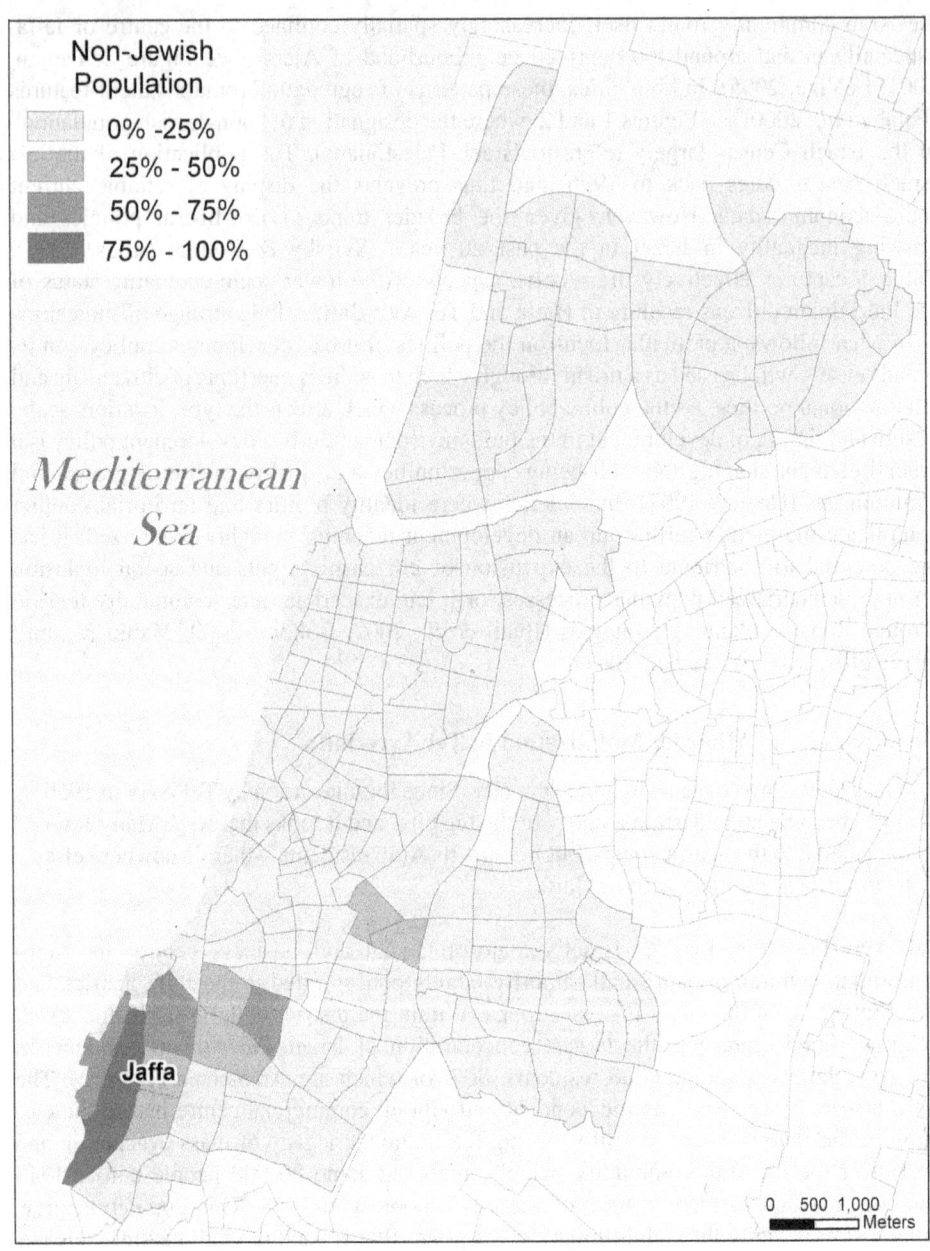

Figure 1. Non-Jewish Population, City of Tel Aviv-Jaffa. *Data source*: Israel Central Bureau of Statistics (1995)

coalitions, or to the emergence of cross-national and cross-community social movements, except for periodical and temporary experiments (see below). Institutional, symbolic and infra-political features have played an important role in structuring the form and substance of political contention among the local Palestinian community.

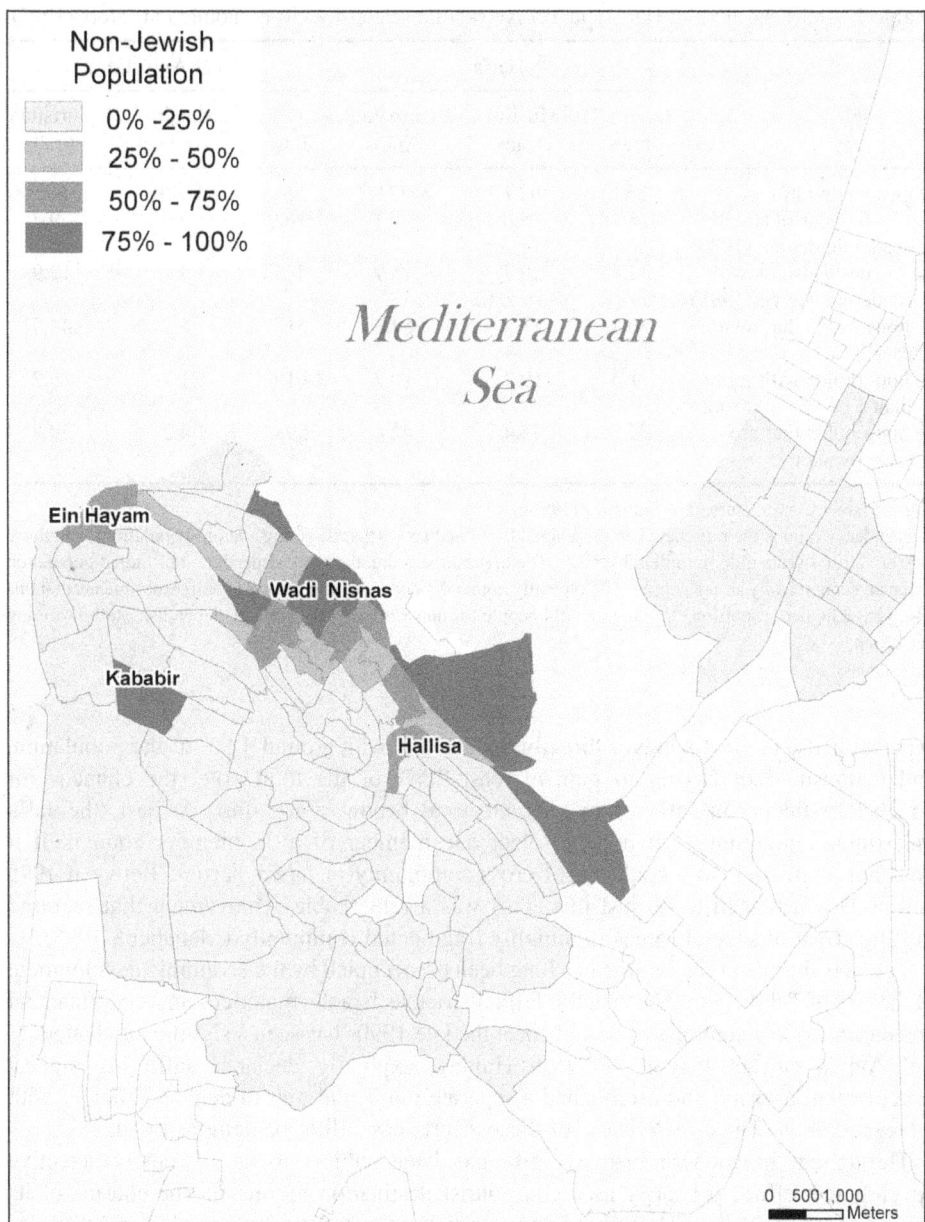

Figure 2. Non-Jewish Population: City of Haifa. *Data source*: Israel Central Bureau of Statistics (1995)

Main Governance Dynamics

First, the dynamics of urban governance have been important in deploying and limiting opportunity structures. The voting system in Israeli municipal elections, which since 1975 have been based on proportional representation for city council members and a

Table 1. Arabs and Jews in Haifa and Tel Aviv-Jaffa: selected socio-economic indicators (1995)

	Haifa			Tel Aviv-Jaffa		
	Jews	Muslim Arabs	Christian Arabs	Jews	Muslim Arabs	Christian Arabs
Dependency ratio*	862	928	721	751	1043	682
% 25–64-year-olds with academic degree (1983)	18.4	5.0	7.1	16.0	2.0	9.3
% 25–64-year-olds with academic degree (1995)	32.8	6.7	15.7	28.6	5.1	12.9
% households that own a car	56.8	43.5	54.3	51.2	38.7	44.5
% households with more than 2 persons per room	1.4	19.2	10.2	1.8	21.7	9.2
% households that are homeowners	72.9	37.4	42.8	59.4	34.2	39.7

Source: Israel Central Bureau of Statistics (1996b)
*Dependency ratio is the ratio between those aged 0–19 and 65+ (that is, young and old population), and those who are 20–64 years old, multiplied by 1000. The highest the score, the more dependent the studied population group on economically active people. The typically higher dependency ratio among Israeli-Arabs means that this group has a higher proportion of young and old people (of non-working age) who are dependent on the working age group.

separate ballot to elect a mayor directly, means that with around 4.5% of the population, and a threshold of having to gain at least 2.5% of the total vote, the chances for Israeli-Palestinians in Jaffa of making electoral headway are slim. At best, the Jaffa Palestinian community can hope to elect one member of a 31 member council, if it does not align itself to a coalition of cross-community or larger parties. Between 1995 and 2003 it managed to do just this. This was a remarkable achievement that required the alignment of several forces in a highly fragmented community (Menahem, 1998).

Tel Aviv-Jaffa's urban regime has long been preoccupied by the economic development of the city of Tel Aviv, rather than the Jaffa district, as Israel's major commercial, financial and entertainment centre. The period since the late 1990s has seen a significant change, as Tel Aviv's current mayor, Mr Ron Hulday, explicitly declared Jaffa his highest development priority, and established a separate municipal unit to deal specifically with its regeneration. The effectiveness of these efforts has still to be demonstrated.

Throughout its modern history, Jaffa has been subject to an extremely selective development effort, primarily as a chic tourist destination relying on the charms of its old port and its mainly Jewish-occupied artistic quarter, a strategy that did little to benefit its Palestinian residents (LeVine, 2005). During the 1980s and much of the 1990s, urban renewal policy encouraged speculative luxury housing development on its attractive seafront, again contributing very little to the welfare of local residents (Montereskou & Fabian, 2003). Redevelopment and gentrification efforts have been accompanied, at times, by forceful eviction of Palestinian residents into new but low-quality public housing projects. In addition, issues of law and order have long dominated the governance of Jaffa, and the relationship between the community and the police force has been contentious. Consequently, Jaffa is often portrayed as a hotbed of criminal, illegal and semi-legal activity. Urban planning in the context of inter-ethnic relations in Tel Aviv-Jaffa suffers from poor communication and lack of trust between planners and residents.

In Israeli local political culture, notions of public participation are relatively young and untested. Municipal politics has been traditionally the domain of elected mayors and their senior professional planners and officials, with privileged positions among civil society given to actors from the property development industry. Yet this has been changing in Tel Aviv-Jaffa, with the last ten year seeing greater discursive emphasis on public consultation and citizen input. It is within this context that public participation exercises have been introduced in relation to urban policy in Jaffa, and carried through the auspices of a new governance machinery, the Jaffa Governance Unit (JGU). Yet this has been a highly selective and strongly controlled process which has "cherry picked" particular actors and specific segments of the community thereby strengthening the public legitimacy of urban policy, co-opting certain communities and leaders among Jaffa's Palestinian residents, and avoiding or isolating elements which have been deemed uncooperative, unconstructive, or extremists.

Palestinian Political Organization and its Infra-politics

Second, in the absence of realistic, explicit and formal political options, the extremely marginalized position of the Palestinian elite in Jaffa has landed greater significance to and complex patters of infra-politics.[7] In 1979 a group of Arab intellectuals in Jaffa established an organization called *Harabitta*—the Organization for Jaffa's Arabs. While the initial impetus for the development of *Harabitta* came from frustration over the long social neglect and severe deprivation of the Palestinian community in Jaffa—especially in manifested poor housing, crime and safety problems, and poorly performing schools—and the failing of the Tel Aviv-Jaffa municipality in these areas, there has always been important infra-ethnopolitical, religious and class elements to *Harabitta*'s activities. From the outset, it objected to explicit forms of collaboration with formal municipal institutions based on the arguments that they represented an extension of the Zionist project of Jewish nation-building and the purposeful disinheritance of Palestinian Jaffa. Its range of activities emphasized the importance of preserving Arab-Palestinian identity in Jaffa through encouraging the use of Arabic language, and it led campaigns *vis-à-vis* the municipality to provide street signs and public announcements in Arabic. They also raised the issue of housing and community survival against a backdrop of state-led gentrification and the "Judaization" of Jaffa, organizing a number of protests in the late 1970s and through the 1980s against house demolitions and new luxury development projects.

In all, the infra-political elements of their activity incorporated a form of localized ethnonationalism, relying on the mobilization of resistance to the Israeli nation-building project as one defined as a Jewish national state (arguing rather that the state should be modelled on a recognition of its bi-national components), and resistance to the eradication of the Palestinian presence in Jaffa. Another important infra-political dimension relates to *Harabitta*'s complex religious and class-based identity. The organization is associated with professional middle-class Christian Palestinians. Christian Palestinians are themselves a "minority within a minority" among the Palestinian citizens of Israel, and even more pronouncedly in Jaffa, where they constitute less than a third of the Palestinian community. The result has been an interweaving of demographic politics among the complex web of political contention in Jaffa. Christian Palestinian elites and community leaders have been concerned with the preservation of this small community, a concern that has impacted both the infra-politics of the whole Jaffa Palestinian community, as well as the articulation of political mobilization agendas. One strategy through which this group's elite has attempted to align itself to the Moslem majority has been through the evocation of strong ethnonational stance in addition to civic demands. As one activist explained:

> *Harabitta* represents a certain Palestinian national sentiment that is not only about resisting the dominant Jewish-Israeli identity ... One of the claims against *Harabitta* ... is that "they are Christians" ... even though [sic] in the past one of their chairman was a Moslem ... and even then there were those who claimed that he was only an instrument at the hand of the Christian community.

In addition to a preservation tactics aimed outwardly, other Christian community activists have turned inwardly, to self-provision of services and internal educational and social activities, and to political moderation as a way of securing the standing of the community. Rather than the conflictual stance of *Harabitta*, these activists have sought to secure informal alliances with local state officials as a way of securing funding to their various community operations (for instance, ex-curricular educational activities, cultural events, and support for various youth organizations). They have shied away from forms of political protest such as demonstrations, claiming that these represented an "outmoded, ineffective and counterproductive approach" (in the words of one activist), and have raised doubts as to the efficacy of municipal electoral or party politics, given the limited influence that such an approach could yield (bearing in mind the small size of the Jaffa Palestinian electorate).

Yet this pattern of political organization and fragmentation has not been an outcome of solely internal dynamics. It has been given further impetus and encouragement by the state, primarily the machinery of urban governance in Tel Aviv-Jaffa. The city's mayor has chosen a strategy of selective incentives and other technologies of regime politics (allocation of resources, coalition politics and symbolic gestures) in order isolate *Harabitta* on the one hand, and co-opt the religiously oriented movements and their political elites in particular. In this, he has been successful in sharpening internal divisions with the Arab-Palestinian community of Jaffa, while buttressing the delivery of his own agenda for the city and for Jaffa in particular.

But it was also an infra-politics of internal representation and strategic choices that contributed to the fragmented nature of the Palestinian community in Jaffa. Different groups within the community have engaged in different territorial politics of citizenship, the result of this has been the production of incompatible visions of citizenship and engagement. The dominant Islamic sect has sought accommodation through informal politics with the city's mayor, and thus broke away from the coalition. It has effectively sought a model of faultline citizenship through which Islamic institutions would provide much of the religious, community and welfare services to the community, while keeping certain levels of dialogue with city officials through informal cooperation and the distribution of selective incentives by the Mayor (mostly through patronage). One segment of the Christian minority sought a strategy of internal preservation of its own identity and presence in Jaffa, given its small numbers (estimated to be around 500). It therefore turned away from collective action and concentrated internally on its own institutions. And yet another segment of the community, represented by *Harabitta*, continued its own distinctive strategy of collective claims towards the state around issues of services, education, crime and housing, but blended it with a radical ethnonational discourse related to Palestinian identity in Jaffa and its connection to the Palestinian nation more generally. Increasingly, however, it found itself isolated, both internally in Jaffa, and by civic institutions in Tel Aviv-Jaffa.

Place-making Politics

It is in the politics of place-making that one could discern the various and complex ways through which political opportunities and hidden intra-movement dynamics are translated into the governance of ethnically fractured communities. In Jaffa the politics of place-making since the 1980s is suggestive of the way through which political opportunities do not necessarily adhere to the expectations raised in the literature regarding their likely effect on the form of contestation.

Since the late 1980s one area of Jaffa, known as the "Jaffa Hip", has become, in the word of one Israeli-Palestinian community organizer, "the nerve centre of our struggle here". The area, in the west of the district and extending to the Mediterranean shore has been designated according to existing city plans to contain low-density housing build. In effect, had these plans were to materialize they would have probably led to another stage in the gentrification of Jaffa, leading to influx of high-income home owners, most probably Jewish rather than Palestinian Israelis (as the Palestinian community as a whole tends to occupy the lower-income brackets). The implementation of the plan would have every chance of complimenting another prestige development in Jaffa, known as Andromeda Hill, which has generated deep resentment by the Palestinian community of Jaffa as it meant a de-facto Judaization of parts of the district (Montereskou & Fabian, 2003).

As events would have it, the city has been unable to implement the "Jaffa Hip" plan as a result of fierce opposition from community organizations such as *Harabitta*, and unfavourable market conditions. Nevertheless, the area served as dumping ground for waste, resulting in an unsightly and ever-growing landfill (hence its name). Given this situation, a number of Palestinian and Jewish community organizations have labelled court appeals against the municipality's use of the area as a waste dumping ground, resulting in a court injunction in 1999 which ordered the city to abstain from this practice. Instead, since 2000 onwards, the city's planning department and the Jaffa Governance Unit (JGU) have been promoting the development of a municipal park in the area. During the period between 2002 and 2006, JGU has been holding a series of public participation exercises to determine the future of the area, designed to help determine the specific design and layout of the planned park. In short, the city has moved from planned housing development and state-supported gentrification (with very probable further displacement of Arab residents and ethnonational conflict over Jaffa's future), to a deliberate neglect and finally towards an environmental improvement policy.

Simply relying on a political opportunity structure approach would have led us to conclude that community organizations deployed their strategy according to available opportunities, protesting against the city, using formal and informal linkages to city council, making use of the courts, and finally taking part and being co-opted towards a public participation mechanism. The most recent opportunity structure orchestrated by JGU—that of publicising the new "Jaffa Hip" plan and opening channels for public hearings and participation—might have led to a more vigorous airing of concerns with and opposition to city plans. It could have provided channels for oppositional discourse and the formation of alternative strategies. In effect, however, the city has been able to make use of the internal divisions within the Jaffa community—both Palestinian and Jewish—to establish legitimacy for its plan to beautify the Jaffa beach areas. It has created a highly structured public participation exercise that was carefully divided to several groups, including Palestinian women, Jewish representatives, youth movements, a local environmental association, representativex of Arab organizations, business representatives and so on. This has effectively sterilized the process, and took advantage of existing cleavages to prevent more spontaneous and free-flowing dialogue between the different segments of the community. In the event, the city policy-making institutions have been able to record a participatory process in which they carefully controlled the agenda and diffused tensions. While activists remained concerned that the beautification of the beach would merely be a stage in "preparing" Jaffa for another round of gentrification in the long term (and thus invoking the danger of further ethnonational motivated policies), they found themselves agreeing to the overall agenda, claiming that "anything is better than the piles of trash which lies at our doorstep" (Jaffa resident).

Thus, political opportunity structures alone have not been solely responsible for the contentious politics of governing Jaffa. The literature on contentious politics pays insignificant attention to the potential interplay of opportunities with infra-politics in particular places. Infra-politics of rivalry, cleavages and the use of selective incentives by city institutions (including co-option and patronage) have combined to reduced levels of contention even when the long-term outcomes of existing policies might eventually exacerbate the tension between Palestinian and Jewish residents, and between Palestinian organizations and the state. Rather, mobilization patterns and mobilizing agendas (the "outputs" of collective action) have been influenced by the interplay of opportunity structures and their changing nature with internal political, cultural and social contestations within Jaffa's various organizations.

Governance and Minority Politics in Haifa

Situated in the north of Israel, Haifa is Israel's third largest city and an important industrial centre. The city grew rapidly during the Inter-World War period due to the construction of its port which was initiated by the British mandate authorities. Its growing economic significance was matched by its enhanced cultural role in mandatory Palestine, serving as a major centre of Palestinian theatre, printing houses, newspapers and the arts. At the same time, it also served as a target for Jewish immigration before World War II due to its strategic location in northern Palestine. Although there were tensions between the Palestinian and Jewish communities of Haifa, there were also remarkable instances of accommodation and political and economic cooperation before and after the establishment of Israel (Goren, 2006). The outbreak of inter-community hostilities during 1947 and 1948 and the war which followed Israel's declaration of independence have been subject to historiographic debate about the dynamics of the conflict and the causes, and indeed the balance, of Palestinian forced evacuation and voluntary abandonment of the city (Morris, 2002). What is clear is that a Palestinian community of about 70 000 people was reduced to a few thousand (Goren, 2004; Morris, 2002). Since then, Palestinian immigration to Haifa from the surrounding villages—searching for economic opportunities—and natural increase have contributed to the growth of the community. In the early 1960s it constituted 5% of the total population of the city, and by the mid-1990s it reached roughly 14% (Israel Central Bureau of Statistics, 1995). It now accounts for 9% of the population of Haifa, numbering about 30 000 people. Close to 60% of this community is defined as Christian Arab, the rest being mostly Moslem.

Haifa has traditionally been cited as an example of Arab-Jewish co-existence (Falah *et al.*, 2000). At the same time, available data indicate that the Arab residents of Haifa tend to have, overall, lower socio-economic status than the Jewish majority, exemplified in poorer housing, segregation, lower income and lower educational attainment levels in the city's public schools (City of Haifa, 2006; see also Table 1). So there has been an interesting tension between *perceptions* and officially supported narratives of co-existence (see below) and *realities* of social, economic and geographic inequalities. Findings from my research point to a number of important factors that underpin the relationship between Haifa's Arab residents and the city's Jewish majority. Three features have been particularly important in mediating the form and substance of contentious Palestinian politics in Haifa.

Governance dynamics: leadership and symbolic politics
First, there is an important historical legacy of strong local political leadership with its traditional emphasis on "co-existence", inter-community accommodation and dialogue as key political and symbolic strategies used by Haifa's civic leaders throughout its modern history (Goren, 2006). The important point is, however, that the strength of political leadership in the form of mayoral charisma extends mostly to the symbolic and discursive spheres—exemplified by public statements about the distinctiveness of Haifa as a model of co-existence that is allegedly different than the reality in the rest of Israel—and much less towards concrete policy initiatives. In fact, the weak policy capacity of Haifa stands in contrast to the situation in Tel Aviv-Jaffa (for instance, the city of Haifa still operates under a statutory Outline Plan prepared in 1934 under the auspices of the British Mandate of Palestine). As one senior city council official has commented in an interview:

> ... we've developed a brand of municipal localism here ... of inter-group accommodation, common life and dialogue, that has set us apart from other places in Israel. Some of the things we've done ... such as the special festivals, could not have been dreamt about elsewhere.

In my interviews and fieldwork in Haifa it became apparent that both the mayor and the senior level of his local government machinery focused much of their resources on symbolic gestures. For instance, during 2001 the then mayor of Haifa appointed a Palestinian "figurehead" to a newly created municipal position of a "Vice Mayor for Arab Affairs", which was in effect devoid of significant power and resources, and was quick to be condemned as an empty gesture by local Palestinian elites. On the other hand, the city's civic leadership has been reluctant to engage in the development of concrete policy initiatives that would target specifically the city's Palestinian residents, or even acknowledge them as a distinctive ethnonational group. There has been thus a latent tension between what the city—through the symbolic efforts of its leaders—has proclaimed to be, and the coherence of urban development policy initiatives which have not matched the prevailing characterization. As a senior Haifa policymaker commented in an interview, the city's official discourse has placed a strong emphasis on a civic (as opposed to an ethnic, culturally collective) form of social rights in terms of its policy agenda:

> In fact, we do not look at the Arab minority as a distinctive group from an identity or a national point of view, but as just another group that deserves the same level of services as everyone else. The purpose of urban planning here is to reduce inequalities.

A landmark event demonstrating the significance of the Haifa model of intermingled leadership and symbolism in mediating between the geopolitics of the Palestinian–Israeli conflict and local circumstances occurred in October 2000. During that time, Israel's Palestinian minority engaged in wide-ranging protests and demonstrations in conjunction with the escalating conflict and violence in the Palestinian Occupied Territories. As in other parts of the country (particularly in northern Israel), Haifa became a scene of confrontation between Palestinian protestors and police forces. During these events, Haifa's mayor at the time, Mr Amram Mitzna, stepped out of his city council chamber and physically put himself between a group of Arab-Palestinian demonstrators in one of the city's prominent Palestinian neighbourhoods—Wasi Nisnas—and the security forces, persuading both sides to step down. He then called on a "summit" of the city's major religious groups in order to restore calm and open dialogue. He was consequently rewarded in local elections with an overwhelming electoral support by the Arab-Palestinian minority. While he subsequently did little to follow up with concrete policies aimed at improving the living conditions or the quality of social services in the city's Palestinian neighbourhood, his symbolic gesture continued to be powerfully ingrained in the memory of local activists and residents.

Palestinian political organization
Second, there is a broader contextual factor which has shaped the terrain on which Palestinian mobilization has materialized in Haifa. The city has been traditionally a considered a bastion of the Israeli left, and has often been referred to as Red Haifa, because of the strength of the Labour party and the power of trade unions, through which there has been significant representation of Haifa's Arab elites. Furthermore, the Israeli Communist Party, in its different incarnations, still regards Haifa as one of its most important local branches, and the city has played an important role in the socialization of Israeli-Palestinian activists and intellectuals into political involvement. Currently part of the Democratic Front for Peace and Equality (HADASH by its Hebrew acronym), the party has traditionally emphasized parity and cooperation between Jewish and Palestinian activists, and has attempted to develop class consciousness as opposed to ethnonational discourse. Yet, both the grip of the traditional left (in the form of the Israeli Labour Party) and the more radical left (in the form of HADASH) on local politics have been seriously weakening in the past 15 years, with challenges coming from right-wing Israeli parties as well as from more radical Palestinian nationalists challenging the viability of HADASH's ideology. What this has meant is that while Haifa's Palestinians have tended to enjoy rather strong and visible forms of formal

political organization (in the form of HADASH), there has been a sense that since the mid-1990s the contestation of different ideological streams has become at once more visible and acute, as well as providing grounds for latent intra-community tensions.

Institutions and symbolic politics
The third element shaping the ways through which ethnic mobilezation and urban governance have interacted in Haifa refers to the symbolic role of key institutions. Multi-culturalism and tolerance can be enhanced, or at least be constructed discursively and symbolically as important local qualities, by the presence of particular local institutions. In Haifa, the Arab-Jewish Centre, located at the edge of the pre-dominantly Palestinian Wadi Nisnas neighbourhood, has played a key role in engaging both communities with each other through a range of social, cultural and political initiatives. For instance, it has initiated the annual "Holiday of Holidays", a common festive to all three major religions represented in the city. The event has helped to support a sense of identity and citizenship that is at once local and regional, by stressing the character of Haifa as a Mediterranean city rather than merely an Israeli or Palestinian city.

Place-making politics
Taken together, the mainly symbolic role of local political leadership, the wider contextual factor of Haifa's distinctive role with an Israeli left politics, and the symbolic actions of distinctive local institutions have funnelled the terrain and the form of Palestinian mobilizing agendas and the particular formation of urban governance around minority–majority relations in the city. What this view enables us to establish is the complex shades of ethnic mobilization and the politics of claiming citizenship. It helps us in avoiding the narrowing down of patterns of mobilization and political campaigns to an overtly simplistic correlation between dependent and independent variables, and to obtain a rich picture of the urban political field as a terrain for the governance of ethnically fractured communities.

For instance, it is precisely the discourse of "co-existence" which has become the target of and opportunity structure for dissenting voices among several more radical Palestinian actors in Haifa. Seeking to challenge the dominant discourse of "co-existence in Haifa", these activists have combined in their strategy, particularly in the struggle over space, with more imaginary, or visionary, counter-discourses about the reconstruction of Lower Haifa as a re-enlivenment of the lost Palestinian City, the centre of the cultural, national and social life of Palestinian identity, which was lost in 1948. The combination of material struggle incorporating liberal civic demands of quality of life and life-chances issues with collective identity and rights demands, and the visionary elements of cultural and nationalist memory has come about at least partly as a result of local elites identifying "crack's" in the local political opportunity structures, as well as in recognition of wider political shifts among the Palestinian citizens of Israel and their relationship to the state (which has manifested in the rise of the Islamic Movement on the one hand, and secular ethnonationalism in the form of the young BALAD Party).

The confluence of discursive and symbolic institutional features in the governance of Haifa, with the tradition of relatively well organized explicit political organization forms, and emerging forms of infra-politics where the privileged position of the traditional Left is increasingly "squeezed" by both Islamic and radical-secular ethnonational politics is now prevalent in the city. For instance, rather than representing an ameliorating space within the broader context of the politics of claim-making among Israel's Palestinian citizens, the governance of Haifa may evolve to an ever closer proxy to its respective national space. And yet local variations continue to matter. In the politics of place that ensued during the first years of the twenty-first century, such variations mattered in the mediation of Palestinian protest and contention.

I have already highlighted the example of the city's mayor intervention during the fatal events of the October 2000 rising. The other example concerns the threat of housing demolition in the mostly Moslem neighbourhood of Halisa in Haifa. Reacting to a threat by the city authority to demolish an illegally built structure, a coalition of activists from the community, Jewish and Palestinian, supported by elites of both HADASH and the nationalist BALAD organizations, and extended to embrace national actors from Palestinian and Jewish Israeli left-wing parties and non-governmental organizations, was able to effectively resist the act. It is important to note that my research in the community revealed that activists sought at once to challenge through their act the notion of Haifa's alleged symbolic local distinctiveness, while also treading a fine line to avoid breaking with the tradition of a local model of accommodation. In the word of one activist, "we knew that things would not deteriorate to violence, or to demolition of homes ... after all, *this is Haifa!*"

My interviews and fieldwork in Haifa have also revealed significant undercurrents of infra-politics, where rivalry and competition between different political, cultural and religious streams were translated to latent forms of neighbourhood politics. For instance, with regards to Lower Haifa—the section of the city where much of the Israeli-Palestinian population reside—campaigns for educational reform between 2003 to 2006 were actually more than just about raising educational standards. Underneath, these campaigns were motivated, in part, by a middle-class elite who wanted to break away from the traditional hold of Christian religious institutions on Arab-speaking schools, and in part by Islamic Movement activists who have sought to weaken church-led institutions in the city. In addition, latent tensions and localized forms of ethnic politics give rise to a geographic pattern of political and religious organization, with the Halisa neighbourhood of the city being increasingly identified with the institutions of the Islamic Movement, while Wadi Nisnas, the other large Israeli-Arab neighbourhood, retaining its more Christian and left-wing orientation (albeit challenged by new secular forms of local ethnonationalism).

It is through struggles over city spaces that the placing of Haifa as a benign and distinctive model of Palestinian-Jewish polity is challenged and called into question. While Haifa's governance elites have sough to construct a polity that projects inter-ethnic accommodation through the discourses of its governing institutions—and primarily through symbolic gestures—it is precisely this discursive polity that has become the object of minority mobilization. Far from successfully constructing a hegemonic citizenship regime, this attempted dominant discourse has manifested itself as a local opportunity structure: a set of hard and soft institutional features that Palestinian activists have sought to challenge. The shaping of fault-line citizenship has thus involved a polity-creating effort by the state on the one hand, and constant resistance to this representation of the city that this project entails on the other.

Conclusion

The empirical discussion in this paper provides an important contribution to the fledgling studies of the urban governance of ethnically mixed cities. Within the context of this volume, one of the important challenges has been to begin to uncover a local level of governance with respect to the contentious politics of ethnic, religious, national and cultural diversity. At the heart of this broad-based and international scope in inquiry are surly normative questions: how far can local models of governing diversity advance various forms of social and political rights? What is the potential of local governance dynamics to advance social justice and enhance democratic practices? But before such questions can be addressed, further empirical and theoretical work needs to be undertaken in order to explore, in the first instance, the very institutional, historical and cultural contexts that may or may not give rise to locally distinctive forms of ethnic politics. To this end, the paper has provided the contribution of empirical discussion of two contested cities in Israel that are themselves situated within a larger geopolitical terrain of ethnonational and territorial conflict.

A relational view of citizenship contributes to overcoming the impasse of static institutionalism manifested in many studies of opportunity structures an political contention on the one hand, and approaches to social movements which have emphasized the organic, or grass root, nature of movement politics on the other hand, but have failed to relate them to the form and apparatus of the state (Koopmans, 2004; Koopmans & Olzak, 2004; Tarrow, 1998). Relational approaches to citizenship studies are particularly appropriate for research concerning the particular role that cities and urban politics play within a wider, complex constellation of territorial politics of rights involving local, national and supra-national dimensions. The implication of an approach that is more explicit about the local context of minority political organization and mobilizing agendas is a detailed interrogation of urban governance dynamics. The institutional features of urban governance combine local dynamics at the same time that they incorporate the crucial role of the nation state. As Lowndes (2005) has argued, the advantage of institutionalist analysis is that it seeks to uncover the informal "rules of the game" that underpin local politics. When augmented by an emphasis on the politics of urban development and place making, we can begin to develop a nuanced view of whether, how and why local politics matters.

It has been shown in this paper that studies of inter-ethnonational relations at the local scale can both illuminate the wider picture of conflict, while also highlighting how city-wide politics of contention and ethnic mobilization can produce their own dynamics of the substance and meanings of citizenship. So while, *prima facie*, the substance of political mobilization by the Palestinian communities of Haifa and Jaffa might come across as very similar, a closer inspection reveals important—albeit at times nuanced—variations. In Table 2, a summary of political claims made by activists in both cities is presented, demonstrating that in both cities civic concerns over housing condition and allocation, the status of the educational system, and public safety have been paramount. Yet, more subtly, collective identity-based claims have featured in the form of an undertone of urban separatism in Haifa and Palestinian community survival in Jaffa.

Those nuanced variations are of great significance to and the subject for considerable efforts of political activists among numerically small and (politically and socially) marginalized minorities. Table 3 summarizes how features of minority politics in the two cities differ from each other, and how they relate to the national scale of state intervention (regime capacity), the prevailing citizenship incorporation discourse, and patterns of minority mobilization. This tentative summary highlights the contingent nature of "scaled" citizenship at the sub-national level. In Haifa, the historical legacy and current

Table 2. The substance of contemporary Israeli-Palestinian political claims in Jaffa and Haifa

Jaffa	Haifa
Housing: conditions, affordability, infrastructure	Housing: conditions, affordability, renewal, construction of new neighbourhoods
Community survival; resisting gentrification	
Education: reform and improvement	Education: reform and improvement
Fighting crime, contentious policing issues, public safety	Public safety
Urban separatism: safeguarding Jaffa's Palestinian past	Urban separatism: safeguarding Haifa's Palestinian past

claims by civic leadership to produce and represent the city's "distinctiveness" are example of the political construction of difference locally. In Jaffa, patterns of conflict and social exclusion seem to re-produce and enhance the subordination of the Palestinian citizens of Israel, which has become an important feature of the country's form of ethnonational politics, producing what Yiftachel (2001) has coined an "ethnocracy". While activists in Haifa could draw on both the city's symbolic gestures and the relative strength of party and non-governmental organizations as important resources for action,

Table 3. The political terrain of minority politics in Haifa and Jaffa, within the context of ethnopolitics in Israel

	Israel	Haifa	Tel Aviv-Jaffa
Regime intensity	+	−	+
	State control through various forms: budget allocation, planning and land policy, surveillance, etc.	Weak local state capacity; weak formal policy	Strong local state intervention in Jaffa; strong local state institutions (Jaffa Governance Unit)
Incorporation discourse	+	+	−
	Selective rhetoric of "equality" and "rights"	Prevalent local institutional discourse of co-existence; Red Haifa localism; strong symbolism	Weak sense of cultural/ethnic recognition; legacy of social exclusion
Minority political mobilization	+	+	−
	Strong, through combination of party and non-governmental organizations	Strong. Historical role of Haifa in the evolution of Israeli left wing; strong political organization	Weak. An internally fragmented, despite experiments. Dominated by infra-politics

+ sign represents a strong factor; − sign represents a relatively weak factor.

activists in Jaffa enjoyed little of either options, and their actions have been further constrained by strong local state interventions.

Both cities highlight the importance of political contestation and ethnic movement politics to an in-depth uncovering of what I have termed "relational citizenship", one that is explored by a dynamic and qualitative assessment of the juxtaposition of state practices, countervailing strategies of minority actors, and the infra-politics of ethnic movements. In this, the paper has provided a contribution towards a dynamic and "scaled" conceptualization of the dynamics of political claim-making and ethnic contention. It has been argued that vintage insight can be gained by highlighting the institutional features of localized minority–majority relations in combination with an emphasis on the politics of space and place, so as to gain a fuller and richer view of how the urban governance of ethnically fractured cities is conditioned by both institutional features (such as political opportunities and the symbolic role of governance arrangements) and concrete struggles over particular places (see also May, 1996; Purcell, 2001).

Cities are important arenas for the study of minority citizenship and rights, even under extreme circumstances of inter-nationalist conflict. It is important to remember, however, that national politics still matter in providing the framework for social cohesion and constitutional rights. The interplay between local and non-local political constellations of opportunities, constraints and circumstances represents an important challenge to which contemporary studies of ethnic politics and the construction of citizenship regimes have yet to adequately respond.

Acknowledgements

The paper draws on research that has been financially supported by grants from the Nuffield Foundation (grant no. SGS/00856/G) and the Economic and Social Research Council in the UK (award no. RES-000-22-0894). This financial support is gratefully acknowledged. The author also wishes to thank Mr Erez Hatna of the Geography Department at Tel-Aviv University for the production of the maps. Earlier versions of this paper were discussed during the international conference of the European Consortium for Political Research, Budapest 2005, and the World Convention of the Association of the Study of Nationalities, New York City, 2006. The helpful comments and suggestions provided by the participants in these workshops, the editors of *Ethnopolitics*, two anonymous referees and Mr Roald Plug are gratefully acknowledged. Responsibility for any mistakes rests solely with the author.

Notes

1. In Israeli discourse the term "mixed cities" refers to those few cities containing a Palestinian minority (Jerusalem, Haifa, Lydda, Ramla, Tel Aviv-Jaffa, Acre and Upper Nazareth). However, due to the segregated nature of these cities I prefer the terms "ethnically fractured cities", or "contested cities".
2. Traditionally, the Arabs within pre-1967 Israel have been referred to as "Israeli-Arabs", although the terms Israeli-Palestinians, or the Palestinian citizens of Israel (PCIs), are increasingly common in use. The term "Palestinians" is usually applied to the population of the Occupied Territories of the West Bank and the Gaza Strip (that is, the territories occupied by Israel since 1967). In this paper I use the terms the Palestinian citizens of Israel, or Israeli-Palestinians, which reflect a current trend in the political identity of this group.

3. Before 1975, mayors were chosen from city council members through post-election coalition-building negotiations between the various political parties.
4. The size of the Israeli-Palestinian population is estimated to be around 1.2 million.
5. Israel unilaterally withdrew its army from the Gaza Strip, which, along with the west back, it occupied as a result of the 1967 war, in 2005.
6. Accordnig to LeVine (2005, pp. 215–216), the Israeli government decision to annex Jaffa was only reluctantly accepted by the civic leadership of Tel Aviv. The decision, according to LeVine (2005), was largely due to the government's ambition to further undermine the Arab nature of Jaffa, and to newly demarcate the new, modern municipality of Tel Aviv-Jaffa.
7. The discussion in the this context is founded on the author's fieldwork in Jaffa.

References

Amin, A. (2002) Ethnicity and the Multicultural City: Living with Diversity, *Environment and Planning A*, 34(6), pp. 959–980.
Archibugi, D., Held, D. & Kohler. (Eds) (1998) *Re-imagining Political Communities: Studies in Cosmopolitan Citizenship* (Cambridge: Polity Press).
Balibar, E. (1995) Is European Citizenship Possible?, in: J. Holston (Ed.), *Cities and Citizenship* (Durham, North Carolina: Duke University Press).
Ball, R. & Piper, N. (2002) Globalisation and Regulation of Citizenship—Filipino Migrant Workers in Japan, *Political Geography*, 21, pp. 1013–1034.
Banton, M. (2000) Ethnic Conflict, *Sociology*, 34, pp. 481–198.
Baubock, R. (1994) *Transnational Citizenship* (Northampton, MA: Edward Elgar).
Beall, J., Crankshaw, O. & Parnell, S. (2002) *Uniting a Divided City: Governance and Social Exclusion in Johannesburg* (London: Earthscan).
Bell, D. & Keil, R. (Eds) (1996) *Global Processes, Local Places* (Montreal: Black Rose Books).
Benford, R. D. & Snow, D. A. (2000) Framing Processes and Social Movements: An Overview and Assessment, *Annual Review of Sociology*, 26, pp. 611–639.
Blank, Y. (2004) The Localisation of the "Local": Local Government Law, Decentralisation and Territorial Inequality in Israel, *Mishpatim*, 34, pp. 197–300 (in Hebrew).
Bollens, S. A. (2000) *Urban Policy and Ethnic Conflict in Jerusalem and Belfast*, (Albany, NY: SUNY Press).
Boudreau, J.-A. & Keil, R. (2001) Seceding from Responsibility? Secession Movements in Los Angeles, *Urban Studies*, 38, pp. 1701–1731.
Bousetta, H. (2000) Institutional Theories of Immigrant Ethnic Mobilisation: Relevance and Limitations, *Journal of Ethnic and Migration Studies*, 26, pp. 229–245.
Bulmer, M. (1998) Conceptualising Fractured Societies: The Case of Israel, *Ethnic and Racial Studies*, 21, pp. 383–407.
City of Haifa (2006) *Statistical Yearbook* (Haifa: Municipality of Haifa, Department of Strategic Planning and Research).
City of Tel Aviv-Jaffa (2005) *Statistical Yearbook* (Tel Aviv-Jaffa: Municipality of Tel Aviv, Department of Social and Economic Research).
Della Porta, D. & Diani, M. (1999) *Social Movements* (Oxford: Blackwell).
Dowding, K. (2001) Explaining Urban Regimes, *International Journal of Urban and Regional Research*, 25, pp. 7–19.
Ehrkamp, P. & Leitner, H. (2003) Beyond National Citizenship: Turkish Immigrants and the (Re)construction of Citizenship in Germany, *Urban Geography*, 24. pp. 127–146.
Ellis, G. (2001) The Difference that Context Makes: Planning and Ethnic Minorities in Northern Ireland, *European Planning Studies*, 9(3), pp. 339–358.
Fabian, R. (2001) Yaffo (Jaffa): A Commentary on Urban-political Insight, *Mikarov: A Social-Literary Journal*, 6, pp. 26–49.
Falah, G. (1996) Living Together Apart: Residential Segregation in Mixed Arab-Jewish Cities, *Urban Studies*, 33, pp. 823–857.
Falah, G. (1997) Ethnic Perceptual Differences of Housing and Neighbourhood Quality in Mixed Arab-Jewish cities in Israel, *Environment and Planning A*, 29, pp. 1663–1674.

Falah, G., Hoy, M. & Sarker, R. (2000) Co-existence in Selected Arab-Jewish Cities in Israel: By Choice or by Default?, *Urban Studies*, 37(4), pp. 775–796.

Ghanem, A. (1998) State and Minority in Israel: The Case of Ethnic State and the Predicament of its Minority, *Ethnic and Racial Studies*, 21(3), pp. 428–448.

Ghosh, S. & Wang, L. (2003) Transnationalism and Identity: A Tale of Two Faces and Multiple Lives, *The Canadian Geographer*, 47, pp. 269–282.

Goren, T. (2004) The Judaization of Haifa at the Time of the Arab Revolt, *Middle Eastern Studies*, 40, pp. 135–152.

Goren, T. (2006) Hassan Bey Shukri and his Contribution to the Integration of Jews in the Haifa Municipality at the Time of the British Mandate, *British Journal of Middle Eastern Studies*, 33, pp. 19–36.

Harding, A. (1994) Urban Regimes and Growth Machines: Towards a Cross-national Research Agenda, *Urban Affairs Quarterly*, 29, pp. 356–382.

Harney, N. D. (2006) The Politics of Urban Space: Modes of Place-making by Italians in Toronto's Neighbourhoods, *Modern Italy*, 11, pp. 25–42.

Healey, P. (1997) *Collaborative Planning: Shaping Places in Fragmented Societies* (Basingstoke: Macmillan).

Hepburn, A. C. (2004) *Contested Cities in the Modern West* (Basingstoke: Palgrave-Macmillan).

Hooghe, M. (2005) Ethnic Organisations and Social Movement Theory: The Political Opportunity Structure for Ethnic Mobilisation in Flanders, *Journal of Ethnic and Migration Studies*, 31, pp. 975–990.

Horan, C. (2002) Racializing Regime Politics, *Journal of Urban Affairs*, 24(1), pp. 19–33.

Israel Central Bureau of Statistics (1995) *Population and Housing Census*, (Jerusalem: Government of Israel Publishing).

Jacobs, D. (2000) Multinational and Polyethnic Politics Entwined: Minority Representation in the Region of Brussels-Capital, *Journal of Ethnic and Migration Studies*, 26, pp. 289–304.

Jamal, A. (2002) Beyond "Ethnic Ddemocracy": State Structure, Multicultural Conflict, and Differentiated Citizenship in Israel, *New Political Science*, 24(3), pp. 411–431.

Kimmerling, B. & Migdal, J. S. (2003) *The Palestinian People: A History*, London: Harvard University Press.

Koopmans, R. (2004) Migrant Mobilisation and Political Opportunities: Variation among German Cities and Comparison with the UK and the Netherlands, *Journal of Ethnic and Migration Studies*, 30, pp. 449–470.

Koopmans, R. & Olzak, S. (2004) Discursive Opportunities and the Evolution of Right-wing Violence in Germany, *American Journal of Sociology*, 110, pp. 198–230.

Krause, S. (2003) Lady Liberty's Allure: Political Agency, Citizenship and the Second Sex, *Philosophy and Social Criticism*, 26, pp. 1–24.

LeVine, M. (2005) *Overthrowing Geography* (Berkley, CA: University of California Press).

Lowndes, V. (2005) Something Old, Something New, Something Borrowed ... How Institutions Change (and Stay the Same) in Local Governance, *Policy Studies*, 26(3/4), pp. 291–309.

Mabin, A. & Smit, D. (1997) Reconstructing South Africa's Cities? The Making of Urban Planning 1900–2000, *Planning Perspectives*, 12(2), pp. 193–223.

Martin. (2003) "Place-framing" as Place-making: Constituting a Neighbourhood for Organising and Activism, *Annals of the Association of American Geographers*, 93, pp. 730–750.

May, J. (1996) Globalisation and the Politics of Place: Place and Identity in an Inner London Neighbourhood, *Transactions of the Institute of British Geographers*, 21, pp. 194–215.

McAdam, D. (1982) *Political Process and the Development of Black Insurgency: 1930–1970* (Chicago, IL: Chicago University Press).

McAdam, D., McCarthy, J. D. & Zald, M. N. (Eds) (1996) *Comparative Perspectives on Social Movements, Political Opportunities, Mobilising Structures and Cultural Framings* (Cambridge: Cambridge University Press).

McAdam, D., Tarrow, S. & Tilly, C. (2001) *Dynamics of Contention* (Cambridge: Cambridge University Press).

McCarthy, J. & Zald, M. N. (1977) Resource Mobilisation and Social Movements: A Partial Theory, *American Journal of Sociology*, 82, pp. 1212–1241.

Menahem, G. (1998) Arab Citizens in an Israeli City: Action and Discourse in Public Programmes, *Ethnic and Racial Studies*, 21, pp. 545–557.

Menahem, G. (2000) Jews, Arabs, Russians and Foreigners in an Israeli City: Ethnic Divisions and the Restructuring Economy of Tel Aviv, 1983–96, *International Journal of Urban and Regional Research*, 24, pp. 634–654.

Mesch, G. S. & Manor, O. (2001) Ethnic Differences in Urban Neighbour Relations in Israel, *Urban Studies*, 38(1), pp. 1943–1952.

Montereskou, D & Fabian, R. (2003) "The Gilded Cage": Gentrification and Globalisation in the *Andromedah Hill* Project, Jaffa, *Theory and Critique*, 23, pp. 141–178 (in Hebrew).

Morris, B. (2002) *The Birth of the Palestinian Refugee Problems, 1947–1949* (Tel Aviv: Am Oved Press) (in Hebrew).

Mossberger, K. & Stoker, G. (2001) The Evolution of Urban Regime Theory: The Challenges of Conceptualisation, *Urban Affairs Review*, 36, pp. 810–835.

Page, E. & Goldsmith, M. (1987) *Central and Local Government Relations*, Beverly Hills, CA: Sage.

Phalet, K. & Swyngedouw, M. (2002) National Identities and Representations of Citizenship: A Comparison of Turks, Moroccans and Working-class Belgians in Brussels, *Ethnicities*, 2, pp. 5–30.

Purcell, M. (2001) Neighbourhood Activism among Home owners as a Politics of Space, *Professional Geographer*, 53, pp. 178–194.

Purcell, M. (2003) Citizenship and the Right to the Global City: Reimagining the Capitalist World Order, *International Journal of Urban and Regional Research*, 27, pp. 564–590.

Rabinowitz, D. (2001) The Palestinian Citizens of Israel, the Concept of Trapped Minority, and the Discourse of Rransnationalism in Anthropology, *Ethnic and Racial Studies*, 24, pp. 64–85.

Savitch, H. V. & Kantor, P. (2002) *Cities in the International Market Place* (Princeton, NJ: Princeton University Press).

Schnell, Y. & Alexander, M. (2002) *Urban Policy Towards Migrant Workers: Lessons from Tel Aviv-Jaffa* (Jerusalem: Floersheimer Institute for Policy Research) (In Hebrew).

Schöpflin, G. (2000) *Nations, Identity, Power: The New Politics of Europe* (London: Hurst & Company).

Smith, M. & Beazley, M. (2000) Progressive Regimes, Partnerships and the Involvement of Local Communities: A Framework for Evaluation, *Public Administration*, 78, pp. 855–878.

Smith, S. (1995) Citizenship: all or Nothing?, *Political Geography*, 14, pp. 190–193.

Smooha, S. (2002) The Model of Ethnic Democracy: Israel as a Jewish and Democratic State, *Nations and Nationalism*, 8, pp. 475–503.

Snow, D., Rochford Jr, E. B., Worden, S. K. & Benford, R. D. (1986) Frame Alignment Processes, Micromobilisation, and Movement Pparticipation, *American Sociological Review*, 51, pp. 464–481.

Soysal, Y. (1994) *Limits of Citizenship: Migrants and Post-National Membership in Europe* (Chicago, IL: University of Chicago Press).

Staeheli, L. A. (2003) Cities and Citizenship, *Urban Geography*, 24, pp. 97–102.

Staeheli, L. A. & Thompson, A. (1997) Citizenship, Community, and Struggles for Public Space, *The Professional Geographer*, 49, pp. 28–38.

Stone, C. (1993) Urban Regimes and the Capacity to Govern: A Political Economy Approach, *Journal of Urban Affairs*, 15, pp. 1–28.

Svirsky, S. & Connor-Attias, E. (2006) *A Report on Social Conditions in Israel: 2006*, Tel Aviv-Jaffa: ADVA Centre (in Hebrew), available online at: http://www.adva.org/UserFiles/File/ADVA_ISRAEL_2006_H EB1.pdf

Tarrow, S. (1983) *Struggling to Reform: Social Movements and Policy Change During Cycles of Protest*, Western Societies Program Occasional Paper No. 15. New York Center for International Studies, Cornell University, Ithaca, NY.

Tarrow, S. (1996) States and Opportunities: The Political Structuring of Social Movements, in: D. McAdam, J.D. McCarthy & M.N. Zald (Eds), *Comparative Perspectives on Social Movements, Political Opportunities, Mobilising Structures and Cultural Framings*, pp. 41–61 (Cambridge: Cambridge University Press).

Tarrow, S. (1998) *Power in Movement: Social Movement and Contentious Politics*, (Cambridge: Cambridge University Press).

Tilly, C. (1978) *From Mobilisation to Revolution* (Reading, MA: Addison-Wesley).

Tzfadia, E. & Yiftachel, O. (2004) Between Urban and National: Political Mobilisation among Mizrahim in Israel's "Development Towns", *Cities*, 21, pp. 41–55.

Urry, J. (2000) Global Flows and Global Citizenship, in: E. Isin (Ed.), *Democracy, Citizenship and the Global City*, pp. 17–28 (London: Routledge).

van den Berghe, P.L. (2002) Multicultural Democracy: Can it Work?, *Nations and Nationalism*, 8(4), pp. 433–449.

Vermeersch, P. (2003) Ethnic Minority Identity and Movement Politics: The Case of the Roma in the Czech Republic and Slovakia, *Ethnic and Racial Studies*, 26, pp. 879–901.

Yacobi, H. & Tzfadia, E. (2004) On the Formation of Territorial Citizenship: Nationalism and Space Among Immigrants in Lydda (Israel), *Theory and Critique*, 24, pp. 45–71 (in Hebrew).
Yiftachel, O. (1997) The Political Geography of Ethnic Protest: Nationalism, Deprivation and Regionalism Among Arabs in Israel, *Transactions of the Institute of British Geographers*, 22(1), pp. 91–110.
Yiftachel, O. (2001) Centralised Power and Divided Space: "Fractured Regions" in the Israeli "Ethnocracy", *GeoJournal*, 53(3), pp. 283–293.
Yiftachel, O. (2002) The Shrinking Space of Citizenship: Ethnocratic Politics in Israel, *Middle East Report*, 32, pp. 38–45.
Yuval-Davis, N. (1999) The Multi-layered Citizen: Citizenship at the Age of "Glocalisation", *International Feminist Journal of Politics*, 1, pp. 119–136.

The Future of Kirkuk

DAVID ROMANO

Department of International Studies, Rhodes College, USA

Since the ouster of Saddam Hussein's regime in 2003, the city of Kirkuk's status has emerged as one of the thorniest issues in need of resolution. Iraq's Kurds, Turkmen, and Arab communities have all made claims on Kirkuk and its surrounding oil fields. Kurds and Turkmen even go so far as to portray Kirkuk as their "Jerusalem," implying a quasi-religious and inalienable attachment to the city. Iraq's Kurdish groups in particular expended a great deal of effort trying to advance their claims on Kirkuk, including demanding provisions in Iraq's constitution regarding the city. Neighboring Turkey, in turn, has periodically demanded that Kirkuk not fall under Kurdish control, and that its Turkmen population and identity be preserved as an integral part of a unified Iraq.

In the post-Saddam sectarian struggle for power, the fate of Kirkuk will continue to play a very important role. The analysis below provides an overview of the modern history of the city of Kirkuk and its surrounding area, its role in Iraqi politics, and the risk of sectarian conflict over control of the Kirkuk region breaking out. This paper also assesses the broad outlines of various strategies for mitigating sectarian conflict over Kirkuk, as suggested by a number of observers. More specifically, it is argued that Article 140 of Iraq's Constitution (which promises to hold a referendum on the status of Kirkuk no later than 31 December 2007), should be respected. Should the referendum results indicate a desire to join Kirkuk governorate to the Kurdish Autonomous Region, such inclusion should occur along with a number of federalist resource and power-sharing provisions, and the city of Kirkuk itself should possibly receive a special independent administrative status.

Kirkuk's Mixed History

Kirkuk lies in the plains adjacent to the Zagros mountain range, and abreast of some of Iraq's most important oil fields. The city is situated on ruins dating back some 5000 years, and its history as a city goes back at least to the time of the Assyrians (tenth century BC). Under the Ottoman Empire, Kirkuk functioned as an important garrison town. Over the years, Oguz Turks (in the eleventh century AD) and Ottoman officials came to form Kirkuk's large Turkmen population, at the same time that Kurds of the adjacent Zagros Mountains, Arabs from the south, and Christians from the earliest days of Christianity contributed to the city's ethnic mix. By the nineteenth century, Kirkuk became a very important cultural, economic, and political center for especially its Turkmen and Kurdish population. The discovery of oil around Kirkuk in 1927 also dramatically increased the city's strategic importance from the multi-ethnic market town it used to be.

After the British created Iraq in 1920 and then attached predominantly Kurdish northern Iraq (the Mosul Villayet,[1] including Kirkuk) to the new country in 1925, periodic Kurdish revolts broke out until 1991. While Iraq's Turkmen population remained too small to seriously entertain secessionist or irredentist ambitions, Iraqi Kurds never embraced their inclusion in the new Arab state. After the 1968 Arab nationalist Ba'ath Party's ascension to power, counter-insurgency campaigns and ethnic cleansing of non-Arabs from strategic areas (especially Kirkuk) preoccupied the government in Baghdad. Iraq's 1970 Agrarian Reform Law (Law 117), mandating that land in excess of a new maximum hectare limit (depending on the type and its crop) be expropriated and redistributed, was likewise disproportionately applied to Kurdish large landowners. The redistributed land was turned over especially to Arab small farmers. A 1970 Autonomy Accord, between Mullah Mustafa Barzani's Kurdish rebels in the north and the government in Baghdad, largely failed over disagreements on the borders of a Kurdish autonomous region. Barzani insisted on Kirkuk's inclusion within the Kurdish region, while Baghdad (represented in the negotiations by then Vice-President Saddam Hussein) categorically refused to allow Kirkuk and its surrounding oil fields to fall out of its control. The Ba'athist government instead changed the administrative boundaries of Kirkuk governorate, creating a new governorate of "Ta'amim," (meaning "nationalization") with new boundaries designed to lessen the Kurdish demographic majority of the Kirkuk region.

After crushing Mustafa Barzani's revolt (the last revolt of many for the elder Barzani) in 1975, Baghdad embarked upon a serious Arabization program for the Kirkuk region. Kurds, Turkmen and even Christians were expelled from Kirkuk and other areas, and replaced with mostly poor Shiite Arabs from the south, who were encouraged to settle in newly vacated lands in the north with grants of up to 10 000 Iraqi Dinars (roughly $35 000 USD at the time). After Iraqi Kurdish collusion with Iranian forces during the 1980–1988 Iran–Iraq War, the Arabization and counter-insurgency policies degenerated into the genocidal *Anfal* campaigns, during which 100 000 to 200 000 Iraqi Kurdish civilians were killed in northern Iraq.[2] After Iraqi Kurdistan gained autonomy from Saddam's Iraq in late 1991,[3] expulsions from Kirkuk and other areas south of the Kurdish safe haven continued at the rate of approximately 1000 expulsions a month until 2003.[4] All together, from the time of the Ba'ath Party's 1968 ascension to power until the March 2003 fall of Saddam's regime, some 200 000 to 300 000 people (mostly Kurds) were expelled from the Kirkuk area (Baker, 2004).

After the 2003 removal of Saddam's regime from power, many of those expelled from Kirkuk and other regions wished to quickly return to their former homes. Coalition authorities attempted to address the return and restitution issue in a neutral, legal, and uniform manner. In an attempt to buy time to devise a policy and avoid retribution by the displaced against Saddam's settlers, they tried to stall returns and pursued a "stay-put" policy.[5] Nonetheless, some 100 000 IDPs (internally displaced persons) returned to Kirkuk alone by 2005, generally taking up residence in new camps around the city or abandoned buildings.

As of 2005, Kirkuk contained approximately 710 000 inhabitants. A lack of any reliable census based on sectarian identities makes it difficult to know Kirkuk's exact ethnic make-up. In 2004, US Military officials estimated the city's make-up to be about 40% Kurdish, 35% Arab, 20% Turkmen, and 5% Christian.[6] Results from the January 2005 and December 2005 Iraqi elections, however, suggest a higher proportion of Kurds in Kirkuk governorate as a whole, given that Kurds won a significant majority (60% and 53.4% respectively) of the Kirkuk governorate vote.[7] Members of each major sectarian community routinely claim that they form the large majority of Kirkuk's population, however, and undertaking any ethnically sensitive census risks quickly becoming an explosive task. The last semi-reliable census of the area was taken in 1957 (see Figure 1). This census showed Turkmen comprising the largest single group in Kirkuk city, while Kurds formed the majority of the governorate as a whole.

The Post-Saddam Contest Over Kirkuk

With the downfall of Saddam Hussein's government in 2003, a myriad of political actors began struggling over the configuration of power in post-Saddam Iraq. The contest included religious forces, tribal groups, ethnic blocks, secular political parties and even various layers of Iraq's newly emerging post-Saddam bureaucracy.

The original intent of Ba'athist-era Arabization policies and ethnic cleansing around Kirkuk was to solidify central government and particularly Arab claims to the area, particularly in the event that sectarian conflict weakened the state. In this sense, settling

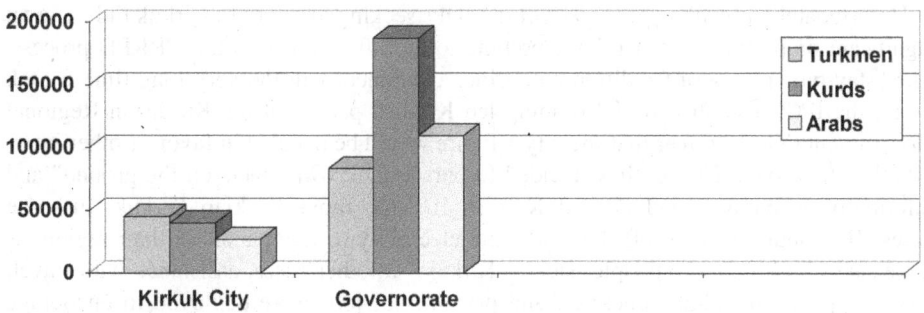

Figure 1. 1957 Census of Kirkuk City and Governorate. *Source:* 1957 census figures taken from O'Leary (2005, p. 84)[18]

Arabs from southern Iraq (to the tune of 200–300 000 thousand settlers since the 1970s) aimed to establish "facts on the ground". Iraqi Kurdish groups argue that the hundreds of thousands expelled from the Kirkuk area must be allowed to return, and restitution granted. Additionally, the vast majority of Saddam's "10 000 Dinar Settlers" must return south, lest his policies of ethnic cleansing be rewarded with a permanently altered demography around Kirkuk.

Forcibly expelling settlers, who were mostly poor Arab Shiites ordered or induced by Saddam to settle in the north, would amount to correcting an injustice with a new injustice, however. Further complicating matters, many settlers have also intermarried within the pre-existing population of Kirkuk and have children and even grandchildren born in Kirkuk. Forcing such people to move south will be perceived by many as "exile" rather than "return." The Coalition Provisional Authority that ran Iraq in the year after the invasion also wanted to avoid making, and taking the blame for, difficult decisions about the future of Kirkuk. They perceived no quick or easy answer that would satisfy all of the important sectarian groups with a stake in Kirkuk, and therefore tried to postpone the issue with their "stay-put" policy and a formal, fair and extremely slow legal process for determining competing claims for property in Kirkuk: the Iraqi Property Claims Commission (IPCC).

The IPCC describes itself as "... an independent agency of the Government of Iraq, established to redress certain wrongful takings of real property (or interests in real property), by confiscation, seizure, expropriation, forced sale, or otherwise, in Iraq during the period 17 July 1968 to 30 June 2003" (CPA, 2006). The IPCC envisions providing compensation for returnees deemed to have been deprived of property, as well as settlers ordered to vacate properties, although it remains unclear if sufficient funding will be made available for this kind of redress on a significant scale. The passage of time, loss of documents, and multiple overlapping and contradictory claims for property make the organization's task exceedingly complex. The IPCC only established its regional offices one year after the war (March 2004), and began accepting claims in July 2004. It began rendering judgments in October of 2004. Since March 2006 the IPCC has been renamed the Commission for Resolution of Real Property Disputes (CRRPD), and two important changes in the compensation law were made. First, good-faith secondary owners[8] now have the right to compensation from the government if the property they currently live in is returned to the primary owner. Second, property estimates are made according to the value of the land today, rather than at the time of their expropriation (Internal Displacement Monitoring Centre, 2006, p. 11).

Unfortunately, it is likely that most of the IDPs seeking to return to Kirkuk did not own significant property, and hence have nothing to look forward from the CRRPD process. The "stay-put" policy of Coalition authorities combined with the very long time it took to get the IPCC established and running led Kurdish parties of the Kurdistan Regional Government (KRG) to fear that the city's future would be decided in favor of other interests than their own. Hence, they decided to pursue their own "facts on the ground" and informally encouraged and pushed Kurdish IDPs to move back to Kirkuk. In some cases KRG authorities cut off the water and electricity to IDP camps in their region, as a means of pushing these people back to Kirkuk.[9] In other cases, assistance with travel, some supplies (including concrete), and promises of jobs were deployed to encourage Kurdish IDPs to return to Kirkuk sooner rather than later. Of course, many IDPs needed no encouragement to return. By the end of 2005, some 100 000 IDPs had returned to the Kirkuk area, and, as Figure 2 indicates, the US military estimates that as early as August 2003 the large majority of IDPs around Kirkuk were Kurdish.

Arab and Turkmen groups responded to the influx of Kurdish IDPs by claiming that the Kurdish parties were intent on taking over Kirkuk, or even engaging in "reverse ethnic cleansing."[10] One Arab settler described the situation quite simply: "The Kurds are Kurdifying the area. The Arabs Arabized the area. So we are just suffering the same as them. We came to Arabize the area. It's plain and simple. That was a big error" (interview with Shiite settler family in Kirkuk, 10 May 2004). Sectarian violence around Kirkuk has remained very limited, however, since the summer of 2003 until the fall of 2006. Estaban Sacco, a resettlement expert in Kirkuk, suggests that, unexpectedly, property disputes between Kurds and Arabs have not been paramount; the majority of claims have dealt with property confiscated by the former regime for public work projects (Internal Displacement Monitoring Centre, 2006, p. 10). Nonetheless, ominous statements and predictions abound, such as that of one of Kirkuk's Sunni Arab leaders: "The Arabs will not give up Kirkuk," said Mohammed Khalil, the leader of an Arab bloc within the Kurdish-dominated Kirkuk provincial council. "If America really wants to help Iraq, it will try to stop the Kurds from gaining control over Kirkuk, which would start a civil war" (Fainaru, 2005).

Clearly, the Kurdish parties running the Kurdistan Regional Government (the KDP—Kurdistan Democratic Party, and PUK—Patriotic Union of Kurdistan) wished to strengthen the Kurdish position around Kirkuk for the contest over the city that virtually all Iraqis knew was coming. In addition to promoting IDP returns, they have worked hard to place Kurds in as many positions of authority in Kirkuk City and Ta'amim (Kirkuk) Governorate as possible, including municipal councils, the police force, and the oil fields (of course, Saddam's government had barred most Kurds from such positions for years). In effect, most of Kirkuk's municipal government and various municipal services are run by Kurds today more than any other group. In the provincial elections, the Kurdish list won an absolute majority, holding 26 of 41 council seats. On the other hand, there is a

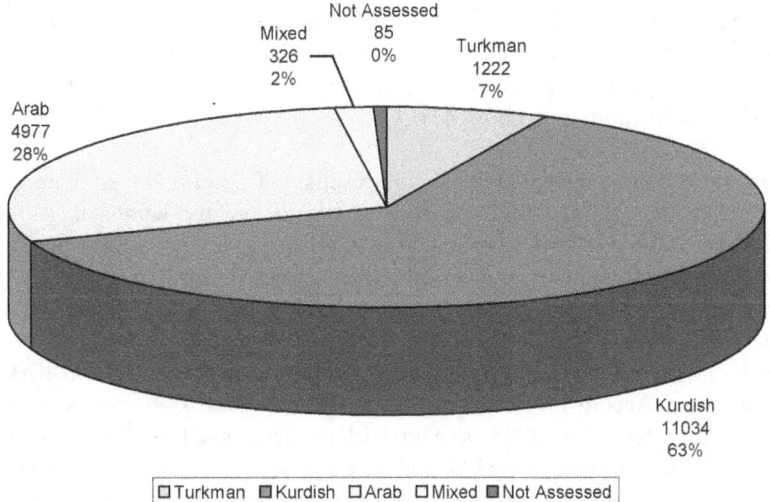

Figure 2. IDP Demographics—August 2003. *Source*: United States Civil-Military Operations Center Kirkuk

good chance that Arab settlers around Kirkuk also came under pressure from insurgents and Arab political forces to the south not to leave Kirkuk. Furthermore, in an attempt to protest against the Kurdish agenda, Arab and Turkoman politicians, while participating in council meetings, have made a habit of being absent for votes (International Crisis Group, 2006, p. 22). With a Kurdish majority controlling the Kirkuk municipal council, it seems these leaders preferred to boycott votes which they could not hope to determine.

The future of the city and its surrounding oil fields have, hence, become a central issue in post-Saddam Iraq, and negotiations over the permanent Iraqi Constitution almost failed over the Kirkuk issue. Kurdish parties successfully insisted that the permanent Constitution reaffirm Article 58 of Iraq's 2004 transitional Constitution, which stipulates that the situation in Kirkuk be normalized (meaning that people expelled from Kirkuk be allowed to return, and settlers would return south), and that a referendum (for everyone residing in Kirkuk) on the future of the city be completed by 31 December 2007. Shia leaders initially resisted these demands, due to a generalized Arab (both Sunni and Shiite) distrust of Kurdish demands for autonomy. Arab Iraqis fear that the Kurds plan on eventually seceding from Iraq, and the oil fields of Kirkuk could make such a Kurdish state more viable. Nonetheless, "... the need to reach consensus to form a postwar government eventually led to an accord, first cemented in Article 58 of Iraq's 2004 transitional constitution, and reaffirmed in the permanent constitution approved in October [of 2005], that falls roughly in line with the Kurdish vision for the city" (Negus, 2006). These stipulations became Article 140 of the permanent Constitution, which states:

> *First:* The executive authority shall undertake the necessary steps to complete the implementation of the requirements of all subparagraphs of Article 58 of the Transitional Administrative Law.
> *Second:* The responsibility placed upon the executive branch of the Iraqi Transitional Government stipulated in Article 58 of the Transitional Administrative Law shall extend and continue to the executive authority elected in accordance with this Constitution, provided that it accomplishes completely (normalization and census and concludes with a referendum in Kirkuk and other disputed territories to determine the will of their citizens), by a date not to exceed the 31st of December 2007. (Iraqi Constitution, 2005, p. 42)

Judging from the December 2005 election results, a Ta'amim Governorate or Kirkuk city referendum will almost surely produce a vote to join the Kurdistan Autonomous Region. In the December 2005 elections, the Kurdish parties got 53.4% of the vote in Ta'amim Governorate (a bit less than the 60% they garnered in the January 2005 elections but still a majority). The Iraqi National Dialogue Front (led by an Arab Sunni but including other communities) received 14% of the Ta'amim vote, followed by 10.9% for the Turkmen Front (the only seat they won in the Iraqi elections came from Kirkuk) and 5.9% for the Iraqi Accord Front (Arab Sunni). Turkmen and Arab groups have already claimed that the December 2005 vote in Kirkuk was rigged, and that many of the Kurdish IDPs who returned to Kirkuk and voted were not actually from Kirkuk.[11] Of course, Kurdish groups can just as easily argue that Arab settlers who voted in the Kirkuk region should not have had that right, as this rewards past Arabization policies. One can only assume that a 2007 referendum will produce even more strident protests.

To date, the IPCC/CRRPD has proven ponderous at best. As the graphs in Figure 3 illustrate, the IPCC from July 2004 until January 2006 received 129 758 claims, but pronounced judgment on only 19 151 of these claims. The majority of claims filed come from the Kirkuk region. According to the *Washington Post*,"... the agency [the IPCC] has failed to provide compensation to Kurds seeking to relocate or to Arabs seeking to return to their homes in southern Iraq, as required under the transitional law and the constitution" (Fainaru, 2005).

If both settlers and returning IDPs widely come to view the CRRPD as ponderously slow and incapable or unwilling to fulfill the promises made to them, this will not bode well for future peace in Kirkuk. IDPs may come to view continued delays and the failure to normalize the situation in Kirkuk as completely unacceptable, and blame Baghdad and Coalition Forces for the failure to fulfill their promises. They may decide to take matters more forcefully into their own hands and look north to the KRG authorities for assistance in doing so. Meanwhile, if they do not receive any assistance settlers may react to encroachments and view the post-Saddam regime as an unmitigated disaster, pushing them into the arms of the insurgency or radicals such as Moqtada [al-]Sadr and his Mahdi Army.

Strategies for Governing Iraq and Kirkuk

In Donald Horowitz' (1985) terms, Iraq would be a "centralized" ethnic system, in which the Arab and Kurdish ethnic groups (as well as the Sunni and Shiite groups) are so large that relations and competition between them become the central themes of politics within the state. Horowitz views such centralized ethnic systems as more prone to polarization and sectarian strife, as group symbols and relative group standing emerge as non-negotiable and incessant sources of conflict.

People in search of security, such as IDPs and settlers in a contest over territory in Kirkuk, tend to turn to whatever networks are available to support them—such as Kurdish political parties, Arab Sunni associations, and Shiite religious organizations. As Azar & Burton (1986) explain, people then often come to increasingly identify with and find much of their own sense of self-worth in the larger sectarian group to which they belong and derive security from. Such contests between sectarian groups can quickly polarize and become violent: as each group arms itself to defend against possible offensive moves from other nearby sectarian communities, the other communities likewise come to feel threatened and begin preparing for the worst. The resulting ethnic security dilemma can lead to pre-emptive violence as soon as one community resolves to act upon a temporary advantage, before the relative power balance shifts out of their favor (Posen, 1993). With the central government in Iraq still unable to provide security, the overall structural condition of anarchy in sectarian relations makes such an ethnic security dilemma a real threat.

In the case of Kirkuk, the city has become both a resource (due to the surrounding oil fields) and a symbol for Kurds and Turkmen, and perhaps Arabs as well. When symbols become markers of group status and worth, it becomes very difficult indeed to negotiate over them. Since oil resources constitute a material, divisible asset, the oil around Kirkuk can be divided and apportioned with less difficulty than non-material symbols. In contrast, which Iraqi sectarian groups get the upper hand in and control over Kirkuk stands out as much more of a zero-sum game. If control of state institutions and resources,

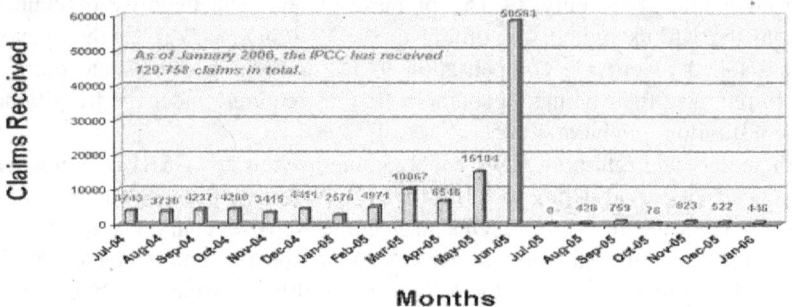

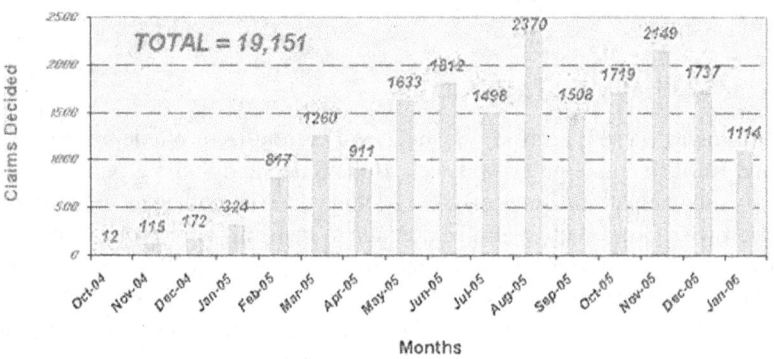

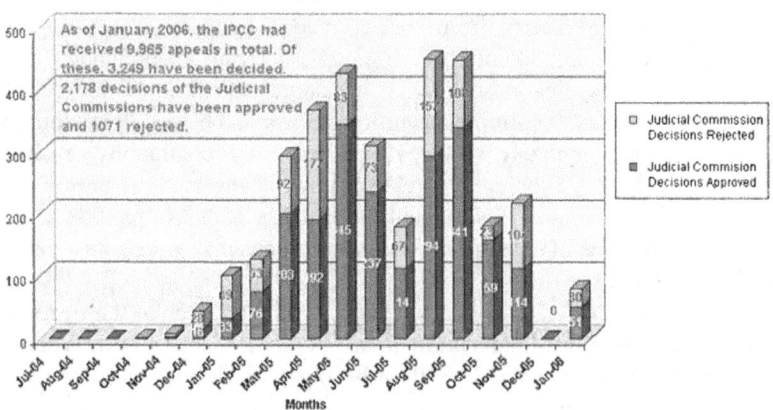

Figure 3. IPCC claims received, determined and appealed between July 2004 and January 2006. *Source:* Commission for the Resolution of Real Property Disputes (formerly the Iraqi Property Claims Commission)—http://ipcciraq.org/en/CRRPDorn09.php

including Kirkuk, come to be viewed as zero-sum games for polarized Iraqi sectarian groups in competition with one another, the potential for large-scale bloodshed across the country (rather than mainly in Baghdad) will rise accordingly.

Strategies for preventing sectarian conflict over Kirkuk thus look a lot like the strategies for preventing civil war in Iraq as a whole. Policies must be constructed so that all the significant political actors "see something in it for them," something more valuable than the risks and costs incurred from exiting the legal political system and resorting to violence. As much as possible, policies that mitigate the security dilemma faced by Iraqi sectarian groups also need to be implemented. Although such a generalization does some violence to the diversity of opinion present within various Iraqi groups, each significant sectarian group in Iraq seems to have certain "red lines" regarding Kirkuk and the administrative arrangements for a post-Saddam Iraq:

- Kurds demand the maintenance of a robust and secure autonomy similar to what they enjoyed before the 2003 war, and the possibility (via referendum) of extending the Kurdish Autonomous Region to include significant Kurdish areas (mainly Kirkuk) that lie immediately south or west of their current autonomous boundaries.
- Sunni Arabs in Iraq appear to have largely accepted Kurdish autonomy, but they have very strong objections regarding Kurdish control of northern oil resources, as well as a Shiite autonomous region in southern Iraq—leaving "Sunnistan" the empty and destitute middle of a new sectarian sandwich. Hence the Arab Sunni red-line could be described as a demand for some of Iraq's petroleum wealth and a political status beyond that of a continuously out-voted minority.
- Turkmen (mainly as represented by the Iraqi Turkmen Front) have a stated red-line of not incorporating Kirkuk into the Kurdish Autonomous Zone. On a more general level, they desire a level of security and autonomy that remains difficult to attain for such a relatively small minority in Iraq.
- Arab Shiites as a whole do not focus on Kirkuk as much as the other aforementioned groups. In general, they need to see the mostly Shiite settlers around Kirkuk treated fairly, and they reject Kurdish secession from Iraq. As far as Kirkuk might provide the economic basis for such secession, they remain weary of (but not dead-set against) the scheduled referendum.
- In addition to the Iraqi communities mentioned above, the view of neighboring states must also be taken into account. While both Iran and Syria appear leery of Kurdish acquisition of Kirkuk, the issue does not appear to be a red-line for them. Turkey, on the other hand, has made numerous protests and threats on this issue: "Turkish officials have warned that they may intervene if the vote [Kirkuk referendum] goes against their interests. Gul[12] declined to say what would happen, but he pointedly noted that Turkey currently provides Kurdistan with its electricity and 90% of its gasoline" (Kessler, 2007).

Given the diametrically opposed nature of especially the Kurdish and Turkmen redlines, it will prove impossible to devise a solution that does not tread perilously close to, or over, the limits of some of these groups' preferences.

The most difficult issue to address will likely be Kirkuk's administrative and geographic fate. Leaving the city outside the Kurdistan administrative region would be viewed as a defeat for the powerful Kurdish parties, who are set on its acquisition or restoration (depending on who you ask) and wield considerable influence in the new Iraq. Just as the 1970 Autonomy Accord between the Kurds and Baghdad largely failed over the question of administrative boundaries and Kirkuk, post-Saddam Iraq could fail over the same issue. At the same time, it remains unclear how the political boundaries of governorates in Iraq can be changed. The new Iraqi Constitution provides no guidance on the issue, which is likely to be very contentious. In the 15 October 2005 referendum on the issue, 37.09% of voters in Ta'amim governorate also rejected the Permanent Iraqi Constitution. It seems reasonable to assume that this figure amounts to most of Ta'amim Governorate's Arabs and Turkmen (Kurds were overwhelmingly supportive of the document, and the aforementioned election results seem to indicate that Kurdish voters amount to around 55% of voters in Ta'amim). It remains difficult to know if the Ta'amim Arab and Turkmen refusal of the Constitution stemmed largely from their antipathy towards Article 140's promised Kirkuk referendum or other factors, however.

If all of Ta'amim Governorate were to be attached to Kurdistan following a referendum, in addition to Kirkuk this would include towns such as Altun Kopre and Hawija, both of which have mostly non-Kurdish populations hostile to the Kurdish political parties. While returning to the pre-1974 Kirkuk Governorate boundaries might help the situation, it would not completely solve this problem. Smart Kurdish leaders might also think twice before becoming occupiers of unwilling towns and villages, given available examples of what this can lead to just a few miles south of Kurdistan. Some Kurdish politicians have considered allowing majority Arab regions such as Hawija to break away from the governorate to join neighboring governorates rather than fall under Kurdistan authority (International Crisis Group, 2006, p. 22). Additionally, a referendum that produced a bare majority in favor of joining the KRG region would not bode well for such a transition.

Hence there are a number of different routes for governing Kirkuk that can be followed, none of which will perfectly satisfy all of the interested parties, and some of which are certain to provoke conflict. All of the following potential options assume Iraq will follow through with the broad outlines of a federal system enshrined in its constitution.

Option 1. Let the Local Majority Decide

The first option is to do as the Kurds desire and abide by Article 140 of the Permanent Iraqi Constitution: conduct a census and hold a referendum in Ta'amim governerate by December 2007, over whether or not to join the Kurdistan region. David L. Phillips of the Center for Preventive Action and US Council on Foreign Relations provides several suggestions for the future of Iraq and Kirkuk, one of which could be a result of such a referendum:

> Iraqi Kurdistan would be established as one federal unit encompassing Dahouk, Suleimaniya, Erbil and Kirkuk provinces. Consistent with "geographic and historic facts," the 1974 decree would be reversed thereby restoring the historical boundaries of Kirkuk province. All nationalities, including Kurds, Arabs, Turkmen, and Assyrians, would have equal rights as citizens of Iraqi Kurdistan. To avoid population flows resulting in ethnically homogenous regions, individual and group rights would be enshrined in both the State and Iraqi Kurdistan constitutions. (2004, p. 12)

Arriving at such a happy outcome, however, may prove more difficult than might appear at first glance. Extremely sensitive obstacles must be crossed before referendum day. As mentioned previously, the borders of Kirkuk (Ta'amim) governorate must be determined.

Governorate borders under Saddam's regime were gerrymandered to produce a smaller Kurdish demographic around Kirkuk. Returning to pre-1974 or pre-1968 borders present problems of their own, however: most importantly, redrawing one set of borders produces pressure to redraw others. For instance, the current Kurdish Autonomous Zone (an accident of the 1991 Gulf War[13]) encompasses more than the majority Kurdish provinces of Dohuk, Erbil, and Suleimaniya—it also includes chunks of Nineva province, Ta'amim, and Diyala provinces. Kurdish leaders expect these areas to remain part of their region, necessitating a redrawing of governorate boundaries. Presumably, authorities in these provinces as well as the central government will in turn demand that, at a minimum, areas with predominantly non-Kurdish populations around Kirkuk (Ta'amim governorate), not be included in a Kurdish autonomous entity.

Additionally, a census would likely be boycotted by those groups lacking a plurality in Kirkuk (non-Kurds). The Turkoman population, for example, is much smaller than the millions they cite (judging from election results) and they are loath to have that confirmed. Disputes over what constitutes a Kirkuki, and thus makes an eligible voter, also risk igniting conflict. For instance, IDP Kurds (ostensibly from Kirkuk) living in Suleimaniya and Erbil provinces were allowed to vote in the Kirkuk provincial elections. Upset, some Arabs threatened that in the event of a referendum they might bus in their kin from the south to vote (International Crisis Group, 2006, pp. 7, 18). Furthermore, Kurdish politicians don't believe that Arab settlers should be allowed to participate in the referendum, despite many being born and raised in Kirkuk.

It also seems unclear whether or not all sides will accept the results of a referendum. If the result of a referendum is the union of Kirkuk and Kurdistan, the "red-line" of Sunni Arab and Turkomen groups, as well as of important neighboring states, will have been breached. All sides have alluded to the possibility of violence or intervention if their particular "red-lines" are crossed. Nonetheless, some scholars and most Kurds maintain that allowing Kurdistan the Kirkuk prize is the only geographically, historically, demographically and morally sound action (O'Leary, 2005, p. 85). Additionally, Kurdish leaders of both the KDP and PUK have made so many strident statements regarding the need for a referendum on Kirkuk that they may now be incapable of conceding this issue, lest they lose control of their respective constituencies. From a security perspective, Iraqi Kurds may also fear leaving control of all of Iraq's major petroleum producing land in central government (meaning Shiite) control. Hence for the Kurds at least, controlling the oil fields around Kirkuk would help alleviate their security worries.

An additional obstacle to Kirkuk's inclusion into Iraqi Kurdistan lies outside Iraq—Syria, Iran and especially Turkey continue to closely watch any political or economic gains made by Iraqi Kurds. Ankara is particularly fearful that Kirkuk's oil resources could serve as an Iraqi Kurdish platform from which to secede from Iraq in the future, as well as pursue irredentist policies towards Turkey's majority Kurdish-populated south-east.

Option 2. Give Kirkuk City a Special Status

This option is actually a variant of, or add-on to, the first option of letting the Kirkuk referendum run its course. While the majority-Kurdish rural areas around Kirkuk could be added to Kurdistan following a referendum result to this effect, the city of Kirkuk itself would receive special status. This would avoid a symbolic loss for non-Kurdish groups in Iraq (particularly the Turkmen), and increase the sense of security for non-Kurdish residents of Kirkuk. In this scenario, Kirkuk city would not be subject to Iraqi Kurdish Regional Government jurisdiction, but would instead enjoy the status of a free-standing municipality (Phillips, 2004, p. 12).[14] Both Navarra in the Basque region of Spain and Brcko (an administrative unit that is shared between the Croat-Muslim Federation and the Serb Republic within Bosnia) exist as precedents for such an arrangement. Such an arrangement might also go a long way toward removing Turkey's main rhetorical justification for intervening in Iraq—protection of the Turkmen minority. As discussed above, Kirkuk's Turkmen population resides primarily within Kirkuk city, rather than in the governorate's countryside outside the city.

Option 3. Leave Kirkuk to the Central Government

Those who fear growing Kurdish affluence combined with separatist aspirations would prefer that the Kirkuk region remain under the control of the central government. This would be in the interest of the majority of Sunni and Shiite Arabs as well as the Turkish state. Such a policy would completely ignore the major red line of the Kurdish parties, however, and threaten stability in the only currently peaceful and secure region of the country (Iraqi Kurdistan). Just as they did in 1970 over Kirkuk, Kurdish parties under such a scenario would most likely take to the battlefield to claim Kirkuk.

Option 4. Try to Avoid "Red-lines" but Leave Nobody Happy (Except Maybe the Turkmen)

The Kurds played an astute political game during the drawing up of the Transitional Administrative Law and the Constitution, and on the issue of Kirkuk, received the nominal promise of satisfaction. However, the outcome of a census and a referendum might include aggravated ethnic conflict and Turkish intervention. The constitution really amounted to a deal between Shiite Arab political leaders and the Kurdish parties, meaning that many other political parties and ethnic groups may not feel bound by all of its articles, particularly regarding Kirkuk. Some leaders of Sunni Arab and Turkmen groups have in fact suggested boycotting a potential referendum and rejecting its results (International Crisis Group, 2006, p. 28).

The ICG therefore suggests the following option for the future of Kirkuk: create a region, or federal unit comprised solely of the Kirkuk province, without the immediate option of joining the Kurdistan region. Instead of a referendum, the Iraqi Council of Representatives would draft a charter to grant the governorate the status of a federal region. In deference to the Kurds, this status should hold only for an interim period (they suggest ten years) after which time a referendum could be held. The ICG plan's proponents hope that by this time Kirkuk's demographic flows will have stabilized and communal relations normalized. To assist this process, a power sharing structure should be constructed (which would deal with the near-total Kurdish control of the Kirkuk municipal government, currently causing so much angst and ill-feeling among Arabs and Turkmen).

Unfortunately, taking this route entails breaking another promise to the Kurds. As discussed above, it is not even clear if Kurdish leaders will be able to control popular Kurdish sentiment over the Kirkuk issue, should it be announced that promises for a referendum on the city's status will be delayed yet again, or even for ten years. The ICG report implicitly recognizes this risk by stressing that it is important to start implementing the suggested plan immediately, so that the Kurdish leadership has time to soften the blow to its people and avoid the fall out from disappointing popular Kurdish expectations of holding a referendum in Kirkuk by 2007's end.

The plan hopes to prevent ethnic conflict over Kirkuk, but more likely postpones such conflict until a later date, when fighting over the issue may prove even bloodier. One can easily imagine conflict festering around Kirkuk as each sectarian group jockeys for advantage ahead of a referendum ten years from now. Leaving the Kirkuk issue unresolved would in fact greatly exacerbate the viscous dynamic of Barry Posen's (1993) ethnic security dilemma, as Iraqi Arabs, Kurds and even Turkmen pursue defensive preparations out of a fear of a looming conflict over the delayed referendum. A consolidated Kurdish region would eventually (probably well before the ten-year mark) enter into the most bitter conflict with "Arab Iraq," as both Arab and Kurdish leaders misperceive the intent of the other and/or try to buttress their popular support by adopting a bellicose attitude towards "outgroups" and the symbolic issue of Kirkuk. Turkmen would also likely cry out for Turkish intervention, which would in turn spark unrest in Turkish Kurdistan.

In Search of a Governing Roadmap

Unfortunately, none of the plans outlined above seem to provide a satisfactory way forward for the Kirkuk issue and Iraq as a whole. Recent scholarship on the general issue of solutions to ethnic conflict also fails to provide much guidance: while scholars such as Kaufman argue, in some cases, for partition as the most tenable solution to ethnic wars, others such as Sambanis marshal evidence that the separation of ethnic communities does not reduce violence (Kaufman, 1996; Sambanis, 2000). Since it seems impossible to ascertain if high levels of violence lead to partition and then continue to fester, or if partition itself causes the continuation of such violence, policymakers remain without adequate guidance. None of the plans detailed above envision the creation of homogenous ethnic regions and forced population movements in any case—ethnic settlement patterns in Iraq, and particularly in and around Kirkuk, are simply too diffuse to envision such a situation except perhaps as the result of particularly intense civil war rather than conscious government policy. Even Saddam's genocidal *Anfal* campaigns and Arabization policies of the 1970s, 80s, and 90s failed to produce ethnically homogenous regions.

Azar & Burton's analysis of protracted social conflicts may provide some guidance for future arrangements in Kirkuk and Iraq as a whole, however: "Societies which have undergone decades of violence and hate retain very little trust for any sort of government—local or central and distant. They become cynical. They transform even benign systems into deformed political and economic entities and they show very little inclination to participatory politics" (Azar & Burton, 1986, p. 151).[15] Azar & Burton argue that the best way to move forward for such traumatized societies involves very decentralized political structures, which can provide a better sense of political participation, autonomy and security for different sectarian groups. In very decentralized political systems, mutually distrustful groups are also freer to identify and pursue their own goals separately, as they see fit. With this in mind, it might be useful to adopt a popular conflict resolution and negotiation strategy to look at the basic needs behind the "red lines" of sectarian groups in Iraq, rather than the well-known positions of each party. In this way, it might be possible to reevaluate the desirability of the various plans outlined above.

Issue 1. Economic Resources

All concerned Iraqi groups have a need for economic security, and thus a strong concern over how the oil resources around Kirkuk are distributed. Because oil is a divisible economic asset, Iraqis have already adopted part of the solution to this issue: according to new Iraqi laws (some details for which are still being worked out at the time of this writing), revenue from all Iraqi oil fields will be shared amongst all Iraqis on a *per capita* basis (Mufson, 2007). Such a resource-sharing arrangement will assure Sunni Arab groups in particular that they will not find themselves locked into a resource-starved "Sunnistan." Neighboring countries, particularly Turkey, will also have less reason to fear that an oil-rich Kurdish autonomous region will declare independence from Iraq and use its oil resources as a base from which to pursue an irredentist challenge aimed at neighboring Kurdish regions. In the interests of both Kurdish and southern Shiites, the new "oil law" would recognize "... the power of regional authorities, such as the Kurdish Regional Government, to award oil contracts," but would also leave the Iraqi central government a role through the establishment of "... a national petroleum commission with the power to review contracts within 60 days" (*ibid.*).

Several difficult issues remain unresolved regarding the new petroleum law, however, including how a national petroleum commission would be managed, under what conditions it could revoke regionally-negotiated contracts, to what extent future oil fields fall under the provisions of the new law (rather than the exclusive domain of regional authorities), and how much oil revenue would accrue to the central government. Nonetheless, the general principle of the new law appears encouraging—precisely the kind of guaranteed resource sharing that could allay many of the fears of Iraq's various sectarian communities. If resource-sharing arrangements are also established for minority groups within Iraqi Kurdistan (mainly Turkmen, but also Arabs), both these groups and the Kurds will likewise have assurances that they will finally benefit from Iraq's oil wealth.

Issue 2. The Administrative Status of Kirkuk

The Iraqi-Arab position on Kirkuk comes primarily from a concern over the area's oil resources and the threat of Kurdish secession rather than symbolic, spiritual or historic ties to the city. Hence an arrangement to have a national petroleum commission (run jointly by Iraq's regions and the central government) receive and coordinate oil revenue derived from the area would make both Shiite and Sunni Arab political parties more willing to concede administrative control of Kirkuk city and non-majority Arab parts of Ta'amim province to the Kurdistan Region. The worsening civil strife between Sunnis and Shiites in Iraq also means that these groups currently have more pressing issues on their agenda than the status of Kirkuk, particularly once the question of Kirkuk's oil resources is settled. December 2007 is therefore precisely the time to have a referendum in Kirkuk to determine the future of the city and province, rather than a few years down the road when the Arab position on the issue may be much less negotiable.

The current presence of Coalition troops in Iraq, as well as Turkey's ongoing efforts to join the European Union, also lessen the chance of Turkish intervention if the referendum is held as scheduled (as opposed to later, when both conditions may no longer hold). As for Kurdish aspirations for a separate state, the Kurdish leadership has already made a huge concession on this point by agreeing to remain part of Iraq. If the Kurds are forced to also concede on issues of federalism and Kirkuk, the conditions under which they agreed to remain willing partners of the Kurdish-Arab union that is Iraq will have disappeared. Iraq will find itself condemned to either division or dictatorship, as well as a resumption of the series of Kurdish revolts that bedeviled the country from 1919 until 1991.

Some Turkmen parties based in Kirkuk would present the most serious opposition to a referendum that could likely result in Kirkuk's incorporation into Kurdistan. Because Turkmen lack sufficient numbers to have their own region in Iraq, their choice seems to involve either being a minority in Iraq as a whole, or a minority within Iraqi Kurdistan. It may be possible to make the latter option more appealing in several ways. First, the city of Kirkuk could be offered a semi-autonomous status as discussed in option 2 above. Second, together with the sizeable Turkmen population in Erbil province of Iraqi Kurdistan, Turkmen in Kirkuk could be offered a number of community rights and power-sharing arrangements to effectively provide them with more autonomy as a group than they would enjoy as a relatively smaller component of Iraq as a whole. As discussed below, these would include greater recognition for the Turkish language than that offered by the central government in Baghdad. Not all Turkmen parties even object to being included within Iraqi Kurdistan—such objections come primarily from the Turkey sponsored Iraqi Turkmen Front, while groups such as the Independent Turkmen Movement already participate in the Kurdistan Regional Government in Erbil. Hence the Turkmen red line may be more negotiable, especially if Turkey can be convinced to revise its position on Kirkuk.[16] The above-mentioned possibility of promising these communities a guaranteed share of oil revenue might also work wonders. It should also be noted that since the emergence of the Kurdish Autonomous Zone in 1991–1992, Turkmen in the zone have faired quite well. Finally, the most important Turkmen security guarantee comes from Turkey, which has since 1991 adopted the role of protector for this community.[17]

Issue 3. Community Rights and Power-sharing Guarantees

The need for decentralization and strong guarantees for minority rights becomes central in situations where groups lack trust in each other, and dispersed settlement patterns preclude easy separation of these groups. Decentralization of power is especially crucial to avoid perceptions of zero-sum political contests between sectarian communities, wherein controlling the state apparatus means taking "the whole pie" for yourself (Azar & Burton, 1986; Horowitz, 1985). This is true in both Iraq as a whole as well as in an autonomous Kurdistan that includes nervous Arabs, Turkmen, and Christians, who may be apprehensive about becoming to Kurdish nationalism what Kurds became to Arab nationalism.

Hence for the same reason that federalism and decentralizing power-sharing mechanisms are essential to keep Iraqi Kurds a willing part of Iraq, similar arrangements will be necessary to reassure Turkmen, Arabs, and Christians under an Iraqi Kurdish autonomous government—federalism within federalism, if you will. Since Turkmen, Arabs, and Christians in Iraqi Kurdistan and Kirkuk do not enjoy majority status in any geographic area of sufficient size, they could be offered guaranteed rights and positions within a Kurdish regional government along the lines of consociational political arrangements in the Netherlands, Lebanon, Brussels, South Tyrol, Northern Ireland, and Bosnia and Herzegovina. Turkmen and Christians in the current Kurdistan Regional Government already enjoy some of these rights, including a Turkish language educational system for the Turkmen, their own community associations and a guaranteed number of seats in the Kurdistan Assembly (five seats for Assyrian representatives).[18] In their treatment of the issue (*The Future of Kurdistan in Iraq*), O'Leary et al. (2005) outline more details of what such an administrative system should look like.

In return for not contesting the genuine nature of Kurdish IDPs physically present in Kirkuk, Arab settlers in the Kirkuk area should also be allowed to vote in a referendum on the region's future. Moreover, Arab settlers should be allowed to remain in and around Kirkuk if they choose to, while those wishing to return south would be offered assistance to do so. Due to intermarriage and the birth of several generations of children in northern Iraq, Kurdish parties must offer a compromise that accepts and guarantees the safety and rights of those settlers who remain in Kirkuk. It also seems clear that the IPCC/CRRPD land dispute resolution process must be made to function more quickly, and must offer the compensation for IDPs and resettlement assistance for settlers that it promised. During the first few weeks after the fall of Saddam's government, a one time "take it or leave it" offer of a few thousand dollars to settlers willing to surrender their properties and return south immediately might have significantly reduced the magnitude of the problem. The number of remaining disputes for the CRRPD to settle might have been significantly reduced, Kurdish and Turkmen IDPs would have perceived a genuine willingness on the part of Coalition Forces to deal with the issue, and settlers would have received needed assistance to re-establish themselves in southern and central Iraq. It might not even be too late for such an *ad-hoc* offer to be made. If a combination of the IPCC/CRRPD determination process and such an *ad-hoc* settlement can sufficiently reduce the number of settlers remaining in Kirkuk, Kurdish parties could likely sell such a compromise (of allowing settlers to vote in the Kirkuk referendum) to all but the most hard-line of their constituencies.

Issue 4. A Clear and Negotiated Framework for Various Referendum Outcomes, Before any Referendum

Common sense dictates that the stakes of a game of dice must be negotiated before the dice are thrown, lest serious disagreements arise. By this same logic, all important involved parties must negotiate all the various possible results of a referendum on Kirkuk's status well before such a referendum is held. While any determination regarding the roadmap for Iraq and Kirkuk's future must come from Iraqis themselves, the international community and the US in particular have and can continue to offer influential advice and support for some courses of action over others. The window of opportunity to arrive at a negotiated and positive plan of action for Kirkuk's status is now, at a time when no sectarian group in Iraq feels sufficiently secure or hegemonic to try and force its preferences on other groups. Postponing a resolution of Kirkuk's status, as well as the distribution of Iraq's oil resources, until a later date when things are less fluid will only allow disagreements to worsen and fester. A referendum on Kirkuk's status should therefore be held by December 2007, as promised in Iraq's constitution.

Given the election results of 2005, the Kurds will likely win such a referendum in most parts of Ta'amim province. A specific, negotiated plan of action for all possible referendum outcomes and including all major interested groups will go a long way towards removing the "all or nothing" sense that would otherwise come with such a referendum. The general outline of such a plan of action should even look similar for a referendum outcome that leaves Kirkuk outside of Kurdistan—oil revenue sharing, community rights, and a quasi-autonomous city-state status for urban Kirkuk would remain desirable even if the city and province remain part of "Arab Iraq." It would also be desirable to negotiate beforehand on how parts of Ta'amim province that voted overwhelmingly for a result contrary to the referendum outcome (e.g. an Arab town such as Hawija voting to remain part of federal Iraq while the overall Ta'amim vote approves of joining with Kurdistan) can have their preferences honored – in which case some minimum size threshold would have to be agreed upon for such breakaway districts.

Conclusion

While the new Iraqi Government, Coalition Forces, and the Kurdistan Regional Government should all be commended for avoiding serious violence over the Kirkuk issue so far, the future remains perilous. No plan for determining the future of Kirkuk appears free of the risk of sectarian conflict. While some plans such as that of the ICG prefer to further postpone resolution of the Kirkuk question, this will likely only push serious conflict over the issue to a later date, without necessarily reducing strife in the interim period. The analysis presented here suggests that it would be preferable to try and resolve the issue sooner rather than later, and therefore recommends abiding by the 2005 Permanent Iraqi Constitution's promise of a referendum on Kirkuk by 2007. The right mix of policies negotiated at the right time, particularly regarding Kirkuk's administrative status and the IDP/settler issue can produce an arrangement that sufficiently satisfies the basic needs of all significant parties. Although such an arrangement will likely produce some violent sectarian conflict, the alternatives involve greater risks of much more serious violent conflict and even sustained civil war spreading beyond Baghdad.

From the analysis presented here, the rough lines of such an arrangement correspond to the above-mentioned "Option 2", and should include the following: After the 2007 Kirkuk referendum, and assuming a Kurdish victory in the referendum, most of Ta'amim (Kirkuk) province joins the Kurdistan Autonomous Region. Depending on the vote in Kirkuk city, however (some threshold should be negotiated ahead of time), the city acquires its own special administrative status separate from the Kurdish region. Finally, a number of power and resource sharing arrangements are instituted to satisfy and secure Arab, Kurdish, Turkmen, and other communities involved in the process. These policies would be aimed at guaranteeing to these groups, as much as possible, that their basic needs will remain secure in the new Iraq and the new Iraqi Kurdistan.

Acknowledgements

The author would like to thank the CERIUM (Centre d'Études et de Recherches Internationales), Université de Montréal, and the Canadian Department of National Defence R. B. Myers Post-Doctoral Fellowship program for research support which made this paper possible.

Notes

1. An Ottoman administrative district, roughly equivalent to a province.
2. For more on the *Anfal* campaigns, see Makiya (1992).
3. For more on the creation of the Iraqi Kurdish Autonomous Zone, see Romano (2004).

4. For more on this, see Fawcett & Tanner (2002).
5. For more on this, see Romano (2005).
6. These estimates are based on my discussions with US military personnel in charge of Kirkuk in 2003 and 2004. The estimate includes the approximately 100 000 mostly Kurdish IDPs that returned to Kirkuk between March 2003 and March 2005, as well as at least 10 000 Arabs who fled the city in the Spring of 2003.
7. In Ta'amim (Kirkuk) governorate, the January 2005 election results placed the following parties in the top three: Kurdistan Alliance List—237 006 votes; Turkmen Iraqi Front—65 614; and the Iraqi List—22 494 (see http://www.epic-usa.org/Portals/1/UpdatedElectionResults.pdf). The December 2005 election, which was not boycotted by significant Sunni Arab groups, had the following results: Kurdistan Alliance—312 800; Iraqi National Dialogue Front—80 000; and the Turkmen Iraqi Front—63 000 (see http://middleeastreference.org.uk/iraq051215results.html).
8. "Good-faith secondary owners" refers to those who were given, or took possession of, the properties of people expelled from the area and currently live in the property in question.
9. Author's interview with Kurdish IDPs near the Kirkuk International Football Stadium, 6 February 2004. The IDPs interviewed stated that they returned to Kirkuk when they did (November 2003) because "the U.N. had cut off the electricity and water in their camp." The KRG was the authority responsible for electricity and water in their camp, however.
10. Human Rights Watch reports that forced evictions of Arab settlers were rare, however, and hence the charge of "reverse ethnic cleansing" appears unjustified. See Human Rights Watch (2004).
11. The author was unable to locate any credible sources, including international election observers, to confirm claims that the vote in Ta'amim governorate was rigged, or that non-Kurds boycotted this December 2005 election in significant numbers.
12. Abdullah Gul is the Foreign Minister and Deputy Prime Minister of Turkey.
13. When Iraqi Kurds heeded George Bush Senior's call to rise up against Saddam in March of 1991, Baghdad's counter-attack led to a rush of some 2.5 million Kurdish civilians towards the Turkish and Iranian borders. Embarrassed as CNN cameras taped columns of fleeing Kurdish civilians being strafed by unimpeded Iraqi helicopter gunships, and worried that Turkey would be overrun by Iraqi Kurdish refugees, the Gulf War allies (mainly the US, Britain, and France) created a protective safe haven in northern Iraq to encourage Kurdish refugees to return home. This safe haven, under its protective northern Iraq "no fly zone," became the Kurdish Autonomous Zone of Iraq. For more on this, see Romano, (2004). Kirkuk lies just south and east of this Autonomous Zone.
14. Phillips' paper includes a wide range of interesting suggestions on federalism, power-sharing, and other strategies for post-Saddam Iraq.
15. For more on the application of Azar and Burton's views to the Kurdish issue, see David Romano, *The Kurdish Nationalist Movement*, Cambridge: Cambridge University Press, 2006.
16. If Iraqi Kurds made a commitment to secure their border with Turkey and act against PKK/KADEK armed units based in Iraqi Kurdistan, Ankara might in turn acquiesce to the possibility of Kirkuk's inclusion in Iraqi Kurdistan, in a kind of quid pro quo that has a long political tradition.
17. Turkmen may worry, however, as to whether or not Turkey's interest in their welfare is genuine and hence long term—during the 1970s and 80s, Saddam expelled Turkmen as well as Kurds from the Kirkuk area without a word of protest from Ankara.
18. In the 1992 and subsequent elections in Iraqi Kurdistan, Turkmen parties were likewise offered seats in the Kurdish Assembly. At the probable behest of Turkey, the Iraqi Turkmen Front refused.
19. O'Leary adds the following observation about Kirkuk's demographics: "The most objective summation of the 1957 demography is that Kirkuk was a multi-ethnic city surrounded by a larger and heavily Kurdish population in the governorate. What the situation is in 2004 no one knows for certain. All the populations have probably grown in size, but Kurds and Arabs have likely had higher birth rates than Turkomen and Assyrians, although it is a fool's game to project demographic data from fifty years ago" (p. 83).

References

Azar, E. & Burton, J. (Eds) (1986) *International Conflict Resolution: Theory and Practice*, (Boulder, CO: Lunne Rienner Publishers, Inc.).
Baker, L. (2004) Returning Kurds, Turkmen Threaten Iraq Crisis, Reuters, 28 January, available online at: http://www.irak.be/ned/nieuws/hotnewsJanuary04.htm

Coalition Provisional Authority (CPA) (2006) About the IPCC, available online at: http://www.ipcciraq.org/01_about.htm
Energy Intelligence Research (2004) Iraqi Oil and Gas; Bonanza Still in Waiting, available on-line at: www.energyintel.com
Fainaru, S. (2005) Kurds Reclaiming Prized Territory in Northern Iraq, *Washington Post Foreign Service*, 30 October, p. A01, available online at: http://www.washingtonpost.com/wp-dyn/content/article/2005/10/29/AR2005102901396_pf.html
Fawcett, J. & Tanner, V. (2002) The Internally Displaced People of Iraq, Brookings Institution-SAIS Project on Internal Displacement Occasional Paper.
Horowitz, D. (1985) *Ethnic Groups in Conflict*, (Berkeley, CA: University of California Press).
Human Rights Watch (2004) Reversing Ethnic Cleansing in Northern Iraq, 16(4E), available online at: http://hrw.org/reports/2004/iraq0804/
International Crisis Group (2006) Iraq and the Kurds: The Brewing Battle of Kirkuk, *Middle East Report* 56, 18 July, available online at: http://www.crisisgroup.org/home/index.cfm?l=1&id=4267.
Internal Displacement Monitoring Centre (2006) Iraq: Sectarian Violence, Military Operations Spark New Displacement as Humanitarian Access Deteriorates, 23 May, available online at: http://www.internal-displacement.org/8025708F004BE3B1/(httpInfoFiles)/5FF5134F8672E698C125717700492CAC/$file/Iraq%20Overview%2023%20May%202006.pdf
Iraqi Constitution (2005) available online at: http://www.export.gov/iraq/pdf/iraqi_constitution.pdf
Kaufman, C. (1996) Possible and Impossible Solutions to Ethnic Civil Wars, *International Security*, 20(4), pp. 136–175.
Kessler, G. (2007) Turkish Official Warns against Vote on Kirkuk, *Washington Post*, 9 February, p. A12 (accessed via the website of the Patriotic Union of Kurdistan, available online at: http://www.puk.org/web/htm/news/nws/news070209.html).
Makiya, K. (1992) The Anfal: Uncovering an Iraqi Campaign to Exterminate the Kurds, *Harper's Magazine*, May, pp. 53–61.
Mufson, S. (2007) Iraq Struggles to Finish Oil Law, *Washington Post*, 27 January, available online at: http://www.washingtonpost.com/wp-dyn/content/article/2007/01/23/AR2007012301534.html
Negus, S. (2006) Kirkuk Dispute Bedevils Iraq's Political Crisis, *Financial Times*, 11 March, available online at: http://www.ft.com/cms/s/ef17ef92-b0a3-11da-a142-0000779e2340.html
O'Leary, B. (2005) Power-sharing, Pluralist Federation, and Federacy, in: B. O'Leary, J. McGarry & Salih, K. (Eds), *The Future of Kurdistan in Iraq* (Philadelphia, PA: University of Pennsylvania Press).
O'Leary, B., McGarry, J. & Salih, K. (Eds) (2005) *The Future of Kurdistan in Iraq* (Philadelphia, PA: University of Pennsylvania Press).
Phillips, D. (2004) Power-sharing with Iraqi Kurds, Center for Preventive Action and Council on Foreign Relations, available online at: http://www.american.edu/cgp/iraq/PhillipsAUPaperonPowerSharing.doc
Posen, B. (1993) The Security Dilemma and Ethnic Conflict, *Survival*, 35(1), pp. 27–47.
Romano, D. (2004) Safe Havens as Political Projects: The Case of Iraqi Kurdistan, in: P. Kingston and I. Spears (Eds), *States Within States: Incipient Political Entities in the Post-Cold War Era*, pp. 153–166 (New York: Palgrave Macmillan Ltd).
Romano, D. (2005) Whose House is this Anyway? IDP and Refugee Return Policies in Post-Saddam Iraq, *Oxford Journal of Refugee Studies*, 18(4), pp. 430–453.
Romano, D. (2006) *The Kurdish Nationalist Movement: Opportunity, Mobilization and Identity*, (Cambridge: Cambridge University Press).
Sambanis, N. (2000) Partition as a Solution to Ethnic War: An Empirical Critique of the Theoretical Literature, *World Politics*, 52, pp. 437–483.

Personal Interviews

Author's interviews with Kurdish IDPs near the Kirkuk International Football Stadium, 6 February 2004.

Interview with Shiite Arab settler family, Kirkuk, 10 May 2004. Interview conducted in Arabic by Karim Khallaayoun, member of the author's research team in Iraq during 2003–2004.

Living Apart in the Same Room: Analysis of the Management of Linguistic Diversity in Bolzano

ANDREA CARLÁ

The New School for Social Research, New York, USA

Bolzano, the main city of South Tyrol (territory in the north of Italy bordering Austria), does not sound or look typically Italian. Indeed, this town belonged to the Habsburg Empire for centuries and almost all of its population was German-speaking until the 1920s. After World War I, South Tyrol became part of Italy, and since then Italian- and German-speaking populations have lived side by side in the same province. This situation has mainly affected the big cities of South Tyrol, such as Merano, Bressanone, and Bolzano, where the Italian-speaking population has been concentrated. Large cities, in particular, have mixed populations and are the main areas of German–Italian co-existence. Bolzano has become an ethnically mixed city; in 2001 73% of its 94 989 inhabitants spoke Italian as native language, and 26% were German speaking. For most of the territory of South Tyrol, the proportion between the Italian and the German linguistic groups is inverted, and the Italian linguistic group is in the minority. In 2001, South Tyrol overall counted 462 999 inhabitants, and the Italian linguistic group represented 26% of the population (see Table A1 in Appendix).[1]

The relationship between German and Italian speakers has not always been a stable one. The history of South Tyrol has witnessed the attempt of Benito Mussolini to Italianize the region, an international agreement between the Italian and the Austrian government to protect the German-speaking group, a separatist movement that resorted to violence and terrorist attacks, and the intervention of the United Nations. Since 1972 the cohabitation of German and Italian-speakers has been regulated by a special Statute of Autonomy, which provides, *inter alia*, for specific language policies and language rights to manage the linguistic diversity of the South Tyrol population.

The purpose of this contribution is to analyze the special arrangements elaborated by the Italian government to guarantee peaceful cohabitation between German and Italian speakers and protect linguistic characteristics. These arrangements have created a regime characterized by the total separation of the two linguistic groups for most aspects of political–social life, from the organization of city councils to the educational system. My goal is to examine this set of language policies, and, in particular, to examine its consequences for the social–political interactions between the German and Italian inhabitants of Bolzano. Because Bolzano has both linguistic groups well represented, it is a prime example for analyzing German–Italian cohabitation in South Tyrol.

This case study will show that in discussing and judging language policies, it is necessary to consider the impact on relations between linguistic groups. First, I argue that language in itself is not an element of division; rather it becomes a charged issue in light of the psychological conditions of the linguistic groups (Arel, 2001). These conditions are the result of specific historical context that structures the relationship among individuals speaking different languages. Second, I argue that language policies affect interactions within the population, distinguishing between policies that impact power relations and policies that affect social relations among linguistic groups, and I claim that language policies should aim at addressing the mental status that maintains language as a divisive factor within a population. In this context, the South Tyrol institutional arrangements have guaranteed a wide use of minority languages and the protection of the German linguistic minority, which subsequently has abandoned most of its separatist tendencies and lives peacefully in an Italian South Tyrol. However, as an analysis of Bolzano shows, the language policies of the South Tyrol regime do not counter the understanding of language as an element of division. Instead, these policies inadvertently end up reinforcing the idea that language relations are competitive. In this way, language diversity is maintained as a divisive issue. With this paper, I intend to enrich the existing literature on language diversity by exploring an additional dimension of analysis. Indeed, to my knowledge, the traditional literature tends to focus on the relevance of language policies for the cohesion of the national state, the well-being of individuals, the protection of linguistic groups, and the maintenance of language diversity, without emphasizing the impact on the relations among linguistic groups.

This paper is organized into four sections. First, I present a theoretical discussion, in which I outline my approach toward the understanding of language diversity and language policies. Then, using an historical-institutional approach, I review the history of Bolzano and South Tyrol since World War I, elucidating the historical–structural processes through which language diversity has become the main factor of division of the South Tyrol society. Next, I present the South Tyrolean institutional measures, focusing on those provisions that most strongly affect the social relationship between the linguistic groups. Finally, I analyze the impact on the relations among the Bolzano's population today. This analysis will show how from a socio-political point of view Bolzano's population is separated in terms of language, and how South Tyrol arrangements structure this situation.

Theoretical Framework

The main objective of this contribution is to analyze the policies used in Bolzano to manage its linguistic diversity. Linguistic diversity is not necessarily a divisive cleavage and policies to manage it should aim at reconciling language diversity. Thus, policies should be analyzed by considering their impact on the relationships between linguistic groups. From a theoretical point of view, I focus on two issues: first, I clarify my understanding of language as a category of diversity by developing a socio-psychological approach; second, based on my understanding of language diversity, I consider how political institutions shape interactions among linguistic groups.

Language as Mind-set

In the debate concerning the reasons put forth to justify the employment of specific policies and rights to deal with language diversity, attention is paid to the functions of language and its nature, and the value of language diversity. Depending on what function is emphasized and how language is understood, different types of language policies are justified. In this regard, scholars have pointed out that language has three functions. Language is considered as an instrument of communication, as a means that provides access to a specific societal culture, and as key element of identity (Patten, 2001; Weinstock, 2003). In this context, the main debate regards the nature of language as a category of diversity. So-called "primordialists" consider language as an ascriptive inherited characteristic of human beings (Geertz, 1963; Horowitz, 1985). Thus, language is depicted as a pre-political category which requires special attention (Lijpart, 1977). "Instrumentalists" challenge the given fixed nature of language and argue that language is fluid, and is the result of the rational choice of individuals (Bates, 1983). However, this view does not explain the permanence of ethnic identities; it does not make clear why some identity groups mobilize and others not; it contrasts with the fact that members of groups are not rational calculators since their identity includes the belief that it represents a biological given characteristic (Laitin, 1985). "Constructivists" share with instrumentalists the idea that ethnic identity are fluid, but they point out that the social–cultural division that becomes politicized depends on the structural context (Laitin, 1985; Chandra, 2005). From this point of view, language is a political category of mobilization, which should be treated like other political phenomena such as class or ideology (Jung, 2000, 2001, forthcoming).

In the constructivist tradition, I argue that language is not a key element for the development or realization of individuals' identities. Indeed, identities are formed through the relationship between the individual and the supra-natural, that is, "the realm of the sacred and sublime," the individual and power authorities, and the individual and the others (Eisenstadt, 1998, p. 232; Eisenstadt & Giesen, 1995). Within this process, language is only a means of communication, and therefore language diversity does not imply the existence of competitive collective identities, and language in itself is not necessarily an element of division. Indeed, as O'Reilly (2003, p. 20) points out, although Latin American countries and Arab countries share the same language, Spanish and Arabic respectively, they express different collective identities. Moreover, the inhabitants of Ireland or Wales that speak respectively Gaelic or Welsh do not have a different collective identity from that of their fellow Irish or British citizens. Therefore, language is neither a necessary nor a sufficient element for the development of collective identities.

Language should not be considered as a thing possessed by individuals, an innate factor that characterizes individuals. Language diversity is not a factor of division of the society. Instead, I propose to regard language as a *mind-set*, namely a mental attitude caused by belief and perception regarding the category of language and the relationships among the individual, his/her language and his/her environment.[2] Mind-sets are not static, but can evolve, causing the emergence of different linguistic issues. Variations of mind-sets depend on structural changes, which affect the experience of relationship among individuals speaking different language. As pointed out by Billig (1976), social identification is a process, which has social nature and occurs in historical context at a definite time. Group categories and social identities do not arise spontaneously; rather they are the product of social activities in a historical context. In this regard, the author refers to a laboratory experiment of intergroup relations showing that "the division of rewards on a group basis in a intergroup situation produces strong intergroup attitudes" (Billig, 1976, p. 333). Therefore, shared similarities do not account for the subjectively felt unity of social groups; instead, it is necessary to refer to Lewin's notion of "interdependence of fate," or what Campbel calls "common fate" (cited in Billig, 1976, pp. 332, 333).

Studies of racial policies, whose authors often refuse to consider race as a given, usually tend to refer to processes through which racial identification is formed. According to Guinier and Torres (2002), asymmetries of power between black and white people lead to the racial understanding of the self. This understanding of the process of social identification also characterizes some of the literature on nationalist movements. Brubaker (1996) considers nations not as substantial entities, but as contingent events. According to Greenfeld (1992), national identities are generated by "ressentiment," namely a psychological status rooted in inequalities between subjects and objects, which are believed to be equal. Similarly, Gellner (1983) argues that a category of persons becomes a nation not because of shared attributes that separate that category from non-members but as the result of common experiences, which cause individuals to recognize each others as fellows, and teach them to be aware of culture.

Like race and nationalism, I propose that language as an element of identity is the result of collective experiences. This situation is caused by structural changes, which affect the relationship among individuals speaking different languages. Indeed, structural changes put in motion what Petersen (2002, p. 22) calls "belief-formation," namely "processes of conceptualization and evaluation." When structural changes threaten personal status and security of individuals related by same characteristics (same language), these individuals develop a self-awareness of their diversity. Indeed, this common experience generates profound changes in the understanding of the self and of the role played by the discriminatory factor in this understanding of the "I." The "I" identifies with the discriminatory factor, and thus with the "We" characterized by this factor. In this way, macro-structural dynamics activate micro-mechanisms at the individual level, which in turn spark macro-dynamics at the collective level

(Bloom, 1990). Several scholars of ethnic relations have emphasized the role played by threats to status and security in enforcing ethnic identification and thus in exacerbating ethnic tensions (Young, 1976; Horowitz, 1985; Posen, 1993; Lake & Rothchild, 1996; Petersen, 2002). According to Young (1976, p. 161), "social cues carrying cultural symbols are likely to be perceived in communal terms at moments of threat and insecurity." Threats, derived by an alteration in power relations within a polity, cause an increase in group solidarity (pp. 161–162). Arel (2001) develops a psychology of group perception, which focuses on the social status of cultural groups. According to the author, threats to cultural security cause secessionist movements and political instability. Structural changes that bring traumatic experiences of threats to the self-esteem of individuals belonging to the same linguistic groups foster shared beliefs among those individuals and shape the understanding of language, transforming it from a means of communication to a main element of identity.

Structural changes that affect the experiences between majority and minority linguistic groups involve factors such as the numerical strength of groups, demographic balance, the socio-economic conditions of the groups' members, which affect the social status of the linguistic group, and the social prestige of the language.[3] However, belief and perception can also be influenced by political institutions (Arel, 2001). Indeed, language policies can affect the development of language understood as a mind-set, by emphasizing or de-emphasizing language as a factor of identity, and thereby encouraging or discouraging contacts and competition between languages.

Based on this socio-psychological understanding of linguistic identity, I argue that language becomes politically salient in a specific context as a result of structural changes that produce peculiar mind-sets. Further, I propose that it is possible to distinguish two types of mind-sets: *mind-set of discrimination* and *mind-set of minorization*. With the former, language becomes *racialized*, in the sense that it is considered a biological characteristic of people. The latter points to a dynamic in which language is not only racialized, but relations between majority and minority languages are represented as a zero-sum game. Therefore, threats to the language itself are seen as reflecting a general threat to the survival of the linguistic group and its members. The mind-set of discrimination and mind-set of minorization transform language into a critical social cleavage, thereby affecting the day to day relations between linguistic groups. Thus, within this context, language and language policies become salient.

These parallel processes of racialization and minorization can be illustrated by way of the following example. Imagine five children in a room; three children speak language A, while the other two speak language B. In the center of the room, as the only toy available, there is a foosball game, the game that simulates soccer also known as table football. The children will probably play together peacefully at the foosball table. Let's assume that one day the foosball is substituted by a language A version of Trivial Pursuit, the popular game where players take turns answering questions. In this case the three children speaking language A will grab the game and play by themselves. Meanwhile, the other two children speaking language B will find themselves marginalized and, through this common traumatic experience, will acquire awareness of their linguistic diversity, developing a mind-set of discrimination. Moreover, let's assume that additional children speaking language A will enter the room, to join the game, thereby reducing the space available to the children speaking language B. In this context, any new voice speaking language A will be considered by children speaking language B as a threat to their placement in the room, leading to a mind-set of minorization.

Language Policies and Regimes

With this understanding of language as a mind-set, I consider how political institutions and language policies shape interactions among linguistic groups. In this regard, I distinguish between two types of language policies. On the one hand, I consider language policies that regulate power relations among linguistic groups (*power language policies*), where policies address access to political institutions, such as parliaments and governments, and the decision-making process. On the other hand, I consider language politics that regulate the use of language in the social relations among linguistic groups (*relational language politics*), within institutions such as schools and media. Most of the literature on the management of linguistic diversity focuses on the former policies, or tends to elide the analysis of the latter with it, treating these kinds of policies as secondary. Indeed, there are countless studies on how party systems, electoral voting systems, federal systems and other institutional designs regulate power relations among groups (Ljipart, 1977; Jung & Shapiro, 1995; Horowitz, 1985, 1991; Chandra, 2005). The goal of this body of literature is to identify which institutions favor the democratic process and moderate politics among linguistic groups. The main argument is whether this goal is best achieved by institutions that provide security to each group by guaranteeing to parties attached to one specific identity group access to power, or by institutional designs that aim at depoliticizing ethnic issues and encourage the creation of integrative political organizations. For example, Reilly (2001) distinguishes between consociational electoral systems, which replicate and maintain the existing divisions of the society in the legislature, and centripetal electoral systems, which encourage inter-group cooperation and accommodation through a "vote-pooling" effect, namely giving incentives to candidates to attract the preference of voters that belong to the various groups that make up the society.

In this contribution I focus on the second category of language policies, which, to my knowledge have been analyzed mainly from a normative point of view (Kymlicka, 1995; Patten, 2001; May, 2001; Van Parijs, 2002; Kymlicka & Patten, 2003). Relational language policies concern four main areas of social life: communication with public authorities, the toponymy of geographical and personal names, the language of public media, and the organization of the education system. In this context, scholars argue over whether, in these four areas, linguistic minority groups should be recognized as having collective language rights in order to protect and preserve their distinctive idiom. One debate is centered on the notion of the neutrality of the state, what Kymlicka calls a "benign neglect" approach. According to this idea, modeled on policies concerning religious diversity, states should only guarantee freedom of linguistic choice in the private sphere and should not support any particular language in the public sphere. The question is whether this approach is enough to satisfy the needs that arise from language diversity, or further language policies and the recognition of specific language rights are necessary (Kymlicka, 1995). Language rights imply treating people differently based on their linguistic membership, thereby clashing with basic individual rights such as the principle of individual equality. In this regard, "communitarians," who give priority to minority rights rather than to the principle of individual equality (Johnston, 1995; Herz, 1993), argue with "orthodox liberals," who deny most of the special arrangements to manage diversity, because they clash with general principles of liberal democracies (Barry, 2001, 2002; Hartney, 1995). Another group of scholars, who can be defined as "multicultural liberals," have tried to explore a middle way by justifying special arrangements for minorities inside the liberal tradition (Taylor, 1994; Kymlicka, 1995; Kukathas, 1997).

In this context it is possible to distinguish four different approaches, depending on the ordering of priorities of the author. These priorities are: the well-being of the state, the maintenance of language diversity (Patten & Kymlicka, 2003), the well-being of the group, and the well-being of the individual. Various scholars point out that an approach that emphasizes the need to guarantee the well-being of the state as a cohesive entity would raise objections to language policies that can put in danger the unity of the state (Coulombe, 2001; Arel, 2001; May, 2001; Patten & Kymlicka, 2003). Some authors instead aim at encouraging the existence of language diversity, considered to have an intrinsic value (Skutnabb-Kangas, 2000; Nettle & Romaine, 2000; Boran, 2003). In the third approach, the existence of linguistic groups and the need to protect their identity are the main priorities (Coulombe, 2001; Taylor, 1994; Hogan-Brun & Wolff, 2003). In other cases, at the center of analysis is the well-being of individuals. On the one hand, it is endangered by language policies that do not respect individual rights (Hartney, 1995; Barry, 2001; Appiah, 2005), and, on the other hand, it needs to be protected from the discrimination that comes from being part of a minority (Kymlicka, 1995; Patten, 2001; Levy, 2003; de Varennes, 1996). Scholars have focused on the state, language diversity, the individual or the linguistic group, and depending on their approach, they have elaborated different normative principles to justify (or deny) and evaluate language policies. Therefore language policies and language rights raise objections because they threaten the existence of the state or discriminate among individuals; or they are supported because they encourage language diversity, protect the existence of linguistic groups, or compensate individuals for being part of a minority.

Works on relational language policies diverge from works on power language policies due to a difference of focus. Most of the latter literature emphasizes the impact that constitutional engineering has on the relationship between linguistic groups and tries to design solutions to avoid group conflicts and sustain peace. In contrast, works on relational language policies focus on the state, language diversity, the individual, or the linguistic group, without considering the impact of relational language policies on group relations, and avoiding this dimension of analysis. In this way, these scholars forget the simple facts of life that pushed them to study and analyze language issues, namely that individuals living in the same territory speak different languages, and this condition affects the way they interact and their relations. In my opinion, relational languages policies, like power language policies, should be analyzed and evaluated according to their impact on the relations among the various linguistic groups that compose the society.

Since I consider language as a mind-set, I argue that relational language policies can impact the way individuals experience and understand language diversity, and this understanding affects the relationship between linguistic groups. In a prescriptive vein, language policies should not only have the goal of protecting linguistic diversity, but should also aim to neutralize mind-sets of discrimination and minorization. By encouraging the idea that majority–minority languages do not belong to two different arenas and do not compete in a zero-sum game, relational language policies can positively influence majority-minority relations, reducing the potentiality of seeing language as the main factor of division of the society. In this regard my position stands apart from that of Arel. As stated above, the author points out that cultural insecurity can bring instability. In his analysis of linguistic dynamics in Barcelona, Brussels, and Montreal, he argues that in order to promote stability it is necessary to reduce this insecurity, even by using "'politically incorrect' means," such as closing Castilian language schools in Barcelona

(Arel, 2001, p. 89). His account seems to imply that the goal of language policies is to make linguistic groups feel secure about their survival. In contrast, I argue that relational language policies, more than assuring the survival of linguistic groups, should neutralize the fact that language has been racialized and has long been considered the main element of division of the society, with majority-minority languages understood as competing in a zero-sum game. When speaking of linguistic survival, it is useful to refer to the terms used generally in international relations and national security studies. According to Buzan *et al.* (1998, pp. 23–24), the process of *securitization* arises when an issue is considered as an "existential threat," which cannot be handled in "the normal bargaining processes of the political sphere" and requires "emergency measures." Similarly, I argue that with mind-set of discrimination and minorization, *language becomes securitized*, and any factor that can endanger its purity as a unique tongue is thus translated as a threat to the survival of the linguistic group and its members. The goal of language policies and language rights is therefore to de-securitize language, bringing language issues out of emergency mode. Language policies should be evaluated based on their ability to change attitudes and perceptions and thus reconcile language diversity.

Based on this evaluation, it is possible to distinguish two types of relational language policy regimes: a *parting-regime*, which encourages individuals to consider majority and minority languages as two separate entities that are situated in a precise hierarchy of values and cannot be contaminated; and a *pooling-regime*, which promotes the joined use of majority and minority languages, considered on an equal basis. Whereas a parting-regime maintains language as racialized and maintains an understanding of majority–minority language relations as a zero-sum game, a pooling regime facilitates the disregarding of language as a factor of division of the society. For instance, returning to the example of kids playing in a room, a parting regime solution would trace a line on the floor and provide a language B version of Trivial Pursuit. In this way language A and language B children would be able to play and enjoy their time, but they would not have incentives to interact. In contrast, a pooling-regime solution would bring back the foosball table, so the children would be induced to bridge the linguistic barriers.

To summarize, I analyze relational language policies not only in view of their relevance for the cohesion of the national state, the maintenance of language diversity, the well-being of individuals, and the protection of linguistic groups, but also by considering their impact on inter-group relations. A comprehensive evaluation of language policies will emerge from considering their role in neutralizing the consequences of mental attitudes towards the experience and understanding of language diversity, by looking at their pooling or parting-effects. In this regard I have to make a clarification. A language group's mind-set is created and altered through context and structural changes. If the structure maintains this mind-set, a supposed pooling regime can provoke contrary effects. For instance, in the example of the children in the room, the solution to put back the foosball will not work if one group monopolizes its use. To resolve this situation it is necessary to return to power language policies that regulate power relations among groups, such as measures regarding the decision-making process on which games should be in the room and how their access should be regulated. In this way this "relationship" approach points out the interaction between language cleavage and political institutions. Indeed, the effects of institutions depend on the conditions of the society. An important consequence of this approach and of thinking of language as a mind-set is that it allows us to avoid formulating theoretical normative principles, which claim to determine which language policies should be employed or denied (Carens, 2000). Actually, the concept of language as mind-set also allows avoiding the assertion that the recognition of linguistic diversity "is a universal human need" (Fraser, 1996, p. 34). Indeed, if structural dynamics have not caused language to become an element of identity and a factor of division, language policies are not required. For example, in the case of the numerous dialects that exist in Italian society, some of which could claim the status of language, the use of dialect maintains a folkloristic connotation and can remain in the private sphere, without raising any tension. This approach requires the contextualization of each situation and a consideration of the history of the relations between the linguistic groups in order to understand how language diversity affects group relationship and how language policies can eventually modify this situation.

Below, I use this approach to analyze the South Tyrolean language regime and its impact on the inhabitants of Bolzano. This analysis will show how language in Bolzano has been racialized and has become the main element of division of the society. While the South Tyrol power language policies have guaranteed equal access to power to the linguistic groups, its relational language policies form a parting-regime that does not counteract this mind-set or reconcile language diversity, maintaining language as a divisive factors within the population. In this way the study of a city like Bolzano emphasize the usefulness of disaggregating the concept of language policies in power and relational aspects and of considering their impact on the local level. Studies that emphasize power aspects and how access to power is regulated provide an incomplete understanding of the effects of language diversity on the society and of the means to manage it. Instead, in discussing language policies and language rights it is necessary to support analysis of power language policies with studies of relational language policies, which affect the way individuals experience and understand language diversity influencing linguistic relations within the population.

Historical Background of South Tyrol[4]

Bolzano and South Tyrol are a typical example of a territory in which structural changes have caused the rise of mind-set of discrimination and minorization. With the 1919 Treaty of St Germain, South Tyrol, which had been part of the Hapsburg Empire for centuries and had an almost entirely German-speaking population, became part of Italy. After a short time, during which Rome carried out tolerant politics for the South Tyrol inhabitants, Fascism took power in Italy and the new government started a program for the Italianization of the territory. The German-speaking public officers were fired or transferred; in schools, teaching in German was forbidden and punished; only Italian was allowed in offices, public places, and in public inscriptions. According to Ettore Tolomei, the fascist counselor for the issue of South Tyrol, the local population was composed by Latins, who had forgotten their origin and had become Germans. Therefore, he invented a Latin root for each local German name and imposed the use of Italian toponymies.

Moreover, industrial zones were created in the biggest South Tyrolean towns, i.e. Bolzano, Merano, and Bressanone, in order to encourage Italian immigration. This process, which involved the main Italian industries, such as Falk, Montecatini, and Lancia, transformed the economy of the region. Traditional agriculture and small commerce were replaced by the creation of the modern chemical, metallurgic, and hydroelectric sectors. In the new industrial factories, the German-speaking population could not find jobs, and in this way lost the control of the most vital economic sectors and was excluded from the process of modernization.

Instead, Italian families from the rest of the peninsula received incentives to come in South Tyrol to work in public administration and the new industries. As stated by Mussolini, the goal of this program was to "modify the physical, political, moral, demographic character" of South Tyrol, replacing, or at least mixing, the German-speaking majority with an Italian-speaking majority (cited in Peterlini, 1996). The Italian population grew from 7000 in 1910 to more than 100 000 in 1943, becoming one-third of the South Tyrol inhabitants (Pristinger, 1978). This process especially affected urban centers such as Bolzano, which was previously a small pre-industrial city. Bolzano became an important industrial center and expanded its boundaries noticeably with the creation of new neighborhoods inhabited by Italian families. Between 1935 and 1941, 2800 houses were built, of which only 5% were given to German-speakers.[5] Due to the arrival of Italian elements, who in 1921 amounted to 30.3% of the 32 679 inhabitants of the city, its population grew to 65 553 in 1943 (Table A1 in Appendix reports the demographic trends of the German and Italian linguistic groups in South Tyrol and Bolzano in the 20th century).

Meanwhile, Hitler had taken power in Germany and in 1938 annexed Austria. Many South Tyroleans wished the same destiny for their land. However, Mussolini and Hitler did not want to ruin their alliance over a few thousand South Tyroleans and decided to resolve the South Tyrol question by moving the German-speaking population to the other side of the border. German-speaking South Tyroleans could choose between German citizenship, and immediate expatriation, and Italian citizenship, with the acknowledgment that they would not be protected (the so called *opzioni*—options). Of 266 985 German speaking South Tyroleans, 185 085 chose to move to Germany. However, the war slowed down the expatriation process, and at the end "only" 70 000 South Tyroleans left Italy (Vedovato, 1971).

After World War II, renewed discussions about the future of South Tyrol began. The German-speaking population and the Austrian government asked the Allies to unite South Tyrol and Austria. The Italian government opposed this plan, maintaining that the ethnic composition of the region had changed because a large number of Italians now lived in the region. The Allies refused the request for self-determination and pushed Rome and Vienna to conclude an agreement that would eliminate the conflicts between the two governments and the abuses of the Fascist past. On 5 September 1946, the Italian Prime Minister A. De Gasperi and the Austrian Minister of Foreign Affairs K. Gruber signed an agreement, which was attached to the 1947 Italian Peace Treaty. The *De Gasperi–Gruber Agreement* (also called the *Paris Agreement*) provided for the creation of an autonomous regional government under the Italian state with special measures to protect the German-speaking group.

The Paris Agreement is fairly generic, and thus there arose a number of interpretative issues. In particular, problems about the dimension of territorial autonomy surfaced. The German-speaking group wanted it limited to South Tyrol, where German-speakers comprised a majority of the population; the special Statute of Autonomy, approved by the Italian government to put the Paris Agreement into practice, gave territorial autonomy to the whole region of Trentino Alto-Adige, where the German-speaking group is in sum a minority, providing for the possibility to delegate some political functions to the two Provinces of Trento and Bolzano (South Tyrol).

After a short period of cooperation between the Italian- and German-speaking groups, the Italian government gradually neglected the Statute. Moreover, the influx of Italian speakers did not abate. Between 1953 and 1961, the population of Bolzano increased from 74 600 to 88 980, and by 1961 the Italian linguistic group amounted to 78.6% of the population of the city (see Table A1 in Appendix). A climate of mistrust emerged. German speakers dubbed the arrival of Italian-speaker immigrants the "Todesmarsch" (March of Death), that is the demise of the German-speaking group. The German-speaking population started to accuse the Italian government of having diluted its protection granted by the De Gasperi–Gruber Agreement, and claimed the right of self-determination. When the Italian government planned to build 5000 new houses in Bolzano, the German-speaking group considered it an attempt to further Italian immigration, and organized mass protests. Meanwhile, initial acts of terrorism began to be perpetrated targeting symbols of Italian presence, and included destructive attacks against electric power pylons and railways. In 1960 and 1961, the Austrian government brought the South Tyrol question to the United Nations' General Assembly. The Assembly clarified the impossibility of changing national borders and urged the parties to find a solution through the peace instruments provided by the UN Charter.

The UN intervention did not produce immediate results, and one of the most violent periods followed. Through 1969 there were 330 terrorist attacks (Agostini, 1985). However, the situation changed when the Italian government decided to give voice to the local population, setting up a research commission (called the *Commission of the Nineteen*) with representatives of the South Tyrol linguistic groups. In 1964 the commission issued a final report that suggested new measures in favor of the South Tyrol minority. These measures provided the basis for negotiations held at Geneva between Italian and Austrian experts, but were contested by the largest political party of German-speakers in South Tyrol, the Südtiroler Volkspartei (SVP). Subsequently, Rome engaged direct negotiations with the SVP, which modified the suggestions of the commission. In 1969, the Italian government enacted a final document of 137 measures (the so called *Pacchetto*—Package), which represented a new political basis for autonomy (Wolff, 2003). The principal elements of the Package provided for the transfer of legislative and executive functions from the region down to the individual provinces of Trento and Bolzano, where the German-speaking population was (and is) the majority, representing three-quarters of the South Tyrol inhabitants. Moreover, the package increased the number of special measures to protect the German-speaking population. An Operational Calendar for the implementation accompanied the Package, which the Italian government began to execute by enacting a new Statute of Autonomy on 20 January 1972.

This new statute has guaranteed the protection of linguistic differences, reducing remarkably separatist tendencies and ending terrorist attacks, and has had important effects on the relations between the Italian and the German-speaking groups. This process can be especially seen in Bolzano, where most of the Italian-speaking South Tyroleans live, and where there is extensive interaction between the German and the Italian-speaking groups. In the next section, I present South Tyrol's institutional arrangements focusing especially on the relational language policies that most affect the relationship between the German-speaking and Italian-speaking inhabitants of Bolzano.

South Tyrol Institutional Arrangements

The renewed 1972 Statute contains several institutional arrangements to manage the linguistic minority population of South Tyrol. These arrangements include both power language policies, which guarantee to the linguistic groups access to power and political decision-making processes, and relational language policies, which regulate the use of minority language in several aspects of social life.[6]

Power Language Policies

Numerous power language policies have re-equilibrated the power relations among the linguistic groups, eliminating threats to status and security of the German-speaking population. First of all, the province of Bolzano, with its German-speaking majority, is given territorial autonomy.[7] The autonomous authority has all the legislative and executive power in matter of local concerns. The only exception is the recognition of limited power of collecting taxes; but the local authority receives enormous financial allocations from the central state.

Besides the concession of territorial autonomy, certain regulations give some special rights to members of minority groups, in order to eliminate the effects of past discriminations and the possible disadvantages caused by the minority status. Thus, German speakers enjoy not only the same rights as the Italian-speaking population (so called *negative protection*), but also a system of special rules for so called *positive protection*. The goal of this system is to protect German-speakers' characteristics and to enhance their economic, political and social development (Pizzorusso, 1993).

First of all, the South Tyrolean linguistic groups are guaranteed a presence in the legislative, executive and judiciary bodies of the autonomous authority (Casonato, 1998). The members of the Provincial Parliament (Consiglio Provinciale), who are elected by a proportional system of representation, are distinguished not only by their political positions but also for their linguistic membership. In this regard, candidates must indicate their linguistic group when they run for elections. Moreover, minority veto rights are recognized. The majority of the deputies of each linguistic group has the power to request *the vote by linguistic groups*, if *a bill is considered prejudicial for the equality of rights between citizens of the different linguistic groups or for the ethnic and cultural characteristics of the groups themselves* (art. 56 translated from the Statute of Autonomy; Giunta provinciale di Bolzano, 1996).

Linguistic groups are also considered as the basis for the constitution of executive bodies. The composition of the Provincial Government (Giunta Provinciale), which is elected by the Provincial Parliament, *must reflect the numerical strength of the linguistic groups as represented in the Provincial Parliament* (art. 50).[8] The proportional representation of the linguistic group is guaranteed as well in the organization of local public bodies. Indeed, *each linguistic group has the right to be represented in the City Government, if there are at least two members belonging to that group in the City Council* (art. 61). Regarding judiciary bodies, judges are nominated in proportion to the numerical strength of the linguistic groups (see below), and the members of the Autonomy Section of the Administrative Justice Regional Court must belong in equal number to the Italian- and German-speaking groups.

Moreover, the South Tyrol Statute also regulates access to public employment. Article 89 of the 1972 Statute affirms that all the posts in government administration should be distributed among citizens belonging to each linguistic group in proportion to the numerical strength. These figures are drawn from an apposite declaration of membership that is given at the time of the official census of the population. The mechanism is called *proporzionale etnica* (ethnic proportion). Additionally, the principle of proportionality extends to all the judicial appointments, except the police force. The ethnic proportion in public employment is a rectifying measure and has the goal of eliminating the results of past negative discriminations. It satisfies the need of rebalancing access to work, creating a reflective image between the linguistic composition of population and that of civil servants in South Tyrol (Winkler, 1997).

Relational Language Policies

Besides the minority autonomy, the system of protection of South Tyrolean minorities is characterized by several relational language policies which guarantee: usage of minority languages in interactions with public administration offices and judiciary authorities; access to electronic media products in minority language; and primary and secondary education in students' mother tongue.

The Statute and its implementing rules have broad implications for the use of Italian and German languages, guaranteeing wide protection for minority language speakers. The local language, although not official, is *parificata* (made as equal) to Italian, the official language of the State, and the right of freedom of language is recognized (art. 99). The Statute provides special measures regarding topographical names. All public signs, such as road markings, should be bilingual (De Vergottini, 1986). Moreover, minorities have the right to use their own language in interactions with public offices. In order to guarantee these linguistic rights, the employees of public offices have to be bilingual. Even employees of private offices that provide public services must be able to converse in both languages. Regarding judiciary authorities, the principle of bilingualism applies to all judicial appointments, and part of the police force has to be bilingual. Since 1993, there are specific regulations regarding language use in interactions with police officers and courts. Interrogatories are done in German when this is the mother tongue of the individual arrested, and there is the possibility to have a first-and second-degree monolingual trial in German language. In order to guarantee these rights, there is the possibility to take in front of the Bolzano's Autonomy Section of the Administrative Justice Regional Court those acts considered as clashing with the measures on the linguistic rights (art. 92).

Regarding language rights, the Statute guarantees access to electronic media products. Indeed, the local branch of the public radio-television network (RAI 3), which has its headquarters in Bolzano, must transmit programs, including news, in German. What is interesting to note is the fact that in South Tyrol two versions of RAI 3 are broadcast on two different frequencies. One version of RAI 3 broadcasts programs exclusively in Italian; the other version of RAI 3 offers programs in both Italian and German. Moreover the Statute provides that the South Tyrol government must install and administrate a network to guarantee the reception of foreign radio-television programs from German-speaking countries.

One of the fundamental pieces of the South Tyrol system is the organization of the school system. The 1972 Statute and the relating implementing rules provide for the teaching in nursery, elementary, middle and high schools in the Italian or German mother tongue of students. The Statute also makes compulsory the teaching of the second language beginning from the second year of the elementary school (art. 19). Consequently, two school systems have been created: one uses as teaching language only German; the other uses only Italian. In this way, there is a total separation between the Italian and the German groups, which characterizes the entire school system, and which segregates students by language (Daniele, 1986; Lampis, 1997; Millian i Massana, 1994). The practice used in South Tyrol has been justified by the need to avoid the risk that, even if under bilingualism rules, unified schools would become an instrument for assimilating minorities. However, this system has not created a true bilingual population. Indeed, especially the Italian speakers have serious difficulties in learning the other language.[9] Therefore, many Italian-speaking parents have asked for new didactic methodologies, such as the introduction of the teaching of the second language in nursery schools and the so called "immersion teaching," namely the teaching of different topics in the second language. The representatives of the German-speaking group have blocked most of these initiatives, because they worry that these experiments could put in danger the integrity of the German language schools. In 1988, teaching of German language in the first year of Italian elementary schools was permitted. Instead, only since 2004 Italian language is taught in the first year of German elementary schools. In 1997, after long debates, Italian nursery schools in Bolzano, Bressanone, and Bolzano have been allowed to teach the second language in the last year of school with the limitation that this experiment cannot be extended to German nursery schools. The immersion teaching is seen as clashing with the Statute and is highly contested. In the current 2006–2007 academic year, there is limited experimentation in a few classes of an Italian elementary school of Bolzano.

Furthermore, to facilitate the learning of the second language, many Italian-speaking parents have enrolled their children in German schools. This phenomenon has been defined as an "assault" on German schools by Italian students, and it has caused many debates over the right of parents to select their children's schools (Winkler, 2005, p. 201). The statute recognizes the right of parents to choose what school to enroll their children. However, since students should be taught in their mother tongue, the freedom of choice is limited by this reciprocity. In this way the South Tyrol rules imply that the freedom of choice should respect the necessity of keeping the linguistic characteristics of schools. In 1988 a provincial law has clarified that if students do not have enough knowledge of the language of teaching, which does not allow them to follow the lectures and threatens the efficiency of the school, they should be enrolled in the school of the other linguistic group. This measure has raised many concerns, because it is used also in nursery schools, where knowing the language is not necessary for attendance, since learning the language is the aim of the school (Pizzorusso, 1990, p. 16).

Some South Tyrolean institutional mechanisms, such as the ethnic proportion, refer explicitly to the division of the South Tyrol population into different linguistic groups, and require knowing the exact affiliation of individuals. In the 1981, 1991, and 2001 censuses, the declaration of membership has been used to determine not only the numerical strength of linguistic groups, but also the individuals' membership. In this way the census has acquired an extreme value, and it has become an individual count with important juridical effects on many aspects of the social life of South Tyrol inhabitants. For this reason, the declaration of membership has been at the center of virulent debates about various aspects, such as the secrecy of the statistical data, the truthfulness of declarations, and the status of some categories of person such as minors, bilinguals and foreigners. Indeed, the 1981 census recognized only the official groups, forcing bilinguals and foreigners to declare forgery. The 1991 and 2001 census offered the possibility to identify with the term *altro* (something else), and to release a declaration of aggregation to the official groups. However, the data regarding the numerical weight of those who check this term are not published.[10]

Language Diversity and Relational Language Policies in Bolzano: Analysis

Since the end of World War I, South Tyrol and in particular its main city Bolzano has experienced demographic changes due to the immigration of Italian-speaking population, which led to the cohabitation of different linguistic groups. Today, German- and Italian-speaking groups represent respectively about three-quarters and one-fourth of the population of the province; this proportion is inverted in the city of Bolzano (see Table A1 in Appendix).

The South Tyrolean institutional arrangements have been particularly successful in guaranteeing peaceful cohabitation among the linguistic groups and ending a conflict situation. Through the establishment of substantive territorial autonomy to South Tyrol, where the German-speaking population is the majority, this linguistic group is in control of almost every aspect of its political, economic, and social life. In Rubio-Marín's words (2003, p. 59), the concession of powers of self-government has enabled the German-speaking minority to protect its linguistic environment. The ethnic proportion and the recognition of numerous linguistic rights have guaranteed access to public employment and the use of German language in all the local public and private spheres. In this way, most of the separatist tendencies have faded away because being a German speaker in an Italian South Tyrol does not imply any inconvenience. Indeed, the new Statute has re-equilibrated the power relations among the linguistic groups, eliminating any threat to the status and security of the German group. This has been recognized, even by the representatives of the German-speaking group, as Magnago (1993), former leader of the SVP, which stated that in South Tyrol the most extended autonomy of legislative power in the economic, social, and cultural sectors has been realized. With the new Statute, the conditions of the German-speaking population have remarkably improved, and this system brings so many benefits that this population has given up its desire to be united with Austria. As recognized by Brugger, former "Obmann" (president) of the SVP, "South Tyroleans are not Italian and they do not want to be Italian, but they are really well. I do not believe they want to change the national borders."[11]

However, regarding linguistic relations between the Italian and the German linguistic groups, the South Tyrol system cannot be considered as successful. These relations have been characterized by both the presence of mind-sets of discrimination and minorization. Historically, the first contact between the Italian- and the German-speaking groups was characterized by competition and the attempt of the Fascist regime to assimilate the region. The Italian-speaking community received favorable treatment, whereas the German-speaking population, which considered the Italians to be invaders, was highly discriminated against. Besides discrimination, the German-speaking group experienced the Fascist attempt to Italianize the region. This process of assimilation was a complete attack on the existence of the German-speaking group carried out with ideological means, namely Tolomei's claims of the Latin roots of South Tyrol, legislative instruments, such as the abolition of German schools and the laws against speaking German in public spaces, as well as physical methods, such as the "options" and Italian immigration. In this context, the betrayal of the first Statute of Autonomy by the Italian democratic government and the continuous arrival of Italian immigrants during the 1950s and 1960s radicalized the situation, convincing the German-speaking population that the attempt to Italianize South Tyrol was not an isolated accident due to Fascism.[12] In addition, under Mussolini the process of modernization and industrialization of the region began. The new industrial factories of Bolzano limited employment to Italian immigrants coming from the rest of the Peninsula. Thus, not only public administration but also industry spoke Italian. In contrast, most of the German-speaking population was employed in the agricultural sector. Speaking German was not given a prestigious status, and the Italian group did not have incentives to learn the local language.

Because of these historical experiences language in South Tyrol has been racialized; it is considered to be a biological characteristic of people, which represents the core element of identity and the main factor of division of the South Tyrol population. Being a German-speaker means not being Italian and vice versa, and any contact between the two languages is considered a danger to the existence of each. The relations between majority and minority languages are represented as a zero-sum game, and their being in danger is believed to reflect a general threat to the survival of the corresponding linguistic group and its members. Since the division between German and Italian speakers is considered primordial, linguistic assimilation and language shift are perceived as unnatural and illegitimate. In this regard, ethnic intermarriages are seen as a hidden form of ethnic erosion, slowly wearing away the linguistic groups.

Whereas the South Tyrol power language policies have eliminated any threat to the status and security of the German linguistic groups, its relational language policies have produced contradictory effects. It is true that the cohabitation among the linguistic groups has notably improved and the South Tyrol population has accepted living in a bilingual society. Indeed, according to *Barometro linguistico dell'Alto Adige 2004* (Provincia Autonoma di Bolzano-Alto Adige, 2006), a survey published in 2006 on the use of language and linguistic identity in South Tyrol, the majority of both the linguistic groups evaluates the other language positively and considers its knowledge important. It also considers cohabitation satisfactory, and sees it as a lesser problem respect to the past. Moreover, an increasing proportion of the South Tyrol population do not see the cohabitation as a problem at all, and a majority of both the German- and Italian-speaking population considers the presence of more than one linguistic group in the territory positively. However, according to this same survey, regarding the knowledge of the other language, the South Tyrol population has problems particularly in the area of oral usage, namely in activities that are characterized the most by interpersonal relations; the majority of both the linguistic groups rarely speak the other language in private life; and the other language is used mainly for necessity or for politeness. Moreover, the population of both the linguistic groups feels at a disadvantage and feels a different sense of identity. According to the survey, 85.6% of the German-speaking population feels "South Tyrolean." In contrast, half of the Italian speaking group feel "Italian" tout court, or alternatively as "South Tyrolean of Italian language" (14.4%), and as "Alto-Atesino"—an Italian term for South Tyrolean (10.1%). Only 2.6% of the Italian linguistic group shares the same feeling of identity of the German-speaking group as "South Tyrolean." Therefore, in the words of the survey, although there are contacts and openings between the linguistic groups, there is the impression that South Tyrol is a divided society, where the language of the other group is spoken mainly for practical needs rather than personal desire (Provincia Autonoma di Bolzano-Alto Adige, 2006, p. 135). It is a suspicious society, where fears of mixture, assimilation, and losing one's identity have not disappeared, and the idea that accepting the other language does not imply any renunciation has not taken root (Provincia Autonoma di Bolzano-Alto Adige, 2006, pp. 262–265, 284).

The problem resides in the fact that South Tyrol relational language policies have not done much to reduce an understanding of language diversity characterized by mind-set of discrimination and minorization. Actually, this mind-set is embedded in some of the South Tyrol policies and is reflected in the words of the Statute of Autonomy, which, by not giving German the status of official language, considers Italian language as the standard, emphasizing in turn the necessity to recognize and protect the right to use German. Furthermore, the system is based on the principle of linguistic separatism, according to which linguistic minorities and the use of minority languages are guaranteed and protected through the separation of the linguistic groups for many significant aspects of social life and through obstacles for the mixed use and contaminations between majority and minority languages. This system imposes on the South Tyrol population the recognition of linguistic differences, thereby encouraging language segregation. It puts forth the idea that language should not be mixed because using a language threatens the existence of the other language, endangering the identity of its speakers. This situation especially affects Bolzano, and the consequences of this system can be observed in the city's political life, where parties that are attached to either one of the two groups and emphasize the linguistic divisions prevail.

Political Life of Bolzano

In Bolzano, German and Italian speakers live together peacefully; but this cohabitation happens for the most part in a segregated environment that fosters linguistic confrontation. The city's political life of the past ten years reflects this condition. Indeed, the strongest party in Bolzano is usually the nationalist Alleanza Nazionale (AN), bearer of the Fascist heritage. In contrast, the German-speaking population, which counts for one-quarter of the electorate, votes predominantly for the SVP, which primarily represents the interests of the German group. The promotion of these two parties for only one linguistic group is symbolically confirmed by the fact that neither of the parties offers a bilingual version of their website.[13] Tables 1 and 2 present the results of the local elections for the AN, the SVP, the third most successful party, and the Verdi-Grüne-Verc, which is the biggest party with a cross-linguistic-group political platform.[14]

As shown by the tables, the SVP and the AN are the two most successful parties of Bolzano in the election of the Provincial Parliament, which has extensive power and

Table 1. Results of elections of Bolzano's City Council in percentages

Year	AN	SVP	Party in third position	Verdi-Grüne-Verc
1995	30.8	18.0	17.4	NA
2000	23.9	18.9	13.3	7.3
2005 (05/08)	20.0	17.7	12.2	5.6
2005 (11/06)	17.7	21.8	10.1	4.3

Table 2. Results of elections of South Tyrol Provincial Parliament in the electoral district of Bolzano in percentages

Year	AN	SVP	Party in third position	Verdi-Grüne-Verc
1998	25.8	18.6	10.7	8.9
2003	25.8	20.4	12.2	8.2

handles important issues, including those regarding the protection of linguistic rights and the relations between linguistic groups. The two parties are also the most successful political forces in the elections of the City Council, which does not have legislative power and only has the task of administering the city. I need to clarify that the decrease of the AN's vote between 1995 and 2005 does not indicate that the linguistic vote is remarkably declining. Indeed, half of it went to a new nationalist right-wing party, Unitalia, which in 1998 obtained 5.6% of votes, 3.8% in 2000, 5.4% in 2003, 4.6% in the May 2005 election, and 3.2% in the November 2005 elections.[15]

Save the 1995 election, the party in third position scores between 10 and 13% and is more than 5 points percentage below the AN and the SVP. Most of the time this party is a left party that is voted by those Italian-speaking inhabitants contrary to the nationalist and right tones of the AN, and is usually allied with the SVP in the government of the Province and the city. Those parties, such as the Verdi-Grüne-Verc, which appeal to both the linguistic groups and present candidates that belong to both the Italian and the German linguistic groups, remain in the shadow. The Verdi-Grüne-Verc is always at least 10% below the AN and the SVP and its electoral results are declining.

As shown in Table 3, it is revealing that the electoral successes of both the AN and the SVP vary depending on the neighborhood. The SVP is stronger in the oldest part of the town, where most of the German-speaking inhabitants live, whereas its vote plummets in the modern neighborhood, especially those built under Fascism, where most of the Italian-speaking inhabitants live. The AN presents an inverse trend. Indeed, in the above elections the SVP obtained between 34.6% and 43.8% of votes in the electoral district "Centro-Piani-Rencio," which includes the old town, whereas it has obtained only between 5.9% and 9.0% of votes in the district "Europa-Novacella," which corresponds to that part of the town built during Fascism. Vice versa, the AN vote has

Table 3. Disaggregation by neighborhood of the electoral results of the AN and the SVP in Bolzano for the elections of the City Council and the South Tyrol Provincial Parliament in percentages

Year	AN			SVP		
	Total	Centro-Piani-Rencio	Europa-Novacella.	Total	Centro-Piani-Rencio	Europa-Novacella.
1995	30.8	18.3	38.7	18.0	37.8	6.2
1998	25.8	14.3	31.5	18.6	34.6	6.7
2000	23.9	16.3	31.6	18.9	37.4	6.1
2003	25.8	13.6	33.8	20.4	37.8	9.0
2005 (05/08)	20.0	9.9	26.2	17.7	36.3	5.9
2005 (11/06)	17.7	8.5	24.1	21.8	43.8	7.8

varied between 9.5% and 18.3% in the district "Centro-Piani-Rencio," and between 24.1% and 38.7% in the district "Europa-Novacella."

Both sets of members of the Provincial Parliament and Bolzano's City Council are elected with the open list proportional electoral system. Some scholars might argue that the political division between the Italian and the German linguistic groups depends on the electoral system and, would therefore ask whether a different system for the elections of the Provincial Parliament and the City Council, which could push parties to form coalition across linguistic groups, would break this dynamic of the linguistic vote. However, the goal of this paper is not to analyze power language policies, such as the concession of the territorial autonomy and the organization of the local political bodies; rather this paper focuses on relational language policies, which more directly affect the social life and the social relations among linguistic groups. In my opinion, political arrangements, such as the electoral system, shape the distribution of power among political forces that play the "language card" as the main element of division of the South Tyrol population. What this paper argues is that South Tyrol relational language policies make playing the language card appealing, because these policies have not reduced the existence of a mind-set of discrimination and minorization. In this sense, the above electoral results do not depend only on the electoral system but are also the consequence of the division of the inhabitants of Bolzano in many aspect of social life; a division that maintains language diversity as the main element of politics. Bolzano's population is institutionally trained to think of itself as divided into German- and Italian-speaking groups. Consequently, although it has accepted to live in a bilingual society, the population easily buys the propaganda of parties that aim at emphasizing divisions and misunderstandings.

Parting-effect Aspects of South Tyrol Relational Language Rolicies

The political life of Bolzano is the result of the South Tyrol relational language policies, which exercise parting-effects by essentializing language diversity and segregating the population in terms of language. The clearest example of this segregation and essentialization of language is given by the system of separate schools.[16] Various devices, such as the limits on the freedom of choice of schools in which children enroll and the opposition to introducing the teaching of the second language in nursery schools, protect the language of schools from any form of "contamination." Moreover, in these separate schools, because the other language is taught as a foreign language and it is not used for teaching other topics, South Tyrolean scholars learn that there is a specific hierarchy between their first language, which defines their identity, and the second language of the other linguistic group. In this way, Italian and German languages are kept separated in a specific hierarchy of values, in which the first language should be used in any form of daily interactions and the second language should be used only in case of necessity.

A further example is given by the way the access to electronic mass media is organized. Foreign channels and the German version of RAI 3 provide a service that exclusively targets the German-speaking group. Therefore, these channels keep separate the majority and minority populations. Indeed, the German-speaking and the Italian-speaking groups have the possibility of watching respectively a German and an Italian version of RAI 3, and each group rarely watches the other version. Moreover, most members of the Italian-speaking group do not watch foreign channels, because South Tyrol is not the main priority for these media outlets. The region is also portrayed with a foreign perspective, which does not consider the local reality and does not represent the local Italian-speaking population. Thus, the Italian-speaking population continues to watch the majority mainstream Italian programs and is not encouraged to change the channel. According to *Barometro linguistico dell'Alto Adige 2004* (Provincia Autonoma di Bolzano-Alto Adige, 2006), 80% of the Italian-speaking population never or rarely watches programs in German language. Vice versa, the proportion of German speakers that does not watch or rarely watches Italian television amounts to 67%. In this way this system reinforces the understanding of the Italian and German language as belonging to two different arenas and the groups' sense of distinctiveness and their disengagement from the rest of the South Tyrol society.

In addition, the declaration of membership by refusing the term bilingual and the recording of the number of people that identify themselves with this term, crystallizes linguistic divisions, which are considered primordial, and maintains a strict separation between the linguistic groups, hurting the relations between the South Tyrolean populations. Since the census has an instrumental dimension, it has become a political battleground for achieving the right proportion (Kertzer & Arel, 2002). Each group fears a reduction in its numerical strength, and each census was followed by discussions and analyses of group demographic trends. The census, by precluding the use of categories that represent shared use of languages, strengthens an understanding of the relations between the South Tyrolean linguistic groups as a zero-sum game, where the growth of one group is believed to be a threat to the other linguistic community.[17]

South Tyrol Management of Linguistic Diversity: Living Apart in the Same Room

The South Tyrol policies exercise a parting-effect. Italian and German languages are kept separate as if they belong to two distinguished spheres that should not be contaminated. This parting-regime fosters a divided society, where the linguistic element is still perceived as the main factor of opposition among organized social groups. In this way, language policies and the recognition of language rights in South Tyrol impose separateness that affects the relational situation among the linguistic groups. Although nobody can deny that majority-minority relations in Bolzano are peaceful, there remains a certain degree of tension among the linguistic groups. To confirm this fact, one needs only to look briefly at the first pages of local newspapers, which at least once every one/two weeks report polemics regarding various aspects of the relations among the groups. These polemics often have nationalistic tones and give extreme importance to the linguistic differences of the South Tyrol population.

Moreover, because South Tyrol language policies foster an understanding of language as racialized and have maintained a potential mind-set of minorization, this psychological condition has expanded from the German to the Italian linguistic group. One example of this process is given by the intense debate regarding the name of one of the squares of Bolzano, namely Piazza della Vittoria (Victory's Square). Piazza della Vittoria is one of the main squares of modern Bolzano developed under Fascism, and, together with the eponymous monument at the center of the square, was built to celebrate the victory of the Italian state in World War I, and consequently carries on the controversial memory of the annexation of South Tyrol. In 2002, the Provincial Government, formed by members of the SVP and left-wing parties, changed the name to Piazza della Pace (Square of the Peace). The Italian-speaking inhabitants, independently from the political creed, considered this act as an attempt to erase the identity of the Italian-speaking group and called for a referendum, in which 62% of the inhabitants of Bolzano have voted for maintaining the old denomination.

This story confirms that even the Italian linguistic group in Bolzano has developed a mind-set of discrimination and of minorization. It believes its identity is separate from that of the German-speaking population, and has developed competitive oppositional attitudes toward the other linguistic group. Although it represents 73% of the inhabitants of Bolzano, the Italian-speaking population emphasizes its minority status in South Tyrol, as an identity that needs to be protected. The reason for this process lies in the fact that Italian and German languages have been racialized and are presented as belonging to two different arenas, which cannot intermingle. The South Tyrol relational language policies do not tackle this problem and do not reduce the mind-set of minorization of the inhabitants of Bolzano. Instead, it is a parting-regime, which maintains the potential existence of this mental attitude, by institutionally segregating Italian and German languages and freezing them in two separate spheres, which are not supposed to overlap.

In this way, language in Bolzano is still a main element of division of the population, despite the fact that in the past decades the society has gone through many structural changes. On the one hand, since the late 80s South Tyrol has entered a post-industrial phase, in which heavy industries are not any longer the core of economic development. Many of the factories opened during the Fascism years, such as Lancia, through which the Italian-speaking group dominated what was once the most dynamic sector of the economy, have closed. On the other hand, there has been the development of the European Union and the increase of international trade, especially with the German-speaking world. In this new situation the German language is no longer relegated to the rural sector, but has assumed a prestigious status in the most dynamic sectors such as tourism and business. Therefore, the Italian-speaking population is eager to embrace the local language, as is proven by the various proposals and experiments to improve the teaching of the second language in Italian schools. Moreover the Todesmarsch (March of Death) is over; indeed, since the 70s, the proportion of the Italian-speaking group has begun to decrease both in South Tyrol in general and in the city of Bolzano, declining respectively between the 1971 census and the 2001 census from 33.3% to 26.4% and from 77.1% to 73.0% (see Table A1 in Appendix).

These changes, together with the concession of the new Statute of Autonomy and its numerous power language policies, should have removed any potential to maintain mind-sets of discrimination and mind-sets of minorization. However, the language rights recognized in South Tyrol form a parting-regime, which has crystallized language diversity and has introduced a rigid separation between the German- and Italian-speaking groups, impeding the adaptation of the relations among the South Tyrol population to the new context. Language diversity is institutionally recognized as being primordial, and linguistic assimilation and language shift are perceived as unnatural. In this way, although the German- and Italian-speaking populations are willing to share the same room, the South Tyrol linguistic groups live apart.

This fact especially affects the children of inter-group marriages, whose existence is not officially recognized by the South Tyrol institutions (except for the use of term "altro"—something else—in the declaration of membership). This "mixed" group, which supposedly represents between 10 and 15% of the South Tyrol inhabitants and is destined to grow especially in Bolzano, has problems with identification in the rigid language division of South Tyrol.[18] Moreover, in the past decade the process of globalization, in the form of immigration from developing countries, has also begun to affect a small peripheral town like Bolzano. In 2001, there were 4458 foreigners, for the most part coming from developing countries, which corresponded to 4.6% of the inhabitants of the town, and this number is rapidly increasing.[19] The South Tyrol regime requires foreigners to fit somehow in the rigid linguistic division and to make a choice between the linguistic groups. For example, they have to choose which school, Italian, or German, to send their children, and they have to aggregate with one of the official group in order to permit the functioning of South institutional mechanisms, such as the ethnic proportion.[20] The South Tyrol parting-regime clashes with the increasing number of inter-group marriages and foreign population. It represents South Tyrol as composed and divided in the official groups, a representation that does not mirror any longer the reality of South Tyrol society. In this way, it maintains an artificial status quo, refusing to recognize the changing environment.

Conclusion

The case study of Bolzano places debates on issues of managing linguistic diversity in new light. Managing linguistic diversity means addressing the process through which language diversity and language policies become salient. Indeed, language in itself is not a factor of division; rather language should be considered as a mind-set formed by the perceptions of the relationships among people, their language and their environment. Language becomes a charged issue when historical-structural processes lead to the collision between language diversity and group identity. As pointed out by Skutnabb-Kangas (2005, p. 280), linguistic diversity is a normal accident of reality; complications related to linguistic diversity are the result of attitudes. In particular, a mind-set of discrimination, through which language is considered as a biological characteristic of people, and a mind-set of minorization, through which relations between languages are viewed as a zero-sum game, transform language into a critical social cleavage, as in the case of South Tyrol. Through this process language becomes securitized, affecting the day to day relations between individuals that speak different languages as a native tongue, and making language policies critical.

In this context, the case study illustrates the usefulness of disaggregating the power and relational aspect of language policies in order to gain a complete understanding of the situation. Managing linguistic diversity implies not only focusing on the distribution of power among linguistic groups; but also requires us to consider those policies that affect how language diversity is experienced and understood in daily life. In the case of Bolzano, the recognition of political autonomy has enabled the German linguistic minority to keep its linguistic environment. In this way, separatist tendencies have faded away and the South Tyrol population has accepted living in a bilingual society. However, the type of language rights recognized in South Tyrol imposes barriers that affect the relational situation among the German and Italian speaking inhabitants. Thus, power and relational language policies produce separate and different results. Whereas the South Tyrol power language policies provide security for the linguistic groups, the South Tyrol relational language policies form a parting-regime, which, by keeping separate its inhabitants and through obstacles for the mixed use and contamination between majority and minority languages, do not neutralize mind-sets of discrimination and minorization. Moreover, the case of Bolzano shows that relational aspects of language policies interact with dynamics in the area regulated by power language policies. Indeed, South Tyrol relational language policies do not counter the understanding of language as an element of division of the society and maintain the idea that language relationship are competitive. This understanding of language diversity in turn affects the political life of Bolzano, which remains characterized by the prevalence of parties attached to either the German- or Italian-speaking communities. In this sense, this analysis shows how, by affecting the understanding of language diversity, language policies exert important effects both on society and on politics.

Therefore, the issue of managing linguistic diversity is not limited to the question whether the presence of linguistic diversity in the society requires state intervention and the enactment of specific language policies. Nor is the main problem the fact that language policies can imply collective rights and lead to a clash between collective rights and individual rights. Although these points of view raise interesting debates, they are misleading because they do not pay attention to the processes that lie behind the consideration of language as a category of diversity. Each situation needs to be contextualized in order to understand how language diversity becomes a salient issue, how language affects the relationship among the population, and how language policies and language rights interact with language cleavages. Managing linguistic diversity is not just a matter of enacting language policies and recognizing language rights. Instead, it is necessary to consider how these policies and rights affect the understanding of language as a factor of diversity and consequently affect the interactions within the population. Returning to the example of children in the room reported in a previous section of this contribution, the question is not whether children should have a toy; rather the question is what happens among the children when they receive one toy or another.

In this regard, the case of Bolzano highlights the necessity to introduce an additional dimension of analysis for relational language policies. Indeed, at stake is not the necessity of guaranteeing diversity or homogeneity, equality among individuals or equality among linguistic groups. Debates around language policies are incomplete if they focus only on such types of priorities to elaborate principles to justify or deny language rights. Proceeding in this way underestimates the fact that recognizing or denying language rights has critical effects on the role of language diversity in relational life. Instead it is necessary to consider that relational language policies can impact the way individuals experience and understand language diversity, affecting relationships between linguistic groups. Thus, relational language policies should not be debated only regarding their impact on the national community and on the individual, or their ability to protect linguistic groups and linguistic diversity, but also on their effects on relations among individuals that speak different languages as native tongue. Incidentally, this perspective allows us to avoid the so called issue of equivalence, namely the need to identify which linguistic minorities deserve linguistic rights, which usually scholars resolve by distinguishing between national, ethnic, endogenous and immigrant groups (Kymlicka, 1995; May, 2001, 2005). This proposed solution raises the question why some linguistic groups merit more protection than others. This issue fades away because language policies are not about the status and the security of language minorities; rather they are about relationships among individuals that speak different language as native tongue, independently from the type of linguistic groups.

In conclusion I need to clarify that this analysis is not an argument against language rights. What this study points out is that the case of Bolzano demands that we rethink the debate about language policies and recognition of language rights. Language policies have socio-political effects, and should be evaluated based on their ability to de-securitize language, bringing language issues out of the emergency mode and reconciling language diversity. In the case of Bolzano, the type of language policies recognized in South Tyrol has not played out this function and is actually an obstacle for the evolution of the society. Today Bolzano's inhabitants have accepted living in a bilingual society and consider it a positive thing; however, they still behave socially and politically as if they live apart.

Acknowledgements

The author is grateful to Lisa Bjorkman and Karen Coleman for their valuable help, and A. Cosima Budabin for her precious pieces of advice. The author also thanks Dr. Francesco Palermo of EURAC (European Academy of Bolzano) and the anonymous reviewers of *Ethnopolitics* for their comments. The views expressed herein are those of the author alone.

Notes

1. Throughout this paper, when I use the term "minority," without any further specification, I refer to the German-speaking group or to the German language. Moreover, 4% of the population of South Tyrol is composed by Ladins, a small linguistic group, which lives concentrated in three mountain valleys and which, through the centuries, has maintained specific costumes and a distinct romance language. In Bolzano, 0.7% of the inhabitants are Ladins. Unless otherwise indicated, all the demographic data used in this paper are available from ASTAT-Istituto provinciale di statistica/Landesinstitut für Statistik (Provincial Statistic Institute), and are accessible online at: http://www.provincia.bz.it/astat. Some data have been kindly provided by Francesca Speziani of ASTAT.
2. I owe this understanding of language to the lectures of Prof. Mala Htun and Courtney Jung at The New School for Social Research (spring 2005 and fall 2005). In this regard, referring to the concept of ethnicity, Prof. Htun defines it as a behavior. I prefer to use the term mind-set, because it is the mental status that determines behaviors. Moreover, the following account has been extensively influenced by the reading of Roger Petersen's book *Understanding Ethnic Violence*, which explores the role of emotions in causing ethnic conflicts (2002). According to the author, emotions are the results of structural changes, which "produce( ) information that is processed into beliefs". Once arisen, emotions generate "a change in the saliency of a particular desire" and "generate action tendencies to meet that desire" (Petersen, 2002, p. 22).
3. In this regard I also refer to Shafir's brilliant book *Immigrants and Nationalism* (1995) on the connection between nationalism and relations between immigrant population and host countries.
4. For further historical researches see Peterlini (1996); Vallini & Allatri (1997); Vedovato (1971); Corsini (1993); and *Giunta provinciale di Bolzano* (1999).
5. Data available in: Provincia Autonoma di Bolzano-Alto Adige, "Informazioni sull'Alto-Adige," accessible online at: http://www.provincia.bz.it/aprov/alto-adige/censimento.htm
6. As mentioned in note 1, a small part of the South Tyrol population is Ladin. The Ladin linguistic group has also been granted some special measures to protect its linguistic features. However, because it does not enjoy all the measures elaborated for the German-speaking group and it is demographically small, especially in Bolzano, this paper focuses on the German population and its relations with the Italian linguistic group. The provisions for the Ladin linguistic groups are not presented. This omission does not affect the argument proposed in this paper.
7. In 2001 the Statute has been partially modified and now the term third Statute of Autonomy is used. However, these changes regard especially the political power of the Province of South Tyrol and its institutional relations with the region Trentino Alto-Adige, and are not important for the goal of this paper.

8. The 2001 reform of the Statute allows for the direct election of the president of the Provincial Government.
9. One of the challenges faced by the Italian-speaking group in learning German is the fact that South Tyroleans speak mainly a local German dialect in their daily life, rather than the standard German (Hochdeutsch). Therefore it is difficult to practice the Hochdeutsch learned in classes outside of schools.
10. In 2005, it has been decided that the declaration should be anonymous and should be used only to count the numerical weight of the linguistic groups. Instead the individuals' membership will be determined with declaration *ad hoc* released in case of necessity—i.e. when someone applies for positions in public offices. For the debate regarding the declaration of membership see Winkler (2005) and especially Carrozza (1983).
11. Brugger, translated from quotation in *Alto Adige*, Monday 18 October 1999.
12. Moreover, even after the adoption of the new Statute of Autonomy the Italian government tried to dilute its impact with various devices for some years. For example, between 1972 and 1977 Rome transferred into South Tyrol many public officers from other regions. Through this stratagem, in 1975, despite three years of ethnic proportion, only 14% of the 6000 positions in public offices were held by members of the German-speaking group, which, according to the 1971 census, represented 62.9% of the South Tyrol population. Data in Winkler (2005).
13. See for the AN: http://www.anbolzano.it; and for the SVP: http://www.svpartei.org/bozen. Actually, the SVP website has a link for an Italian version, which, however, is written in German.
14. All the data used in this paper regarding electoral results are available online at: http://www.comune.bolzano.it/prog/elezioni, 12/01/2007. I do not consider the national elections because, in the past, Italy has used a mixed majoritarian-proportional system, which pushed parties to present joint candidates. In these elections the AN was allied with the Right coalition, whereas the SVP was allied with the Left coalition. However, one quarter of the deputies were elected with proportional system and the corresponding results confirm the prevalence of the AN and the SVP. Indeed, in the 2001 national election the AN and the SVP have been the most successful parties receiving respectively 29% and 19% of the proportional vote. In 2005, the proportional electoral system has been (re)introduced. In the 2006 elections the AN and the SVP have obtained respectively 19% and 17% of the vote.
15. In 2005 there were two elections because of discrepancies in the results of the mayoral and City Council races. Indeed, since 1995 the major of Bolzano is elected directly by the inhabitants through a second ballot system. The competition in the second turn is usually between a candidate supported by the AN and other right-wing parties and a candidate supported by an alliance between the SVP and left-wing parties, which won in the 2000 and 1995 elections. In the 2005 elections, the candidate supported by the AN won by only seven votes, but the alliance between the SVP and left-wing parties won the majority of the City Council. The right-wing major was not able to form a City Government, which needs to be approved by the City Council. Therefore, in November 2005 new elections were hold, in which the candidate supported by the SVP and left-wing parties won and the SVP has obtained more votes than the AN (21.8% and 17.7% respectively). For the first time the SVP has not presented a candidate in the first turn of the election of the major. However, these facts are just the result of the temporary exceptional political dynamic (the victory of the right-wing candidate for only seven votes), and it is not clear whether this electoral trend and the SVP political decision will persist.
16. I have to point out that in 1997, the Free University of Bolzano was created. This institute for tertiary education differs from the rest of the South Tyrol school system, because it is a trilingual university in which some courses are offered in German, some in Italian and some in English. However, I do not consider this development because it is too early to analyze its impact, and especially because in my opinion the formation of the understanding of language diversity happens especially in primary and secondary schools, whereas the university can play only a later impact.
17. Many scholars that study censuses emphasize especially the role played by this statistical mechanism in bringing into existence new identities and in altering lines of identity divisions. Indeed, Wallerstein speaks of "ethnogenesis by census redefinition" (cited in Abramson, 2002, p. 199, note 16). See also Uvin (2002) and Kertzer & Arel (2002). Instead, the case of South Tyrol highlights the role of census in preventing the formation of new understanding of language diversity. In this sense it is possible to speak of abortion by census definition.
18. Many "mixed" families are organized in the association Convivia, which has taken various actions to try to change various South Tyrol arrangements, especially by appealing to European institutions.

19. In 2004 the foreign population of Bolzano amounted to 6856 with an increase of 53.7% in three years. Data available from Comune di Bolzano (City of Bolzano) and accessible online at: http://www.comune.bolzano.it
20. It seems that most of the foreign population has chosen the Italian version of South Tyrol, probably due to the fact that many foreigners are not sure whether they will settle permanently in the province or will move to other part of the Italian peninsula. Indeed, in 2002, 58.4% of the foreign students attend Italian schools. It is possible to assume that, if this trend continue, the March of Death will start again; this time caused by the South Tyrol language policies, which force foreigners to choose between Italian and German presented as irreconcilable alternatives. Data from Istituto provinciale di statistica, "Astat informazioni," No. 16 (August 2002) available online at: http://www.provinz.bz.it/astat

References

Abramson, D. (2002) Identity Counts: the Soviet Legacy and the Census in Uzbekistan, in: D.I. Kertzer & D. Arel (Eds), *Census and Identity*, pp. 176–201 (Cambridge: Cambridge University Press).
Agostini, P. (1985) *Alto Adige—La convivenza rinviata* (Bolzano: Praxis 3).
Appiah, A.K. (2005) *The Ethics of Identity* (Princeton, NJ: Princeton University Press).
Arel, D. (2001) Political stability in multinational democracies: comparing language dynamics in Brussels, Montreal and Barcelona, in: Al-G. Gagnon & J. Tully (Eds), *Multinational Democracies*, pp. 65–89 (Cambridge: Cambridge University Press).
Barry, B. (2001) *Culture and Equality* (Cambridge, MA: Harvard University Press).
Barry, B. (2002) Second Thoughts—and Some First Thoughts Revived, in: P. Kelly (Ed.), *Multiculturalism Reconsidered*, pp. 204–238 (Malden, MA: Polity).
Bates, R. (1983) Modernization, Ethnic Competition, and the Rationality of Politics in Contemporary Africa, in: D. Rothchild & V. Olorunsola (Eds), *The State Versus Ethnic Claims: African Policy Dilemmas*, pp. 152–171 (Boulder, CO: Westview Press).
Billig, M. (1976) *Social Psychology and Intergroup Relations* (London & New York: Academic Press).
Bloom, W. (1990) *Personal Identity, National Identity and International Relations* (Cambridge: Cambridge University Press).
Boran, I. (2003) Global Linguistic Diversity, Public Goods, and the Principle of Fairness, in: W. Kymlicka & A. Patten (Eds), *Language Rights and Political Theory*, pp. 189–209 (Oxford: Oxford University Press).
Brubaker, R. (1996) *Nationalism Reframed* (Cambridge: Cambridge University Press).
Buzan, B., Waever, O. & de Wilde, J. (1998) *Security. A New Framework for Analysis* (Boulder: Lynne Rienner Publishers).
Carens, J. H. (2000) *Culture, Citizenship, and Community* (Oxford: Oxford University Press).
Carrozza, P. (1983) La dichiarazione di appartenenza ai gruppi linguistici nella provincia di Bolzano, *Le nuove leggi civili commentate*, pp. 1137–1156.
Casonato, C. (1998) La tutela delle minoranze etnico-linguistiche in relazione alla rappresentanza politica: un'analisi comparata: seminario: Trento, 17 novembre 1997, *Quaderni del CDE 1, Centro di Documentazione Europea*, available online at: http://www.cde.provincia.tn.it/prodotti_editoriali/quaderni_elenco.htm.
Chandra, K. (2005) Ethnic Parties and Democratic Stability, *Perspectives on Politics* 3(2), pp. 215–233.
Corsini, U. (1993) Alcide De Gasperi e i "tedeschi" dell'Alto Adige, *CLIO*, 29(1), pp. 97–143.
Coulombe, P. (2001) Federalist Language Policies: the Cases of Canada and Spain, in: A.-G. Gagnon & J. Tully (Eds), *Multinational Democracies*, pp. 65–89 (Cambridge: Cambridge University Press).
Daniele, C. (1986) L'istituzione di scuole nella Provincia dell'Alto Adige, *Rivista giuridica della scuola*, 25, pp. 109–115.
de Varennes, F. (1996) *Language, Minorities and Human Rights* (The Hague: Kluwer Law International).
de Vergottini G. (1986) Profili giuridici della toponomastica nella provincia di Bolzano, *Diritto e società*, pp. 651–659.
Eisenstadt, S. N. (1998) The Construction of Collective Identities: Some Analytical and Comparative Indications, *European Journal of Social Theory*, 1(2), pp. 229–254.
Eisenstadt, S. N. & Giesen, B. (1995) The Construction of Collective Identity, *European Journal of Sociology*, 36, pp. 72–102.
Fraser, N. (1996) Social Justice in the Age of Identity Politics: Redistribution, Recognition, and Participation, *The Tanner Lectures on Human Values*, available online at: http://www.tannerlectures.utah.edu/lectures.html

Geertz, C. (1963) The Integrative Revolution: Primordial Sentiments and Civil Politics in the New States, in: C. Geertz (Ed.), *Old Societies and New States* (Glencoe, IL: Free Press).
Gellner, E. (1983) *Nations and Nationalism* (Ithac, NY & London: Cornell University Press).
Giunta provinciale di Bolzano (1996) *Il Nuovo Statuto di Autonomia*, 5th edition (Bolzano: Giunta provinciale di Bolzano Ed.).
Giunta provinciale di Bolzano (1999) *Manuale dell'Alto Adige* (Bolzano: Giunta Provinciale di Bolzano Ed.).
Greenfeld, L. (1992) *Nationalism: Five Roads to Modernity* (Cambridge, MA: Harvard University Press).
Guinier, L. & Torres, G. (2002) *The Miner's Canary* (Cambridge, MA: Harvard University Press).
Herz, R. (1993) Legal Protection for Indigenous Cultures: Sacred Sites and Communal Rights, *Virginia Law Review*, 79(3), pp. 691–716.
Hartney, M. (1995) Some Confusion Concerning Collective Rights, in: W. Kymlicka (Ed.), *The Rights of Minority Cultures*, pp. 202–227 (Oxford: Oxford University Press).
Hogan-Brun, G. & Wolff, S. (2003) Minority Language in Europe: An Introduction to the Current Debate, in: G. Hogan-Brun & S. Wolff (Eds), *Minority Languages in Europe*, pp. 3–15 (New York: Palgrave Macmillan).
Horowitz, D. (1985) *Ethnic Group in Conflict* (Berkley, CA: University of California Press).
Horowitz, D. (1991) *A Democratic South Africa? Constitutional Engineering in a Divided Society* (Berkele, CA: University of California Press).
Johnston, D. M. (1995) Native Rights as Collective Rights: A Question of Group Self-preservation, in: W. Kymlicka (Ed.), *The Rights of Minority Cultures*, pp. 179–201 (Oxford: Oxford University Press).
Jung, C. (2000) *Than I Was Black* (New Haven, CT and London: Yale University Press).
Jung, C. (2001) The Burden of Culture and the Limits of Liberal Responsibility, *Constellations*, 8(2), pp. 219–235.
Jung, C. (forthcoming) *Critical Liberalism*.
Jung, C. & Shapiro, I. (1995) South Africa's Negotiated Transition: Democracy, Opposition and the New Constitutional Order, *Politics and Society*, 23(3), pp. 269–308.
Kertzer, D. I. & Arel, D. (2002) Censuses, Identity Formation, and the Struggle for Political Power, in: D.I. Kertzer & D. Arel (Eds), *Census and Identity*, pp. 1–42 (Cambridge: Cambridge University Press).
Kukathas, C. (1997) Cultural Toleration, in: I. Shapiro & W. Kymlicka (Eds), *Ethnicity and Group Rights*, pp. 69–105 (New York and London: New York University Press).
Kymlicka, W. (1995) *Multicultural Citizenship* (Oxford: Oxford University Press).
Kymlicka, W. & A. Patten (Eds) (2003) *Language Rights and Political Theory* (Oxford: Oxford University Press).
Laitin, D. (1985) Hegemony and Religious Conflict: British Imperial Control and Political Cleavages in Yorubaland, in: P.B. Evans, D. Rueschemeyer & T. Skocpol (Eds), *Bringing the State Back In*, pp. 285–316 (New York: Cambridge University Press).
Lake, D. A. & Rothchild, D. (1996) Containing Fear: The Origins and Management of Ethnic Conflict, *International Security*, 21(2), pp. 41–75.
Lampis, A. (1997) Recenti sviluppi dello speciale ordinamento scolastico in provincia di Bolzano, *Rivista giuridica della scuola*, pp. 23–33.
Levy, J. T. (2003) Language Rights, Literacy, and the Modern State, in: W. Kymlicka & A. Patten (Eds), *Language Rights and Political Theory*, pp. 230–249 (Oxford: Oxford University Press).
Lijphart, A. (1977) *Democracy in Plural Societies: A Comparative Exploration* (New Haven, CT: Yale University Press).
Magnago, S. (1993) Il mio Sudtirolo, *Limes*, 4, pp. 179–182.
May, S. (2001) *Language and Minority Rights: Ethnicity, Nationalism and the Politics of Language* (London: Longman).
May, S. (2005) Language Policy and Minority Rights, in: T. Ricento (Ed.), *Language Policy: Theory and Method*, pp. 255–272 (Malden, MA: Blackwell Publishing Ltd).
Millian i Massana, A. (1994) *Derechos linguisticos y derecho fundamental a al education* (Madrid: Editorial civitas).
Nettle, D. & Romaine, S. (2000) *Vanishing Voices: The Extinction of the World's Languages* (New York: Oxford University Press).
O'Reilly, C. C. (2003) When a Language is "Just Symbolic:" Reconsidering the Significance of Language to the Politics of Identity, in: G. Hogan-Brun & S. Wolff (Eds), *Minority Languages in Europe*, pp. 16–33 (New York: Palgrave Macmillan).

Patten, A. (2001) Political Theory and Language Policy, *Political Theory*, 29(5), pp. 691–715.
Patten, A. & Kymlicka, W. (2003) Introduction, Language Rights and Political Theory: Context, Issues, and Approaches, in: W. Kymlicka & A. Patten (Eds), *Language Rights and Political Theory*, pp. 1–51 (Oxford: Oxford University Press).
Peterlini, O. (1996) *Autonomia e tutela delle minoranze nel Trentino Alto Adige* (Bolzano and Trento: Ufficio di Presidenza del Consiglio regionale del Trentino Alto Adige).
Petersen, R. D. (2002) *Understanding Ethnic Violence* (Cambridge: Cambridge University Press).
Pizzorusso, A. (1990) L'uso della lingua come oggetto di disciplina giuridica, in *Le Regioni*, 18(1), pp. 7–22.
Pizzorusso, A. (1993) *Minoranze e maggioranze* (Torino: Einaudi).
Posen, B.P. (1993) The Security Dilemma and Ethnic Conflict, in: M.E. Brown (Ed.), *Ethnic Conflict and International Security* (Princeton, NJ: Princeton University Press).
Pristinger, F. (1978) *La minoranza dominante nel Sudtirolo* (Bologna: Patron ed.).
Provincia Autonoma di Bolzano-Alto Adige (2006) *Barometro linguistico dell'Alto Adige 2004. Uso della lingua e identitá linguistica in Provincia di Bolzano* (Bolzano: Provincia Autonoma di Bolzano-Alto Adige, Istituto Provinciale di Statistica—ASTAT).
Reilly, B. (2001) *Democracy in Divided Societies* (Cambridge: Cambridge University Press).
Rubio-Marín, R. (2003) Language Rights: Exploring the Competing Rationales, in: W. Kymlicka & A. Patten (Eds), *Language Rights and Political Theory*, pp. 52–79 (Oxford: Oxford University Press).
Shafir, G. (1995) *Immigrants and Nationalism. Ethnic Conflict and Accommodation in Catalonia, the Basque Country, Latvia, and Estonia* (Albany, NY: State University of New York Press).
Skutnabb-Kangas, T. (2000) *Linguistic Genocide in Education or World Diversity and Human Rights* (Mahwah, NJ: Lawrence Erlbaum Publishers).
Skutnabb-Kangas, T. (2005) Language Policy and Linguistic Human Rights, in: T. Ricento (Ed.), *Language Policy. Theory and Method*, pp. 273–291 (Malden, MA: Blackwell Publishing).
Taylor, C. (1994) The Politics of Recognition, in: A. Gutmann (Ed.), *Multiculturalism*, pp. 25–73 (Princeton, NJ: Princeton University Press).
Uvin, P. (2002) On Counting, Categorizing, and Violence in Burundi and Rwanda, in: D. I. Kertzer & D. Arel (Eds), *Census and Identity*, pp. 148–175 (Cambridge: Cambridge University Press).
Vallini, E. & Allatri, P. (1997) *La questione dell'Alto Adige* (Firenze: Parenti ed.).
Van Parijs, P. (2002) Linguistic Justice, *Politics, Philosophy and Economics*, 1(1), pp. 59–74.
Vedovato, G. (1971) *Il problema dell'autonomia per la minoranza di lingua tedesca dell'Alto Adige* (Sesto Fiorentino: SETI).
Weinstock, D. M. (2003) The Antinomy of Language Policy, in: W. Kymlicka & A. Patten (Eds), *Language Rights and Political Theory*, pp. 250–270 (Oxford: Oxford University Press).
Winkler, I. (1997) *L'Autonomia dell'Alto Adige* (Bolzano: Giunta provinciale di Bolzano Ed.).
Winkler, I. (2005) *L'Autonomia dell'Alto Adige* (Bolzano: Giunta provinciale di Bolzano Ed.).
Wolff, S. (2003) *Disputed Territories: the Transnational Dynamic of Ethnic Conflict Settlement* (New York: Berghahn Books).
Young, C. (1976) *The Politics of Cultural Pluralism* (Madison, WI: The University of Wisconsin Press).

Appendix

Table A1. Total population, and German and Italian linguistic groups in South Tyrol and Bolzano 1910–2001 (absolute number and percentage)*

		South Tyrol				
		German speaking		Italian speaking		
Year	Total population	Number	%	Number	%
1910	251,451	223,913	89.0	7,339	2.9
1921	254,735	193,271	75.9	27,048	10.6
1931	282,158	NA	NA	NA	NA
1943	292,444	NA	NA	**104,750	†35.8
1953	345,046	**216,344	†62.7	**115,936	†33.6
1961	373,863	232,717	62.2	128,271	34.3
1971	414,041	260,351	62.9	137,759	33.3
1981	430,568	279,544	64.9	123,695	28.7
1991	440,508	287,503	67.9	116,914	27.6
2001	462,999	296,461	69.1	113,494	26.4

		Bolzano			
		German speaking		Italian speaking	
	Total population	Number	%	Number	%
1910	30,424	26,558	†87.2	1,605	†5.2
1921	32,679	17,421	68.9	7,675	30.3
1931	37,351	NA	NA	NA	NA
1943	65,553	NA	NA	NA	NA
1953	74,600	NA	NA	NA	NA
1961	88,980	18,671	21.0	69,834	78.6
1971	105,616	23,651	22.4	81,534	77.1
1981	104,975	26,434	25.8	75,528	73.6
1991	98,059	24,975	26.6	68,109	72.5
2001	94,989	†24,888	26.2	†69,342	73.0

NA: not available.
* Data from ASTAT-Istituto provinciale di statistica/Landesinstitut für Statistik (Provincial Statistic Institute), accessible online at: http://www.provincia.bz.it/astat, 11/07/ 2006. Some data have been kindly provided by Francesca Speziani of ASTAT.
** Data in Pristinger (1978).
† Estimated by the author.

Decentralization, Democratic Participation and Authoritarian Dogma: Local Opposition to Minority Integration in France, Italy and the United States

HARLAN KOFF

Political Science Institute, Faculty of Language and Literature, Humanities, Arts and Education, University of Luxembourg

During a conference on the 2005 urban violence that erupted in migrant neighborhoods surrounding Paris and quickly spread throughout France, the mayor of the city of Tourcoing opened a debate on these events by exclaiming, "I fear for the future of Democracy in France."[1] This statement referred to the systemic socio-economic exclusion of ethnic minorities in French cities, the inflammatory statements made by French Minister of Interior, Nicolas Sarkozy that fanned the flames of discontent, and the imposition of a curfew by Prime Minister Dominique de Villepin in response to the violence. In fact, in most of the public and academic discussions of the 2005 urban unrest in France, the analysis focused on different types of "failures" of French democracy.

In general, discussions of ethnic politics identify a correlation between local democratic practices and ethnic integration (see Penninx et al., 2004; Vertovec, 1998; Ireland, 1994). In the last 20 years, many scholars have argued that the conditions of ethnic minorities in European states have improved because of the spread of local democratic practices due to recent trends towards devolution. Functionalist theories of international relations (see Jacobson, 1996; Joppke, 1998) invoke the normative diffusion of human rights ideals, often through ethnic mobilization or the activity of transnational non-governmental organizations (NGOs). Many of these works claim that democratic rights have evolved beyond the realm of nation-state citizenship through the creation of a global civil society. Conversely, realist approaches in international relations (see Baldwin-Edwards, 1997; Cornelius *et al.*, 2004; Spencer, 1995) focus on the limits that international organizations have placed on the behavior of nation-state actors through soft power tactics, defined as non-coercive means (i.e. economic influence) to obtain objectives. Rather than directly examining the spread of ideas, this school concentrates on how intergovernmental bodies restrict the use of power by domestic actors through various policy-making tools (see Alston, 1999).

There can be no doubt that significant advances have been made globally towards the protection of human and minority rights, especially when comparing contemporary events to those that occurred only 50 or 60 years ago. Nonetheless, many scholars (see Collectif, 1997; Cornelius *et al.*, 2004; Wieviorka, 1999) of domestic politics have correctly demonstrated that ethnic exclusion persists even in advanced industrial states, such as the United States or the member countries of the European Union. In fact, the frequent appearance of ethnic violence in urban areas in Europe, especially in Great Britain and France, has led many (see SSRC, 2005) to believe that integration strategies have failed throughout Western Europe.

It is generally assumed that the increasing presence of ethnic marginalization, racism, and xenophobia in Europe reflects a breakdown of democratic practices on the continent. In response, scholars and activists alike have called for further democratization in these arenas through the decentralization of ethnic policy-making to the local level. This paper questions this approach and asks: "Is there a limit to how open democratic practices should be in integration politics?" It argues that democratic principles, such as equality, justice, and solidarity, can be undermined through their implementation in local democratic systems. The article contends that these ideals should be evoked and operationalized as a means to create a common good for all members of democratic communities. Instead, they have recently become ends in many contemporary political debates, and this shift has contributed to socio-economic exclusion because re-distributive policies, such as affirmative action, school mergers, or anti-discrimination strategies, are being opposed with the accusation that they betray color-blind notions of liberal democratic citizenship. Even in the absence of illiberal practices or overt racism, orthodox defences of particular ideological forms of "democracy" in local political debates can further ethnic tensions and undermine ethnic integration by reinforcing the exclusion and isolation of ethnic minorities.

In order to examine this issue in detail, this paper studies ethnic politics under three distinct models of democracy found in the United States, France, and Italy. Rather than focusing simply on national integration systems, the paper studies democratic principles in the three states and their impact on local political systems, where members of ethnic minority and majority groups interact on a daily basis.

The choice of cases for this study reflects contemporary public debates concerning ethnic integration in advanced industrial states. Following the 2005 urban riots in France, much of the international media, especially news outlets in the United States, framed their coverage of these events in terms of the failure of the French Republican model of citizenship and calls followed for the introduction of multiculturalism and ethnic recognition. By selecting one case city from a country with Republican citizenship where group identities are not recognized (France), one from a state with communitarian citizenship, defined as a model of citizenship in which ethnic belonging is recognized in policy-making (the United States) and one from a state which can best be described as mixed because it is characterized by the adoption of traits from each of the above-mentioned systems (Italy), this paper directly addresses the issues raised in contentious, contemporary, real-world debates on citizenship and ethnic integration. It argues that the formal recognition of ethnicity is not the key issue that needs to be addressed in order to facilitate ethnic and racial integration. Instead, the informal structure and use of power in political systems is the critical variable that inhibits the incorporation of minorities and facilitates socio-economic exclusion.

The article is divided into five sections. The first presents the literature on ethnic integration and citizenship in advanced industrial states and examines its focus on the relationship between ethnic politics and democracy. Sections two through four present the general guidelines for integration and their relationship to overall democratic systems in the three national models chosen for this study. They also demonstrate the implementation of integration approaches at the local level in: Durham, North Carolina, USA; Florence, Italy, and Toulouse, France. Each part represents one case. Finally, section five presents theoretical conclusions.

The three case cities are quite different in terms of their overall populations and socio-economic bases representing a "most different" model of case selection. Florence and Toulouse are mid-sized cities with metropolitan populations of around 600 000 people, whereas Durham is considerably smaller (circa 200 000).[2] Moreover, the two former cities are quite wealthy as Toulouse is the home of the European Air-Space industry and Florence's economy has solid bases in tourism, services, and industry. By contrast, Durham is an old tobacco city whose economy has been transformed by the installation of high technology industries in the "Research Triangle Park" that it forms with its neighbors, Chapel Hill and Raleigh. This shift has created clear socio-economic divergences.

In terms of politics, the cities were chosen for this study because their local political systems rigorously implement the democratic models found at the national level. Durham considers itself one of the "most democratic cities" in the south of the United States. Toulouse, vaunts a strong Republican tradition, in part because of the massive arrival of anti-Fascist refugees from Spain and Italy before and during World War II. Finally, Florence is a city with strong civil society and considerable political mobilization from both left-wing and Catholic currents.

Finally, minorities represent roughly 10% of the population in both Toulouse and Florence. In contrast Durham's minority population represents just under 30% of all inhabitants. Moreover, the ethnic composition of minority populations varies from case to case. Toulouse is a city that received Spanish and Italian refugees in the first part of the twentieth century. However, the city's migrant neighborhoods are mostly inhabited by first-generation French citizens who are children of immigrants from the Maghreb or, to a lesser extent, sub-Saharan Africa. By contrast, Florence is a city of recent migration. Minorities found there are non-European Union migrants coming from different countries, such as China, Romania, the Philippines, Senegal, Iran, the United States, and Albania, in addition to Morocco, Tunisia, and Egypt. There is no geographic concentration of migrants is specific neighborhoods to the extent that exists in Toulouse. Finally, Durham is an old plantation city where black slaves harvested tobacco. In the early part of the twentieth century, many African-Americans migrated there as the city was known as one of the black capitals of the United States. Recently, there has also been an increasing flow of Mexican immigrants. Because wealthier populations have moved to suburbs around the city, there is a strong concentration of African-Americans in the poorer city centre. These characteristics are summarized in Table 1.

Democracy and Social Integration: Theories and Principles

Until recently, most ideological discussions concerning the positions of minorities have focused on class or gender, but rarely on ethnicity, which was linked to nationalist agendas. Native Americans, African Americans, Gypsy/Roma and Jews often remained victimized by stereotypes and hatred as democratic debates surrounding their condition were slow to develop. Since World War II this has obviously changed. Even though contemporary theories of liberal democracy often ignored ethnic difference (see, e.g., Rawls, 1971; Nozick, 1974) various ethnic catastrophes placed discrimination, exclusion, and xenophobia squarely on democratic political agendas. Intergovernmental organizations, most notably the Council of Europe, and NGOs such as Amnesty International, *SOS Racisme* and the *Mouvement Contre le Racisme et Pour L'Amitie Entre Les Peuples* (MRAP or the Movement Against Racism and For Friendship Between Peoples in English) pushed the notion of ethnic rights onto domestic political agendas from the international arena.

Numerous political battles have been fought to end ethnic injustice, leading many observers of ethnic politics, especially those in Europe, to question whether the nation-state has lost its predominance in this policy arena. From the civil rights movement in the United States to recent military interventions in the Balkans, both state and non-state actors have been willing to confront ethnic hatred. Often, these struggles have been justified as defenses of liberal democratic principles. As a result, scholars of migration, such as Soysal (1994), Jacobson (1996), Turner (1993) and Bauböck (1998) have argued that ethnic inclusion has become globalized and citizenship has become transnational

Table 1. Demographic characteristics of case cities

Demographic categories	Durham, NC, United States	Toulouse, France	Florence, Italy
Minority proportion of total oopulation	Roughly 25%	Between 15 and 20%*	Between 10 and 12%
Composition of minority population	Predominantly African-Americans	First generation French citizens, mostly of North African descent	Immigrants from numerous countries including: China, the Philippines, Romania, Albania, Iran, Egypt, Tunisia, Morocco, Senegal
Geographic distribution of minority communities	Concentrated in poorer city center	Concentrated in marginalized neighborhoods outside city	No geographic concentration, present in all neighborhoods

*Ethnic statistics are not collected in France. "Foreigners" officially compose about 10% of the city's total population but most ethnic minorities are French citizens and, thus, not included in this figure. Thus, only a rough estimate is possible.

through the spread of democratic values through media, intergovernmental bodies, such as the European Union (EU), and human rights organizations. This school of thought has argued that minority rights and integration policies have converged around generally accepted norms. In fact, Germany has all but eradicated its guest worker doctrine, which had been in place throughout the post-World War II period and other European states, such as Belgium, Italy, and Great Britain have progressively granted more social rights to ethnic minorities, as more attention has been paid to multicultural education in schools, minority-based employment policies have been adopted, and migrants have been given increased access to social housing (see Brubaker, 1989; Zincone, 2001). Even Japan, which traditionally has implemented the most restrictive migrant policies in the advanced industrial world, has slowly begun reforming what many critics have denounced as nativist positions (see Tsuda & Cornelius, 2004).

Theories of democracy have certainly followed these developments. During the 1990s an entire debate over the rights of minorities flourished as scholars such as Walzer (1983), Connolly (1991), Kymlicka (1989), Gutmann (1994), and Carens (2000) examined democratic models within the context of ethnic heterogeneity. Usually, these discussions included two dominant points of view, which have been well documented in the literature on minority rights. Liberals, such as Connolly (1991), Young (1989) and Carens (2000) constructed theories of rights and justice around the understanding of necessary conditions for individual members of ethnic minority groups to control their own life courses. Liberal models focus on the eradication of illiberal practices, such as discrimination, and the defense of individual rights. Moreover, they understand diversity as a resource on which democratic societies can build a common good because it provides a greater spectrum of cultural choices to individual citizens. Thus, while this approach is founded on the rights of the individual, it embraces diversity as a means to improve the common good.

Conversely, communitarian approaches (i.e. Taylor, 1992; Habermas, 1998; etc.) squarely emphasize ethnic affiliations. They argue that citizens cannot be viewed as individuals because they belong to ethnic/racial groups that condition how they are viewed by others and what spaces are available to them within civil society. Thus, group affiliation is the basis of analysis as it affects identity, socio-economic opportunities and cultural understanding. For this reason, multiculturalism and affiliation with ethnic communities replace diversity and individual citizenship.

Despite these basic differences, the thread that ties these two approaches, as evidenced by Kymlicka among others, is their belief that only democratic approaches to governance can adequately embrace the ethnic heterogeneity found in modern societies and guarantee rights to members of ethnic minorities. This thesis is rather accurate (as history has shown communism's and fascism's inability (or obvious disregard in the case of the latter) to integrate multi-ethnic societies) and this article does not intend to refute it. Instead, this piece merely pragmatically recognizes that democratic theory and practices are often quite different things and it attempts to analyze the relationship between these different levels of democracy. Whereas the theoretical literature on liberal democracy often attributes negative situations, such as exclusion and xenophobia to individual moral corruption or institutional incompetence (including market failure), I contend that the seeds of breakdown of the very democratic goal of integration are often found within the very implementation of democratic practice, especially at the local level. When actors pursue the defense of democratic doctrines as a political objective instead of utilizing them as tools with which they can create a common good, these moral positions are converted into authoritarian dogma, paradoxically, betraying democratic principles in ethnically mixed societies, such as mutual respect, individual equality and ethnic group integration.

Democracy and Social Integration: Models and Practices

Social integration models are multi-faceted as the nature of citizenship is complex. For example, immigration is such an important issue internationally because it touches on so many different aspects of politics: economic markets, political systems, identity, welfare state, etc. For this reason, advanced industrial states have emphasized border controls. These highly symbolic strategies demonstrate concern for different "threats" posed by migration. However, border control policies are also followed because states have recently adopted more progressive policies towards the rights of migrants once they enter and legally settle. While the EU and the US have invested heavily in physical barriers and detection technology, they have also granted a wider array of social rights to legal immigrants.

As stated above, many observers of integration politics have drawn a connection between democratic practices and improved ethnic integration because of these general trends. Advanced industrial states have, indeed, improved legal mechanisms for ethnic integration, especially at the local level where authorities have been given greater freedom to implement measures aimed at furthering ethnic integration. However, important differences exist between integration systems in the advanced industrial world. These distinctions are created by variations concerning notions of ethnic identity, core values regarding democracy, state structures and political mobilization.

In *Limits of Citizenship* (1994), Yasemin Soysal classifies models of incorporation by examining the structural differences in European integration regimes. She identifies the following typologies: (1) Liberal,(2) Statist, (3) Corporatist, and (4) Fragmented. Despite the fact that it was written in the 1990s, Soysal's work is still valid and more recent studies of migration and citizenship, such as those published by Joppke (1998), Vertovec (1998), etc., confirm her conclusions. Her book is the most structured comparative work on integration regimes in Europe as it organizes many of the important policy variations identified on a smaller scale by other scholars of migrant integration (see works by, e.g., Brubaker, 1989; Ireland, 1994; Papademetriou, 1996; Bonifazi, 1999; Hollifield, 1992) into coherent comparative models.

These studies correctly recognize that integration models reflect structural differences between advanced industrial states that go beyond ethnic politics. Concepts such as the role of the state, state–society relations, the structure of power, arenas for mobilization, etc. influence all citizens, not just ethnic minorities. Soysal's work is interesting because it examines different models of integration that identify how power is structured in various countries.

In addition to the different concepts of citizenship mentioned in the introduction above, the countries examined in this paper represent different models of government, power-sharing and incorporation. Employing Soysal's framework (which reflects Esping-Anderson's (1991) work on welfare regimes), the United States can best be described as liberal (market dominated), France is statist (high degree of state centralization), and Italy is fragmented (lack of a clear incorporation model leaving integration responsibilities to the third sector). It should be noted that while Soysal classifies the United States as liberal in a market sense, with regard to minority integration it has taken a more communitarian form, given its willingness to recognize group affiliations in policy. In contrast, France's statist structure does not recognize group differences officially, presenting instead a more neutral-state approach to integration in Republican form. Italy is fragemented in both spheres.

Table 2 outlines the structural differences between the three states. Rather than simply focusing on integration, the analysis presented here discusses important characteristics of practiced democracy. The table shows significant differences related to the centralization/decentralization of power, the relationship between citizens and the state and interest representation.

These characteristics of democratic systems are significant because, despite legal progress in the field of integration politics, the actual structure and exercise of power is the key to ethnic inclusion or marginalization. In fact, ethnic exclusion cannot simply be considered a product of the breakdown of democracy. Instead, the characteristics of democratic systems contribute to structural failures because informal barriers to integration play a more significant role today than formal ones. Whereas the above-mentioned evolution of legal instruments aimed at promoting ethnic incorporation has eradicated formal discrimination, systemic exclusion has become embedded in the very democratic systems created to abolish it. This argument is explained in further detail in the following sections.

Social Integration and American Democracy

The American political system most closely demonstrates the relationship between democracy, ethnic marginalization and informal barriers to citizenship. Many international observers of American politics note the clear social paradoxes found within the country. Even though its overall wealth is enormous (and growing), social marginalization among ethnic minorities is also increasing. Recent census statistics clearly demonstrate a widening gap between Asians and whites on one hand, and Latinos and African-Americans on the other.[3] Also, the US notion of citizenship has a liberal foundation based on the notions of individual opportunity and merit. However, at the same time, it is communitarian because minority integration policies recognize group membership as an influential determinant of

Table 2. Forms of democracy

	United States	France	Italy
Interest representation	"Town meeting" based on public discussions	"Delegated democracy" based on elite decision-making	"Indirect democracy" based on parliamentary representation
Structure of political power	Decentralized, separation of powers	Statist (centralized authority)	Parliamentary
Role of welfare state	Complement labor market	Social solidarity/rights	Social solidarity/rights
Level of centralization	Federalism	Limited devolution	Incomplete devolution
Integration philosophy	Communitarian	Republican	Fragmented: Catholic humanitarianism/left-wing solidarity
Agents of integration	Labor markets/schools	The state	NGOs

individual life opportunities (see Horowitz and Noiriel, 1992). In general, the state plays a minimal role in integration politics and social programs are aimed at complementing market forces. In fact, it is the labor market combined with the education system, which has been the traditional motor of social and ethnic integration throughout the nation's history.

Politically, the US federal system of government should create proximity between citizens and their elected leaders. Under the idealistic "town meeting" model, appreciated by de Tocqueville (1991), among others, citizens have the opportunity to offer opinions on local issues and participate in debates on questions that affect their daily lives. This principle lies at the heart of the US political system, which explains the radical decentralization that elevates the role of local actors in the US higher than that found in most advanced industrial states. Moreover, the administrative separation of powers was instituted to prevent domination by any single political force and, at least formally, ensure that the democratic system of government represented the interests of US citizens rather than a restricted group of elites.

The weakness of this system has proven to be the combination of these characteristics. Ethnic minorities, most notably Latinos and African-Americans, have enjoyed less success in the labor market because many lack access to resources which are necessary for success in the post-industrial world, especially education and employment networks. Because of the federal system described in the paragraph above, US education varies significantly from one area to another as school systems are linked to municipalities or counties rather than states or the federal government. This fact further reinforces the ethnic differences created by the labor market (see Kozol, 1992) and creates social isolation (see Wilson, 2002) because it promotes a vicious cycle in which educational attainment is necessary to overcome economic marginalization but it is difficult to achieve because the quality of local schools is often linked to existing wealth in corresponding communities. School budgets are based on local tax bases which reflect existing socio-economic levels. Stated plainly, schools in poor areas receive less money whereas public systems in wealthier communities have access to greater resources.

Politically, this situation is well-known in the US but often ignored. The lack of welfare state policies and the emphasis on individual participation in integration politics has stigmatized poverty and created a cultural as well as ethnic rift in American society. This division is becoming more intense, as the following local case demonstrates how democratic practices at the sub-national level hinder the creation of policy remedies, especially in moments of political crisis.

Durham, North Carolina, and the Politics of Education

For much of the twentieth century, Durham, North Carolina was a quiet, but successful provincial city in the Southern United States. Its economy was based on tobacco and the city's nickname "The Bull City" and its baseball team "The Durham Bulls" derived from the cigarettes produced there. Duke University, begun in 1924, was an excellent regional institution focused on teaching.

Recently, like many cities in the United States, Durham was forced to reinvent itself economically. The tobacco industry suffered from massive public anti-smoking campaigns and successful lawsuits against cigarette manufacturers. For this reason, city leaders, along with officials from the nearby cities of Chapel Hill and Raleigh, attracted investment in high technology and computer industries through the construction of the

Research Triangle Park, which is now the second largest technological research area in the United States, second only to Silicon Valley. For its part, Duke has grown into an internationally renowned research university and a major employer in the area. Obviously, these changes have significantly affected the local population.

In many ways, Durham is a typical American city. It is currently undergoing a process of de-urbanization as the economic changes in the city have led to outward emigration towards the city's suburbs. The poorer areas in the city centre are mostly inhabited by African-Americans. In socio-economic terms, this has created a net racial separation in the city. According to recent census figures from the 1990s, African-American unemployment was 2.5 times higher than that for whites. The median income for African-Americans was $10 000, while that for whites was $18 000. Similarly, there were 9000 more African-American families living under the poverty level in the County of Durham than white families.[4]

Among young people, the socio-economic differences between racial groups were even more pronounced. The number of unemployed African-American youths between the ages of 16 and 19 lacking a high school diploma was 4.5 times higher than the same demographic group of whites.[5] This situation has obviously had social repercussions as homicides, assaults, and drug trafficking have reached alarming levels in the city. For these reasons, local officials looked to school reform as a necessary step to social integration.

In 1989, a task force created to study the differences between the schools in the City of Durham, mostly attended by African-Americans, and those in the County school system, largely attended by whites, released its conclusions regarding the disparities between the two educational systems. From a financial point of view, the city invested more money per student ($4418 versus $3980) but it offered fewer services. The explanation for this discrepancy was that the city schools paid 45% more than the county to maintain physical plants and support administration. By contrast, the County invested 35% more in educational programs. Not surprisingly, in a poll of teachers from both systems, 76% agreed that "the County schools are better."[6]

In terms of the data on student achievement, the task force found that 28% of the students in county school system dropped out without a diploma. The corresponding figure in the city schools was 46%, which was the highest rate in the State of North Carolina. Standardized test scores on the California Achievement Tests, the North Carolina Tests in Writing, Mathematics, and Social Studies, Scholastic Aptitude Tests, and Advanced Placement exams all demonstrated significantly higher achievement in the county schools. This evident discrepancy in education levels created informal obstacles to social integration and facilitated racial exclusion.

For these reasons, the STEP (Students Together With Educators and Parents) program was proposed in 1994 with the objective of integrating the two school systems so that each school would reflect the racial proportions of the county's population within 15%. While leaders should have expected turmoil from the proposal of such an ambitious project, the political storm that followed the proposal was exacerbated by the nature of local politics in Durham, which closely reflects the characteristics of the "ideal" American political system described above.

In fact, Durham political officials often boasted/complained (depending on their point of view) that the city is one of "the most democratic" places in America. During an interview for this piece conducted by the author, a local City Councilor categorically stated "We practice extreme democracy." This fact was demonstrated structurally as the authority of the city's mayor was overshadowed by the influence of the Board of County Commissioners and the City Council. For this reason, all political proposals of significance were publicly debated (a.k.a "town meeting") before being ratified.

Due to the open nature of local politics, the community immediately took sides on the school merger issue and debates were heated. While African-American groups, such as the Durham Committee on the Affairs of Black People, and progressive associations, such as People's Alliance, supported the proposal, conservative bodies immediately opposed it. The members of one group called Education First promised to sue the Board of education "within a week of the implementation of the plan." The city's Chamber of Commerce also opposed the integration project because it claimed that it would cause white flight, thus, hurting the local economy.

Because of the vociferousness of the debates on STEP, the proposal was immediately watered down. Five different reform projects were examined by the Board of Education before they agreed on a plan to redraw the school district lines "to help racial integration" and create magnet schools in the city open to students from both districts. In order to pass the measure, the Board of Education finally left the city and held a private meeting away from public view. In fact, the defeat of the originally proposed legislation to aggressively promote racial integration created such problems in the local political arena that headlines from the *Herald Sun*, Durham's newspaper simply asked, "Is Anyone in Charge?" Consequently, within two years, many of STEP's supporters on the County Board of Commissioners and the Board of Education had lost their positions in different elections that were considered a referendum on their handling of the integration issue. Public pressure significantly altered the face of local integration politics because of the public nature of democratic debates. Too much exposure to public opinion and citizen input rendered lawmakers helpless in front of a social situation that needed urgent attention. Moreover, in order to avoid a direct confrontation along racial lines, much of the opposition to the school merger was grounded in the argument that government authorities were overstepping their bounds by redrawing education districts. Many grassroots opposition forces supported the limitation of government intervention in social issues to minimal involvement. This was justified as a defense of democratic practices. These local community members argued that government officials whether local, state, or national, had no right to further a social agenda without the approval of local citizens.

Because of the "tyranny of the public" that overwhelmed Durham during this period, one could argue that the logical remedy to this situation would be to shield public officials from outside influences, offering them increased freedom to act autonomously for the benefit of the local community. Such a situation is found in other states, most notably in France. The next section will, however, show that the change in institutional setting does not always provide higher levels of integration.

Social Integration and Democracy in France

For most of the last century, the French integration model was deemed to be a success as much as the American model was viewed as severely flawed. While the US was coping with racial segregation and ethnic exclusion, the French *République* represented equality and non-discrimination. Alas, after having been considered one of the most tolerant countries in Europe for most of the last century, the immigration debate has divided

French society during the first years of the new one. The republican tradition, once the basis for assimilation, has fallen victim to the politics of cultural pluralism, leading to vitriolic, political, social, and economic debates. Adrian Favell correctly states: "Truth and relative proportion can be the first victims of politics when it is pursued in highly symbolic ways. This is the great danger in the French debate, in which the overcharged rhetoric of immigration and integration, *nationalité* [nationality] and *citoyenneté* [citizenship], has become a kind of institutionalized *langue de bois* [language of stereotypes]" (Favell, 1998, p. 160).

It may seem surprising that a country such as France should be so divided over immigration given its long tradition of tolerance. However, France has never followed one specific model of integration. Expressed in terms of citizenship, immigration has never received the legitimacy it holds in countries like the United States or Canada, where *jus soli* notions of citizenship focusing on place of birth are prevalent. On the other hand, France has not followed the *jus sanguinis* model traditionally present in Germany, in which ethnicity is a prerequisite for citizenship (see Brubaker, 1989). Therefore, contemporary scholars of French politics, correctly identify France as a country of immigrants but not a country of immigration (see Hollifield, 1992; Papademetriou, 1996; Viet, 1998). Placed in this conceptual vacuum, French politics have been strongly divided by the immigration issue because both pro-integration and anti-immigration forces can make strong claims to their respective notions of identity and citizenship. Maxim Silverman (1991) accurately notes that, "Immigration can represent both the liberal republic and the threat to the liberal republic, it is the embodiment of France's capacity for assimilation and proof of a break-down in assimilation, it is the embodiment of pluralism and proof of the impossibility of pluralism" (Silverman, 1991, p. 15).

According to the republican model of citizenship, individuals are valued by their contribution to the collective public interest. The state, in this regard, imposes a notion of "total citizenship" on the individual citizen in which full social acceptance is directly linked to individual contribution. Thus, *liberté* (freedom), *égalité* (equality), and *fraternité* (brotherhood), the underlying philosophic values of the French Revolution, and the core concepts of French society, are guaranteed to those who contribute to the economic, social, and cultural prosperity of the nation. These rights are conditional on the social contract in which the individual citizen embraces certain responsibilities and obligations in exchange for the protection of civil and human rights. Thus, unlike the United States where the concept of multiple identities (i.e. Italo-American, African-American, etc.) is one of the foundations of the national "melting pot," the republican model aspired to a situation in which the French-born child of foreigners would not be distinguished from a child with French ancestors.

Cultural pluralism, the natural antagonist of republicanism, has created deep schisms in contemporary French politics and society. The rise of the radical right, heightened protests by immigrant associations for increased cultural autonomy, and the contested debate over citizenship rights has radically changed the nature of French immigration politics. The current trend towards the politicization of immigration began in 1973 with the first oil crisis. It escalated during the rest of that decade and erupted in the 1980s and 1990s. On one hand, the economic recession and resulting shift in public opinion provided the extreme right, especially Jean-Marie Le Pen, and the *Front National* (FN) or National Front, with a niche in French party politics (Betz, 1994). Conversely, socio-economic exclusion has led to political and sometimes violent forms of mobilization within the *banlieues* (marginalized neighborhoods) dominated by ethnic minorities. The national riots that occurred in October/November 2005 were the zenith of this form of social rebellion as they contagiously spread throughout France.

As a result of these developments, integration issues have polarized much of the French electorate and they have focused heavily on questions of security. Due to the efforts of the radical right, the word "immigrant" had taken on new meaning as it had been fused with "foreigner," "Muslim," "Clandestine," and "Arab" in public discussions. In response, many immigrant groups have changed their definitions of integration, claiming that economic integration would only be possible through the recognition of group rights and affirmative action programs. Second generation immigrants (who are French citizens) have reclaimed the cultural rights that their parents renounced. They argue that equality can only be considered complete if measured in economic, political, and moral terms. These groups contend that debates over identity and security fail to address severe systematic problems such as high immigrant unemployment rates, youth delinquency, and the attraction of militant Islam. Most significantly, however, these groups argue that, under the republican model, immigrants could never be fully integrated because the community that the foreigner attempts to join is ready to reject him/her on the basis of difference. Hence, they have embraced these differences and renounced the republic. The result has been increased violence in the *banlieues* of major cities, such as Toulouse.

La République, *and Social Integration in Toulouse*

Since the time of the French Revolution, Toulouse has enjoyed a reputation as one of the most "republican" cities in France. When monarchists in different regions plotted a counter-revolution to restore the monarchy, they came to Toulouse, which at the time was the capital of the semi-autonomous region of *Aquitaine* looking for support from elites who could have profited politically from a divided French state. The city's leaders, however, reaffirmed their support for the fledgling republic and supported the government in Paris. Since that time, the city's dedication to republicanism has been almost mythical. In the first half of the twentieth century, anti-fascist refugees from Spain, Italy, and Portugal flooded Toulouse, having chosen the city because of this reputation. More than 100 000 refugees quickly integrated politically and economically and they reaffirmed the city's republican political culture by adopting French republican values.

Like France, Toulouse has historically been viewed as a place of multi-ethnic integration and anti-discrimination. However, like the general French climate, much has recently changed in the city. When urban riots broke out throughout France in October 2005, Toulouse was significantly affected. In fact, the city has been the site of social conflict for some time. The first significant urban violence occurred in 1998, when police officers accidentally killed a young man of North African descent, and riots occurred in a group of neighborhoods collectively known as the *Grand Mirail*, where most of the city's ethnic minorities live. The 1998 violence lasted for four days and the final toll included: the burning of 70 cars, vandalism against public offices, and the destruction of one metro station and one bus. Since that time, the city has witnessed attacks on police and fire fighters, burned cars, and vandalism on a regular basis. Just as the city previously represented the success of the republic that it embraced, it now symbolizes its failures.

In fact, the city has become socio-economically divided into parallel communities. Due to the installation of Airbus and other technology companies within the industrial parks created by local authorities, Toulouse has the third highest concentration of professionals in all of France. It is also the fourth wealthiest city in the country. Conversely, the economic boom created by this growth led to increased immigration, both internal and international. The city's labor market, which has become highly specialized, has not been able to accommodate all of these workers. For this reason, overall unemployment rates have grown to 14%. The city's ethnic minorities have been especially affected.

Socio-economic statistics clearly illustrate the bifurcation of the city's economic markets. In the *Grand Mirail* neighbourhoods the percentage of professional residents is only 6.3% despite the presence of a major university. The city's overall proportion of professional residents is 13.4%. Unemployment in the *Grand Mirail* is 20.1% compared to 13.7% in the city (*ibid.*). A recent study in the neighborhood also showed that the economically depressed situation is especially pronounced for ethnic minorities. According to this research 43.1% of Africans in the neighborhood are unemployed and two-thirds of the African women are working in precarious or part-time jobs (Collectif, 1997).

These economic conditions have had serious social effects on the neighborhood. In a recent poll of *Grand Mirail* residents, over half claimed to have been victims of crime in the 12 months before the poll was conducted. Similarly, the neighborhood has seen more than 200 cars burned every year over the last four years. Drug-related crimes have also increased. (*ibid.*)

In response to these problems, city, regional, and national officials have developed a series of initiatives to improve social conditions in the *Grand Mirail*. Unlike local officials in the US who enjoy great autonomy but receive little support from national agencies due to the localized nature of the policy-making process, officials in Toulouse, like those in all French cities, work within a relatively rigid bureaucratic structure that is highly centralized. State agencies, such as the *Fonds d'Action Social* (FAS) have set up a number of funding opportunities for local government and NGOs to create social action programs but they attach these resources to strict rules concerning their potential uses. Thus, the *Grand Mirail* has one of the most active non-governmental sectors in all of France. Organizations in this neighborhood focus on education, job training, crime prevention, health care, conflict mediation, sports, music, arts, etc. Nonetheless, the neighborhood becomes more and more isolated politically because public funding for these initiatives follows the French republican model and it is tied to geographic neighborhoods, thus excluding the possibility of intra-city partnerships. Because the non-governmental sector is active and separate from the rest of the city, it has developed in a parallel realm in which leaders have embraced their autonomy and a local counterculture has developed. This has created a threat to long-term goals associated with integration and it reinforces ethnic segregation.

Hence, the question that has increasing significance for the city of Toulouse, and for France as a whole, is "What is the relationship between ethnic political exclusion and urban crime?" In the days following the 1998 riots, most observers argued that the *Grand Mirail* exploded because of the lack of political participation amongst most residents of the neighborhood. In fact, the lack of political representation cannot be ignored as a mechanism for violence.

During the late 1990s and early part of the twenty-first century, Toulouse has witnessed numerous political protests that have become a significant part of the city's political landscape and even its collective identity. Many of these events have focused on ethnicity-related issues. When radical right politicians, such as Le Pen, come to Toulouse, more than 20 000 people take part in "anti-hate" protests. Coalitions of unions, students, migrants, left-wing organizations, and various other NGOs mobilize to fight discrimination. While this political opposition to xenophobia is significant, the lack of support for integration has been equally important. When pro-integration rallies are organized by migrant rights' groups, less than 200 people have attended.[7]

Thus, the city's political condition demonstrates why the French republic has failed to integrate ethnic minorities. First, labor market specialization has led to socio-economic marginalization. In order to respond to these problems, the French state has developed a *Contrat de Ville*, or city contract, which has created programs aimed at neighborhood development rather than ethnic integration. This strategy has created policy walls around the residents of poor neighborhoods and economic bridges are not being created with other areas of the city. The isolation of these segments of the population is further completed by a lack of political representation, unresponsiveness on the part of local and national officials, and weak support from other segments of the non-governmental sector. Unlike the United States, the French system has become a victim of its own insulation of public officials. Moreover, the almost blind defense of republicanism at the local and national levels has shifted the responsibility for integration from the state back to the individual. Hence, like the United States, France is now characterized by informal obstacles to ethnic integration related to market exclusion and political isolation that have been constructed in the name of French democratic principles. Some members of ethnic minority groups who cannot overcome these difficulties and live on the edges of France's large metropolitan areas have become outraged and, because they lack instruments to compete in post-modern economies as well as channels for the expression of their political voices, violence has erupted and riots occur all too frequently in France's main cities. Urban revolts have become so common in France that, in the days following the 2005 urban violence, many observers asked: "Can this violence be considered typically French or can it potentially erupt in other European states?" The following analysis of Italian integration politics will address this question.

Social Integration and Democracy in Italy

The contradictions that mark Italian politics have fascinated scholars since the beginning of the Republic at the end of World War II. Seeming paradoxes exist in most arenas of Italian politics and society, often reflecting social, cultural, and economic cleavages that date back many centuries (see Koff & Koff, 2000). Italian immigration politics have followed this pattern. Scholars of immigration have correctly noted that Italy, in its short history as an immigration state (since the early 1980s), has been characterized by neither a tradition of intolerance nor one of integration. Even though most Italians condemn xenophobia and racism, tension between citizens and immigrants clearly marks Italian society. Moreover, immigration has evidenced many of the above-mentioned problems that characterize the Italian political system, such as bureaucratic inefficiency, lack of trust in the government, the north–south divide, and the fragmentation of the non-governmental sector.

Much has been written on anti-immigrant reactions in Italy. Most of these works focus on the cultural and structural changes caused by Italy's shift from an emigration to an immigration state in the 1980s and 1990s. These studies examine public attitudes (Bonifazi, 1999; Balbo & Manconi, 1992), government reactions (Calavita, 2004; Papademetriou, 1996), and political parties, and social movements (Watts, 2000; Della Porta, 1999) at the national level. However, scholars of immigration to Italy, and Italian politics in general, have accurately noted that regional differences are fundamental in Italian society. Differences in local cultures and levels of economic development have created substantial sub-national variance in Italian responses to immigration (Koff, 2006; Pugliese, 2000). Unlike most European countries, xenophobic reactions have often been linked to regional identities rather than nationalism. This is reflected in the positions taken by the political parties of the right on the immigration issue. Whereas the nationalist *Alleanza Nazionale* (AN), whose support is concentrated in the poorer south, has backed away from xenophobic, anti-immigrant platforms at the national level, the northern-based, ethno-regionalist *Lega Nord* has made immigration a central aspect of its political activity. Declarations against immigrants by the Lega's populist leader, Umberto Bossi, have been so strong, that he has been reproached for "going too far" by his right-wing coalition partners (Casa della Libertá), most notably Silvio Berlusconi, the leader of *Forza Italia* (FI), and the former prime minister.

Anti-immigrant activity in the Italian party system reflects two distinct paradoxes which have created friction within the right-wing coalition. First, unlike anti-immigrant reactions in many other advanced industrial states, nativist positions in Italy cannot be explained by socio-economic factors. The success of the Lega, due in part to the presence of elevated anti-immigrant sentiments, is concentrated in Italy's north-eastern regions where the local economies are strong and most in need of immigrant labor. Even though many small industrial factories would close without the influx of migrant workers, many independent businessmen have supported the Lega and its xenophobic rhetoric, and actions for cultural reasons, as the Lega Nord filled a structural void in the party system that attracted devout Catholics in the region when the old Christian Democratic party disintegrated following the *tangentopoli* corruption scandals of the early 1990s. This has alienated *Forza Italia* (FI) to a certain extent, due to its position as a centrist party which represents many business interests.

Second, due to the presence of the Vatican, religion has been a prominent aspect of the immigration debate and the Lega has vociferously attacked Islam. In a recent special issue of *Quaderni Padani*, a Lega affiliated journal, an editorial condemned that religion as one of the "three worst diseases in history" along with communism and imperialism. Statements such as these have created much friction within the Catholic Church and they have led to official criticism of the Lega from Italy's center-right Catholic parties, the *Cristiani Democratici Uniti* (CDU), and *Centro Cristiano Democratico* (CCD), which are also members of the center-right coalition. The presence of these seeming contradictions (1) elevated nativist positions in regions most in need of immigrant labor, and (2) the alienation of the Lega from the Catholic Church due to its virulent anti-Islam, pro-Catholic positions, would suggest that cultural rather than structural variables best explain Italian nativist responses to immigration.

In terms of the politics of integration, Italy's policy strategies have proven incoherent in many ways. Like other policy arenas, immigration has been confronted in terms of emergencies. When large numbers of clandestine migrants arrive in waves, the national government temporarily confronts the immigration issue. When immigrants perpetrate highly publicized crimes, local and regional governments raise security to elevated positions on the government agenda. When immigrants are the victims of racist attacks, local authorities decry the lack of integration programs and the lack of support for them in the national government. Instead of firmly captivating the immigration agenda, Italian responses in terms of integration strategies often follow public opinion and media attention.

Regionally, integration strategies vary significantly. In the wealthy north-east, where labor-intensive industries are dependent on both skilled and unskilled immigrants, regional governments have invested in housing programs and job training. In the north-west, where many cities, such as Milan and Turin, have felt the growth of migrant involvement in criminal activities, government policies have focused on crime prevention. In the center regions, such as Tuscany, Emilia-Romagna and Umbria, left wing traditions have influenced government responses. In these "progressive" regions, integration strategies include health care, migrant political representation and intercultural education. Finally, the southern regions have not established coherent integration programs, despite central government funding which has, until now, been returned unused due to a lack of consensus on what types of strategies should be instituted. Rather than xenophobia, this trend indicates inefficiency.

The outcome of this ineffective and unresponsive policy-making system has been the development of a strong response to immigration by the non-governmental sector. NGOs from both Catholic and left-wing traditions have been the backbone of the Italian integration effort. In the south of Italy, they have met clandestine migrants upon their arrival and provided food, shelter, and even basic services such as temporary employment contracts. In the center and north of Italy, NGOs have adopted expanded definitions of "integration," and established projects that are much more holistic than governmental ones. Whereas official integration strategies normally focus on housing, jobs, health care, and crime prevention, NGOs are active in these arenas, as well as in education, cultural mediation, political mobilization, and social rights. Unfortunately, their activity has permitted the government to disengage and back away from any responsibility in the field of integration politics. The importance of such NGO work and the irresponsible positions that many government officials have adopted in response to this activity can best be illustrated through the following discussion of integration politics in the city of Florence.

Florence and the Politics of Immigration

Florence is a city of art, music and culture known throughout the world. Moreover, it has a political tradition that is also renowned. In the past, names such as Machiavelli, Savonarola, Medici, Guelfe, and Ghibellina marked the political landscape. In recent times, the city's political thought was illuminated by Giorgio La Pira, the progressive Catholic Mayor during the 1950s and 1960s who bestowed the city with an "internationalist" vision of politics.

La Pira's vision for the city included two major characteristics of the local political culture: progressive Catholicism and left-wing ideals. In fact, while Florence is a city of the left, it cannot be considered communist. Despite the prevailing egalitarian ideology, the Christian Democratic Party maintained power in the city until its implosion through political corruption in the early 1990s. Now the city is ruled by the center-left (*Democratici di Sinistra*) who remain loyal to local traditional values related to humanism.

Despite these political characteristics, the integration of non-EU migrants has been problematic for many years. Economically, Florence's different economic sectors that include employment opportunities in tourism, industry, and services, have facilitated incorporation. In fact, immigrant unemployment is the city is lower than the overall unemployment rate (11% compared to 12%[8]). Moreover, Florence has one of the highest concentrations of immigrant entrepreneurship in all of Italy.

The problem of ethnic integration in Florence is related to the city's social fabric. Non-EU immigration is a new phenomenon in the city as flows from countries such as China, Morocco, Egypt, Tunisia, Poland and Senegal began in the late 1980s. In the 1990s, migrants began coming from Eastern Europe, mainly from Romania and Albania. Since 1990, the local population has dealt with issues related to the integration of these new residents without coherent government intervention as a guide. During that year, the atmosphere in the city surrounding immigration was very tense. Local merchants were protesting against the presence of Senegalese peddlers who were selling their goods without permits. A group of businessmen organized a "March of Undefended Citizens" that focused on the question of immigration. In response to this outburst, the local government did nothing and took no political position on the issue. As a result, the climate surrounding immigration in the city worsened and eventually, a group of young Florentines attacked Senegalese migrants during a *Carnevale* celebration, sending many of them to the hospital. Since then, immigration has been one of the most intensely debated issues in local politics.

In fact, the 1990 attacks on immigrants created a situation that could best be described as chaotic. Because local authorities took no strong public position, non-governmental organizations filled the political vacuum and confiscated the immigration agenda. On one hand, groups of the Left and Catholic centre rallied around notions of human rights and ethnic integration. Trade Unions, NGOs, political parties combined to create a policy network around the issue of immigration which included service provision, the creation of political forums, legal assistance, housing, job training, and political representation. Of the almost thirty NGOs active in local immigration politics, eighteen began their activities within three years after the 1990 attacks.

Similarly, anti-immigrant movements created networks in an effort to publicize the threat "that immigration poses to the city." Right-wing parties, such as *Alleanza Nazionale* and *Lega Nord*, grass roots organizations, and economic groups such as *Confindustria* and *Lega degli Imprenditori*, have organized rallies and public meetings in opposition to immigration that have at times, attracted hundreds of participants. Like the radical right in France, their slogans focus on issues related to security and quality of life in the city. These themes have also been highly publicized in *La Nazione*, the city's newspaper which often portrays immigration questions negatively.

The local government has done little to control the energy of migration debates. The regional and provincial governments have created consultative bodies on immigration and the City has an Immigrant Office within its social service system, but these measures have proven ineffective due to a lack of political backing amongst local officials. For example, during his first election campaign, the city's current mayor, Leonardo Domenici's, first actions included the firing of the director of the city's immigrant office who was one of the most recognizable and respected actors in local immigration politics, the passage of anti-Gypsy/Roma statutes and the strengthening of powers that City police could use to apprehend clandestine immigrants (these last two measures were later repealed by judges who deemed them "unconstitutional").

Within this atmosphere, periodic violence against immigrants has erupted in the city. Most recently, the local Chinese population has become the target of increased antagonism. What is interesting about this situation is that economic integration has occurred. Unlike the above-cited cases of Durham and Toulouse, where ethnic marginalization contributed to social tension, Florence's immigrant community is characterized by significant employment, housing integration and political activity in official channels.

The ethnic tensions in the city have occurred because local officials have abdicated their responsibilities in the field of immigration politics. Immigrants are economically integrated but they remain marginalized socially. Successful immigrant entrepreneurship has created serious tensions with local businessmen who perceive newcomers as sources of unfair competition. This claim is particularly pointed at the Chinese, Florence's largest immigrant community, because local industrialists claim that they enjoy an unfair advantage due to the importation of cheap labour. Thus, they have mobilized and utilized their political influence to attempt to combat recent migration.

By withdrawing from direct confrontations with small but powerful actors, such as merchants and industrialists, City and Provincial authorities permitted the non-governmental sector to polarize immigration debates. This is typical of many issue arenas of Italian politics where public distrust of authorities, non-governmental mobilization, and strong ideological convictions have impeded the creation of partnerships for the solution of policy problems. Even within the pro-integration camps, Left-wing and Catholic organizations refused to collaborate throughout the 1990s and cooperation has only begun in the last few years. For this reason, one can point to signs of progress but long-term solutions have yet to be developed as local actors focus on responses to short-term crises, much like Italian national authorities. As long as this strategy is followed, immigration debates will remain charged, and integration politics will rest fully in the informal sector, undermining their overall legitimacy. Thus, like in France and the United States the main obstacles to recognized membership for migrants in the local community remain informal ones linked to the structure and content of local power rather than a lack of formal rights.

Conclusions

The foregoing analysis openly questions whether too much local democratic participation can hinder ethnic integration. The reflections presented have significant policy implications. By choosing local cases that mirror national democratic models, the article attempts to illustrate the impact of integration strategies on minorities in ethnically mixed cities. The empirical evidence provided by these studies indicates that democratic discussions, especially those taking place at the local level, do not always facilitate integration. In fact, when models of democracy are defended as ideologically dogmatic structures within these debates instead of being forwarded as means for individual participation within society, they become authoritarian and consequently betray democratic principles on which corresponding political systems have been constructed.

Many opponents of multiculturalism, defined as ethnically explicit strategies to integrate minority communities, claim that minorities wish to change traditional notions and models of citizenship. It is often argued that ethnic diversity poses a challenge to democratic systems because of the introduction of questions related to cultural recognition and national identity. In France, this criticism of ethnic minorities has been tremendously contentious, especially since the 2005 urban unrest. In the United States, the recent tension surrounding Mexican immigration has raised this issue through allusions to "Mexifornia" and the "inability of Mexicans to integrate (see Huntington, 2004)." The cases discussed in this article demonstrate that urban integration and ethnic mobilization are not challenges to traditional democratic systems. Instead, minorities fight for access to existing models of democracy. While the majority of public and academic attention in these debates is focused on the formal recognition of ethnicity, this article argues that the key mechanism that inhibits the integration of minorities is the informal structure and exercise of power in local and national political systems.

In the three cases presented above, ethnic minorities are not challenging democratic practices in urban contexts. Instead, they seek access to the socio-economic and political systems that govern the communities in which they live. In Durham, African Americans formally participate in local politics through civic organizations, political parties and interest groups. Nonetheless, education represents the key to socio-economic integration due to the city's recent market transformation and, thus far, African-Americans have faced difficulties due to informal racial segregation and unequal school systems. Thus, many members of this community remain marginalized.

Similarly, the two European cases demonstrate mobilization by minorities aimed at accessing democratic systems rather than challenging them. In Toulouse, residents of the *Grand Mirail*, an ethnically mixed neighbourhood, have not mobilized against the French Republican model. Instead, political and social unrest in this group of neighbourhoods has targeted informal barriers to integration within this model, especially geographic and socio-economic segregation. Residents are isolated due to a lack of structural channels for interaction with local government officials and representatives of the non-governmental sector in other areas of the city. Moreover, socio-economic opportunities are often limited by discrimination that is not recognized by authorities, and therefore, it is not addressed.

Finally, Florence represents a very interesting case. Migrants are socio-economically integrated and geographically distributed throughout the city, thus avoiding concentrations in poor neighbourhoods. Despite these positive opportunity structures, immigrants remain marginalized socially and politically and ethnic tensions persist. This would suggest that socio-economic exclusion is not the only informal barrier that obstructs the integration of ethnic minorities in local contexts.

The description of local politics presented above illustrates that the Florentine model of democracy is based on civil society and political participation. As mentioned above, many NGOs in Florence have created a network to defend the rights of migrants. This network, however, demonstrates that civil society is not just a question of quantity, but also one of quality (see Koff, 2005). The non-governmental sector in Florence is significantly paternalistic as it has traditionally excluded migrants from political participation and decision-making. One representative of a migrant rights organization recently stated: "They do not know what is good for them. That is why we need to fight for their rights"[9]. Migrants in Florence have enjoyed socio-economic integration, characterized by employment and access to housing. However, they have not found access to the political system that dictates the terms of local notions of citizenship and democracy. Until migrants are treated as actors, they will remain political objects rather than local citizens, despite their socio-economic incorporation.

For these reasons, this article asks whether open democratic discussions can be detrimental to minority integration in ethnically mixed cities. In response, the empirical evidence suggests that an orthodox defence of particular ideological models of democratic systems can actually betray the values that they were created to implement. The cases above demonstrate that many actors attempt to maintain the status quo in ethnically mixed cities by strictly adhering to established models of citizenship and democracy. Consequently illiberal practices that maintain the status quo and contribute to minority social exclusion are often cloaked in the guise of "upholding democratic traditions" of decentralization or Republicanism. This has created regimes in many advanced industrial states that can best be defined as authoritarian democracies. While formal minority rights have been expanded, as have anti-discrimination policies, the United States and Europe have witnessed a trend against affirmative action and other pro-integration strategies. Thus, ethnic integration discourse at the national and supranational (EU) levels is rarely translated into policy solutions locally, which have converged around a least common denominator: most cities enact strong anti-racism programs but they do not go so far as to promote ethnic integration. This strategy is quite reactive rather than proactive and the resulting vacuum permits radical political camps (such as radical parties, politically driven interest groups, gangs of youths, etc.) to determine the focal points of local integration agendas. As a result, this work suggests that decentralization is not necessarily the key to improving social integration in ethnically-mixed cities. Local actors are nearer to urban residents and supposedly more reactive to their political needs. They are also however, susceptible to political pressures that prevent them from taking strong stands in moments of crisis and presenting long-term visions to local populations concerning minority integration.

Returning to the 2005 urban unrest in France, one of the biggest questions asked in the national media following the riots was: "Why was there no violence in Marseille?" In response, most analysts pointed to Marseille's unique character among French cities. Experts cited the following characteristics which attenuated the potential for interethnic violence: immigrants and ethnic minorities are informally recognized and accepted as part of the social fabric of the city; elected officials cultivate informal communication networks with ethnic minorities; and through these networks, ethnic minorities have effectively mobilized within institutionalized political channels.

These elements make Marseille one of the least "republican" cities in France. Of course many republican traditions are strong in Marseille. However, the city has been recognized for its practical approach to solving informal problems related to social integration. Unlike most other major French cities, Marseille was not affected by the 2005 urban unrest because it has addressed informal barriers to social integration related to power with practical policy solutions that many purists would consider "unrepublican." Such policy compromises may "betray" national democratic traditions, but they significantly contribute to the maintenance of democratic ideals, such as equality, justice, and the common good at the local level. They also represent the difference between an intelligent defence of democratic principles and the creation of authoritarian democratic dogma.

Many European states are proposing devolution in the field of minority integration politics. The U.S. model still firmly supports unmitigated decentralization. These trends have thrust cities into important roles in national and even international integration discussions. They have also exposed local officials to tremendous public pressure in the fields of integration politics. The cases presented in this work suggest that city governments need support from above if they are to successfully promote social and ethnic integration.

Multi-level governance is the only way to promote democratic values and protect local officials from unmediated populism. Decentralization offers a great deal of potential but also much risk. Many national officials are currently utilizing this approach to avoid responsibility in the field of integration politics, in many cases abandoning local authorities when ethnic tensions arise. Increased autonomy at the local level brings heightened responsibility and therefore greater danger that local citizens will contest minority integration programs through both formal and informal channels. Formal barriers to integration have been addressed in most advanced industrial states. However, decentralization has increased the significance of informal obstacles. These barriers can only be overcome through concerted efforts at different levels of government. By spreading responsibility for ethnic integration, a system of checks and balances can be successfully created, spreading responsibility, so that local leaders will not have to face populist pressures alone.

Notes

1. Statement made at meeting: Les Emeutes en France 2005: Considerations Europeennes, organized by CLERSE, Universite de Lille 1, Lille, France, January 2006.
2. Official census data from the United States Census Bureau, INSEE (France), and ISTAT (Italy).
3. United States Census Bureau. Available at www.census.gov/population/www/socdemo/race.html
4. North Carolina State Data Center. Available at http://census.state.nc.us
5. STEP Task Force. Official Report, 1993.
6. *Ibid.*
7. Author's participant observation.
8. Proveditorato Provinciale del Lavoro (2000) Official Statistics.
9. Personal Interview conducted by author.

References

Alston, P. (Ed.) (1999) *The EU and Human Rights* (Oxford: Oxford University Press).
Balbo, L. & Manconi, L. (1992) *I razzismi reali*. (Milan: Feltrinelli).
Baldwin-Edwards, M. (1997) The Emerging European Immigration Regime: Some Reflections for Southern Europe, *Journal of Common Market Studies*, 35(4), pp. 497–519.
Bauböck, R. (1998) *Blurred Boundaries* (Aldershot: Ashgate Press).
Betz, H. (1994) *Radical Right Wing Populism in Western Europe.* (New York: St Martin's Press).
Bonifazi, C. (1999) *L'Immigrazione Straniera in Italia*. (Bologna: Il Mulino).
Brubaker, W. (Ed.) (1989) *Immigration and the Politics of Citizenship in Europe and North America.* (Lanham, MD: University Press of America).
Calavita, K. (2004) Italy: Economic Realities, Political Fictions, and Policy Failures, in: W. Cornelius, T. Tsuda, P. Martin & J. Hollifield (Eds), *Controlling Immigration* 2nd edition, pp. 345–380 (Palo Alto, CA: Stanford University Press).
Carens, J. (2000) *Culture, Citizenship and Community* (Oxford: Oxford University Press).
Caritas (2004) *Immigrazione. Dossier Statistico* (Roma: Anterem).
Collectif (1997) *Ces Quartiers Dont On Parle*. (Paris: Editions de l'Aube).
Connolly, W. (1991) *Identity/Difference* (Ithaca, NY: Cornell University Press).
Cornelius, W., T. Tsuda, P. Martin & J. Hollifield (Eds) (2004) Controlling Immigration 2nd edition (Palo Alto, CA: Stanford University Press).
Della Porta, D. (1999) Europeanization and Protest on Immigration: The Italian Case in Comparative Perspective. Presented at conference on The Impact of Increased Economic Integration on Italy and the Rest of Europe, Georgetown University, Washington, DC, 30 April–2 May.
Esping-Andersen, G. (1991) *The Three Worlds of Welfare Capitalism* (Princeton, NJ: Princeton University Press).
Favell, A. (1998) *Philosophies of Integration* (Basingstoke: Macmillan).

Gutmann, A. (Ed.) (1994) *Multiculturalism* (Priceton, NJ: Princeton University Press).
Habermas, J. (1998) *The Inclusion of the Other* (Cambridge: Cambridge University Press).
Hollifield, J. (1992) *Immigrants, Markets and States* (Cambridge, MA: Harvard University Press).
Horowitz, D. & Noiriel, G. (Eds) (1992) *Immigrants in Two Democracies* (New York: New York University Press).
Huntington, S. (2004) *Who Are We?: The Challenges to America's Identity* (New York: Simon & Schuster).
INSEE. (1995) *Metropole Toulousaine: Profils des nouveaux habitants et territoires d'accueil*. N. 70 Avril.
Ireland, P. (1994) *The Policy Challenge of Ethnic Diversity* (Cambridge, MA: Harvard University Press).
ISTAT (1996) *Toscana: Informazioni Utili*.
Jacobson, D. (1996) *Rights across Borders: Immigration and the Decline of Citizenship* (Baltimore, NJ: The Johns Hopkins University Press).
Joppke, C. (Ed.) (1998) *Challenge to the Nation-State* (Oxford: Oxford University Press).
Koff, H. (2006) Does Hospitality Translate into Integration?: Sub-National Variations of Italian Responses to Immigration, in: T. Tsuda (Ed.), *Reluctant Hosts? Japan as a Recent Country of Immigration in Comparative Perspective*, pp. 173–204 (Lanham, MD: Lexington Books).
Koff, H. (2005) Migrant Participation in Local European Democracies, *Migraciones Internacionales*, 9(3), pp. 5–28.
Koff, S. & Koff, S. (2000) *Italy: From the First to the Second Republic* (London: Routledge).
Kozol, J. (1992) *Savage Inequalities* (New Yorker: Harper Press).
Kymlicka, W. (1989) *Liberalism, Community and Culture* (Oxford: Oxford University Press).
Nozick, R. (1974) *Anarchy, State and Utopia* (Oxford: Basil Blackwell).
Papademtriou, D. (1996) *Coming Apart or Pulling Together?* (Brookings Institution Press).
Penninx, R., Kraal, K. Martiniello, M. & Vertovec, S. (Eds) (2004). *Citizenship in European Cities: Immigrants, Local Politics, and Integration Policies* (Aldershot: Ashgate).
Pugliese, E. (2000) *Rapporto Immigrazione* (Roma: Ediesse).
Rawls, J. (1971) *A Theory of Justice* (Cambridge, MA: Harvard University Press).
Silverman, M. (1991) *Race, Discourse, and Power in France* (Brookfield, VT: Avebury).
Spencer, M. (1995) *States of Injustice* (London: Pluto Press).
Soysal, Y. (1994) *Limits of Citizenship* (Chicago, IL: University of Chicago Press).
SSRC (Ed.) (2005) Riots in France, available online at: http://riotsfrance.ssrc.org/
Taylor, C. (1992) *Multiculturalism and the Politics of Recognition.* (Princeton, NJ: Princeton University Press).
Tocqueville, A. de (1991) *Democracy in America*. (New York: Knopf).
Tsuda, T. & Cornelius, C. (2004) Japan: Government Policy, Immigrant Reality, in: W. Cornelius, T. Tsuda, P. Martin & J. Hollifield (Eds), *Controlling Immigration*, 2nd edition, pp. 439–476 (Palo Alto, CA: Stanford University Press).
Turner, B. (Ed.) (1993) *Citizenship and Social Theory* (London: Sage Publications).
Vertovec, S. (1998). Multicultural Policies and Modes of Citizenship in European Cities. *International Social Science Journal*, 156 (June), pp. 187–199.
Viet, V. (1998) *La France Immigrée* (Paris: Fayard).
Walzer, M. (1983) *Spheres of Justice*. (New York: Basic Books).
Watts, J. (2000) *An Unconventional Brotherhood* (La Jolla, CA: Center for Comparative Immigration Studies, University of California, San Diego).
Wieviorka, M. (1999) *Violence en France* (Paris: Editions de Seuil).
Wilson, W. (2002) *Youth in Cities: A Cross National Perspective* (Cambridge: Cambridge University Press).
Young, I. M. (1989) *Justice and the Politics of Difference*. (Princeton, NJ: Princeton University Press).
Zincone, G. (Ed.) (2001) *Secondo rapporto sull'integrazione degli immigrati in Italia* (Bologna: Il Mulino).

Index

accountability 19, 29
Acre 71
activists 64–5, 73, 78, 80, 82–7, 144
Adaev, A. 49
administration 8, 15–35, 102, 106–7, 109
Administrative Justice Regional Court 124–5
Adolat 46, 48
Advanced Placement exams 151
affiliations 147, 149
African-Americans 8, 145–6, 149–53, 161
Agrarian Reform Law 94
agriculture 46, 121
aid 17, 22, 24, 26, 30–1
Airbus 154
Ajami 73
Ak-Tilek 49
Akaev, A. 46, 48–9, 51, 54–6
Albania 145, 159
Alleanza Nazionale (AN) 129–30, 157, 159
Allies 122
Alto-Atesino 128
Altun Kopre 102
American South 8
Amin, A. 68
Amir Temur 52, 54
Amnesty International 146
anarchy 99
Anderson, B. 25, 44
Andijan 51
Andreev, S. 19
Andromeda Hill 79
Anfal 94, 105
anthropology 2, 19–20, 32
anti-war protests 66
Arab-Jewish Centre 83
Arabic language 77, 116
Arabization 94–5, 97–8, 105
Arabs 7, 9, 71–3, 77, 79
    Iraq 93–9, 101–9
    Israel 81–2, 84
    Italy 116
    opposition 154

Arel, D. 117
Army of Bosnia and Herzegovina 16
Artykov, A. 48, 54
Asians 149
Assembly of the People of Kyrgyzstan (APK) 49
assimilation 126–7, 129, 133, 152–3
Assyrians 94, 102, 108
Austria 113–14, 122–3, 127
authoritarianism 40–1, 50, 55, 143–63
autonomy 42–6, 48–9, 53, 56
    France 153, 155
    Iraq 98, 101, 103, 105, 107
    Italy 122–5, 127, 131, 134
    role 163
Autonomy Accord 94, 102
Autonomy Section 124–5
Azar, E. 99, 105

Ba'ath Party 94–5
Babur Theatre 51
Baghdad 94, 99, 101–2, 107, 109
Bakiev, K. 54
BALAD Party 83–4
Balkans 19, 146
Banja Luka 16
banlieues 154
Barcelona 119
Barzani, M. 94
Basques 104
Batken 40, 45
Batyr-Avia 55
Batyrov, K. 54–5
Batyrov University 55
Bauböck, R. 32, 146
Bechev, D. 19
Belgium 147
belonging 29–31
Berlusconi, S. 157
bilingualism 9, 125–9, 132, 136
Billig, M. 116

birthrate 7
Bishkek 49–50, 52
blacks 116, 146
blind spots 26
Board of County Commissioners 152
Board of Education 152
Bolzano 3–4, 7–10, 113–38
Bonifazi, C. 148
Bonn powers 19
border controls 148
Bosnia 3, 8, 15, 104
Bosnia-Herzegovina (BiH) 15–16, 18–21, 25–7, 30, 32, 107
Bosniacs 8, 15–17, 23–4, 28
Bosnian Serbs 15–16, 23–4, 28, 30
Bossi, U. 157
Bousetta, H. 66, 68–9
boycotts 7, 98, 103–4
Brcko 16, 104
Bressanone 113, 121, 126
British 94, 116
British Mandate in Palestine 70, 72, 80–1
brokers 53–4
Brubaker, R. 20, 116
Brubaker, W. 148
Brugger 127
Brussels 107, 119
bureaucracies 3, 20, 27, 31–2, 95, 155–6
Burton, J. 99, 105
Buzan, B. 120

California Achievement Tests 151
Campbel 116
Canada 153
cantons 16, 25–6, 32
Carens, J. 147
Carlá, A. 3–4, 8–9, 113–38
Carmel Mountain 72
Castilian language 119
categorization 20–7
Catholics 145, 157–8, 160
census data 7, 18, 20, 25, 72–3
   Iraq 95, 102–3
   Italy 126–7, 132
   US 149, 151
Center for Preventive Action 102
Central Asia 39–40, 45–6, 53, 56–7
Central Bosnian Canton 16
centralization 6, 26, 70, 148–9, 155
Centre for Textbook Production 51

centre-periphery relations 8–9, 40, 49, 53, 56–7
Centro Cristiano Democratico (CCD) 157
Chambers of Commerce 152
Chapel Hill 145, 150
cherry picking 77
China 145, 159
Chinese 160
Christians 72, 77–8, 81, 84, 94–5, 107
Chuy 40
citizenship 15–35, 63–87, 122, 144–9, 153, 161–2
city *see* urban areas
city councils 17–18, 30, 52
   Israel 70, 75, 81–2
   Italy 114, 124, 130–1
   US 151–2
city-state status 103–4, 109
civil rights movement 146
civil servants 17–18, 125
civil society 54, 77, 144–5, 161
clans 40
class 28, 77, 82, 84, 115
clientelism 42
Cluj 6
Coalition Forces 99, 106, 108–9
Coalition Provisional Authority 96
Cohn, B. 25
Cold War 43
collective action 27–9, 31, 65–7, 72, 78
colonialism 20
Commission of the Nineteen 123
Commission for Resolution of Real Property Disputes (CRRPD) 96, 99, 108
Communist Party 82
communists 42, 51, 82, 147, 157–8
communitarians 18, 118, 147, 149
communities 30–1, 40, 42, 95
   democracy 144, 147
   France 154
   Iraq 98–9, 107–9
   Israel 65–6, 69, 72, 74, 76–81, 84–5
   Italy 135, 160
   Kyrgyzstan 45, 47, 49–50, 53, 56–7
   US 150, 152
compensation 21, 96, 99, 108
competition 9
conflict resolution 41–2, 53, 105
Connolly, W. 147
conservatives 152
Consiglio Provinciale 124

consociationalism 4
constitutions 15, 93, 98–9, 102, 104, 108–9, 124
constructivists 115
Contrat de Ville 156
core ethic regions 8
corporations 73
corporatists 148
Council of Europe 146
Council of Refugees and IDPs 30
crime 77, 79, 155, 157–8
Cristiani Democratici Uniti (CDU) 157
Croat-Muslim Federation 104
Croatian Defence Council (HVO) 16
Croats 8, 15–17, 23–4, 28, 30
cross-group voting 7
culture 9–10, 17, 19, 94
   democracy 147, 160
   France 153–4
   Israel 64–5, 69, 77, 80, 83, 85
   Italy 115, 117, 119, 124–5, 127, 156–8
   Kyrgyzstan 41–4, 46–9, 51–3
   US 150

Dahouk 102
databases 22
Dave, B. 47
Dayton Accords 25
Dayton Peace Agreement (DPA) 15–17, 21, 27
De Gasperi, A. 122
De Gasperi-Gruber Agreement 122–3
De Tocqueville, A. 150
de-urbanization 151
decentralization 6, 8, 26, 105, 107, 143–63
deconstruction 53
democracy 149–63
Democratic Front for Peace and Equality (HADASH) 82–3
Democratici di Sinistra 158
democratization 144
demography 1–2, 4–7, 9–10, 47
   Iraq 94, 96, 103–4
   Israel 71–3, 77
   Italy 117, 122, 127, 132
   US 151
deprivation 77
desegregation 8
developing countries 134
devolution 6, 8, 144, 162
dialectics 31
dialects 121

diasporas 44
10000 Dinar Settlers 94, 96
discourse trajectory 4–6
discrimination 50, 55, 64, 71
   democracy 144, 146–7, 149, 161–2
   France 152, 154, 156
   Italy 116–17, 119–21, 124–5, 127, 129, 131, 133–4
Displaced movement 5
Displaced Persons and Housing Office 26
displacement 20–7, 29–31, 95–9, 103, 108–9
district councils 17
Diyala 103
dogma 143–63
Dohuk 103
Domenici, L. 159
domicilni 26
Donja Mahala 24
donors 20, 27–30
double discrimination syndrome 71
Duke University 150–1
Durham Committee on the Affairs of Black People 152
Durham, N. Carolina 8, 145, 150–2, 160–1
dynamic statism 67

Eastern Europe 2–3, 9–10, 159
economics 24, 31, 44–5, 52
   democracy 144–5, 147–8, 161
   France 153–6
   Iraq 94, 103, 106
   Israel 64–5, 68–9, 72–3, 76, 80–1
   Italy 117, 121–2, 124, 127, 133, 156–7, 159–60
   US 150–2
education 28, 44, 46, 51
   democracy 147, 161
   France 155
   Iraq 107
   Israel 70–1, 78–9, 81, 84–5
   Italy 114, 118, 125, 158
   US 150–2
Education First 152
Egypt 145, 159
elections 7–8, 17–19, 46–8
   democracy 150, 152
   Iraq 95, 97–8, 102–3, 108
   Israel 69–70, 73, 75–8, 82
   Italy 118, 124, 129–31
   Kyrgyzstan 51–2, 54–6

electricity 17, 96, 101, 123
elites 5, 20, 42–3, 46–7
　democracy 150, 154
　Israel 64, 66–7, 70, 77–8, 81–4
　Kyrgyzstan 51, 53–4, 57
Emilia-Romagna 158
enclaves 6, 8, 10
entrepreneurs 44, 49, 159–60
environment 66, 79–80
equality 3, 18, 28, 50
　democracy 144, 148, 162
　France 153–4
　Israel 64, 66, 68
　Italy 118, 120, 124, 135
equivalence 135
Erbil 102–3, 107
Esping-Anderson, G. 148
ethnic cleansing 25, 94–7
ethnocracy 68, 86
ethnofederalism 44, 49
ethnography 20–31
ethnonationalism 63–87
ethnopolitics 39–58
ethnoreligious dynamics 1–11
Europe 19, 68–70, 143–4, 146, 152, 156, 161–2
European Administration (EUAM) 17, 27
European Air-Space industry 145
European Union (EU) 19, 106, 133, 145, 147–8, 162
evacuation 73, 80
event trajectory 4–6
evictions 76
exclusion 4, 73, 86, 143–6, 149, 151–3, 155–6, 161–2
exhaustion 55

Falk 121
fascists 121–2, 127–30, 132–3, 145, 147, 154
Fattakhov, B. 48
faultline citizenship 63–87
Favell, A. 153
federalism 94, 102, 104, 107, 118, 150
Federation Statistical Institute 25
feedback effects 5
Ferghana Valley 45
festivals 81, 83
First World War 113–14, 127, 132
Florence 3, 9, 145, 158–61
Fonds d'Action Social (FAS) 155
formal institutions 7–8, 10, 40–3, 47–52, 54, 56, 68, 77

Forza Italia (FI) 157
fragmented incorporation models 148–9
framing 10, 66–7
France 4, 143–63
fraud 51
French Revolution 153–4
Front National (FN) 153
frontlines 27–8
Fumagalli, M. 3, 7, 39–58
functionalism 144

Gaelic language 116
gas 51–2, 101
Gellner, E. 116
gender 65
General Assembly 123
Geneva 123
gentrification 76–7, 79–80
geography 2, 49, 65, 71–3
　democracy 145, 155, 161
　Iraq 101–3, 107
　Israel 81, 84
　Italy 118
German language 3, 113–14, 121–35
Germans 8–9
Germany 122, 147, 153
Giunta Provinciale 124
globalization 65, 134, 146
Gorbachev, M. 44
gossip 30
Grand Mirail 154–5, 161
Great Britain 144, 147
Green Line 71
Greenfeld, L. 116
Gruber, K. 122
guest workers 147
Guinier, L. 116
Gul, A. 101
Gulf War 103
Gupta, A. 20
Gypsies 146, 159

Habsburg Empire 113
HADASH 84
Haifa 5–6, 63–87
Halisa 84
Hapsburg Empire 121
Harabitta 77–9
Hawija 102, 109
Hebrew language 82
hegemony 84, 108

Helmke, G. 2–3, 54
Herceg-Bosna 24
heroes 10, 52
Herzegovina 15–16
Herzegovina-Neretva 16
hierarchies 20–7, 31, 44, 120, 131
High Representative 17, 19
Hindus 4
historiography 80
Hitler, A. 122
Hollifield, J. 148
Hooghe, M. 66
horizontal networks 3
Horowitz, D. 99
housing 9–10, 23, 26–30
  democracy 147, 158, 160–1
  Israel 76–7, 79, 81, 84–5
  Kyrgyzstan 39, 46, 49
Hughes, J. 44, 56
Hulday, R. 76
human rights 21, 23, 29, 144, 147, 153, 159
Hungarians 3–6, 9–10
Hussein, S. 93–7, 103, 105, 108

identification cards 26
imagined communities 18
immersion teaching 126
income 72–3, 79, 81
incorporation models 148
Independent Turkmen Movement 107
India 4
industrialization 121, 128
industry 45, 121–2, 128, 133, 145, 158–9
informality 1–2, 39–58, 68
infra-politics 68–70, 74, 77–80, 83–4, 87
Institute of Regional Studies 50
institutions 1–5, 8–10, 17, 19
  analysis 56, 64, 85, 87
  building 18, 29, 32
  collaboration 77
  concentration 78–9
  control 80, 99
  differentiation 71
  discourses 84
  efficacy 42–4
  enhancement 49–50
  failure 147
  formal 7–8, 47–51
  interplay 40–1
  intertwined 52, 54

language 114, 118, 120, 123–7, 134
  planning 71
  public 21, 26, 32
  range 68
  structures 68
  supranational 65
  symbolism 83
instrumentalists 115
integration 143–63
internally displaced persons (IDPs) 20–6, 29–31, 95–9, 103, 108–9
international community 16, 18, 26, 108
International Crisis Group (ICG) 104, 109
international relations 120, 144
investment 29, 150–1
Iran 101, 103, 145
Iran-Iraq War 94
Iraq 7, 93–110
Iraqi Accord Front 98
Iraqi Council of Representatives 104
Iraqi Kurdish Regional Government 104
Iraqi National Dialogue Front 98
Iraqi Property Claims Commission (IPCC) 96, 99, 108
Iraqi Transitional Government 98
Iraqi Turkmen Front 101, 107
Ireland 116
Ireland, P. 148
Irish 116
irredentists 94, 103, 106
Islam see Muslims
Islamic Movement 83–4
Israel 5, 7, 63–87
Israelis 5, 63, 68, 70–3, 77–8, 82, 84
Italian language 3, 113–14, 121–35
Italian Peace Treaty 122
Italianization 114, 121, 127–8
Italians 8–9, 122, 128, 145
Italy 3, 7, 113, 121
  democracy 143, 156–60
  role 123, 128, 132

Jacobson, D. 146
Jaffa Governance Unit (JGU) 77, 79
Jaffa Hip 79
Jalalabad 40, 45, 48–9, 55
Jalalabad Uzbek Culture Centre 54
Jamal, A. 68
Japan 147
Jerusalem 70–2, 93
Jews 5, 68–73, 76–82, 84, 146

170 *Index*

Joppke, C. 148
Judaization 77, 79
jus sanguinis 153
jus soli 153

Kalyvas, S.N. 40
Kamp, M. 44–5
Kaufman, C. 105
Kazakhstan 40, 51
Khalil, M. 97
Kimmerling, B. 72
kin networks 46
Kirghizia 39
Kirkuk 7, 9, 93–110
Koff, H. 3–4, 8–9, 11, 143–63
Kokand khanate 45
Kolak, T. 70
Konjic 23
Koschnick, H. 17
Kosovo 8
Kurdish Autonomous Region 93, 101, 109
Kurdish Autonomous Zone 103, 107
Kurdish Regional Government 106
Kurdistan 103–4, 106–7, 109
Kurdistan Assembly 108
Kurdistan Autonomous Region 98
Kurdistan Democratic Party (KDP) 97, 103
Kurdistan Regional Government (KRG) 96–7, 102, 107, 109
Kurds 7, 9, 93–9, 101–3, 105–9
Kymlicka, W. 118, 147
Kyrgyz 9, 39–40, 44–6, 48–9, 54
Kyrgyz language 47
Kyrgyz Supreme Soviet 51
Kyrgyz-Uzbek University (KUU) 51
KyrgyzGas 52
Kyrgyzstan 3, 7, 39–58

La Pira, G. 158
Labour party 82
Lahat, S. 70
Lancia 121, 133
land 9–10, 39, 46, 49, 94, 103, 108
landfill 79
language 3–4, 9–10, 43–4
  Iraq 107
  Israel 77
  Italy 113–38
  Kyrgyzstan 46–7, 51, 56
Latin America 116
Latinos 149–50

Le Pen, J-M. 153, 156
Lebanon 107
Lega Nord 157, 159
legitimization 18–19
Leibovitz, J. 5, 63–87
Levitsky, S. 2–3, 54
Lewin, 116
liberals 18, 118, 144, 146–9, 153
linguistic diversity 3–4, 8–10, 113–38
linkages 67, 71, 79
living standards 46
local authorities 20–1, 23, 27–9, 70, 124, 158, 163
local authority figures 39–58
localism 1–11, 81
Lowndes, V. 85
Luong, P.J. 53
luxury development 76–7
Lydda 71

McAdam, D. 65–7
Maghreb 145
Magnago, S. 127
magnet schools 152
Mahdi Army 99
Mamasaidov, M. 51–2, 54–5
marginalization 50, 57, 64
  democracy 144, 149, 154, 156, 160–1
  Israel 67, 77, 85
  Italy 117
market failure 147
Marseille 162
mayors 7, 18, 30, 51
  democracy 143, 152, 158
  Israel 69–70, 76–8, 81–2, 84
media 22, 28, 43, 46, 56
  democracy 144, 147, 158, 162
  Italy 118, 125, 131–2
Mediterranean 69, 72, 79, 83
Merano 113, 121
Mexicans 146, 161
Mexifornia 161
micro-credit 52
Miercurea Ciuc 4, 9
Migdal, J.S. 72
migrant workers 71
Milan 158
mind-sets 115–17, 119–21, 127, 129, 131–4
Ministry for Human Rights and Refugees (MHRR) 22, 27
Ministry of Interior 70
Ministry of Internal Affairs 52

minorities 2–4, 6–8, 10–11, 28
  democracy 143, 145, 148, 160–3
  France 154–6
  Iraq 101, 106–7
  Israel 64–71, 80–5, 87
  Italy 113–14, 117, 119–20, 122, 124–9, 131–5
  Kyrgyzstan 42–3, 46–50, 53, 56
  mobilization 63–87
  opposition 143–63
  rights 107, 118, 124, 135, 144, 147
  trapped 71
  US 149–50
  within minorities 77
minorization 117, 119–21, 127, 129, 131–4
Mitzna, A. 82
mixed cities 63–87
Montecatini 121
Montreal 119
Morocco 145, 159
Moscow 45, 55
mosques 52
Mostar 3, 5, 7–9, 15–35
Mostar Implementation Unit (MIU) 17
Mosul Villayet 94
Mouvement Contre le Racisme et Pour L'Amitie Entre Les Peuples 146
Movement Against Racism and For Friendship Between Peoples (MRAP) 146
multiculturalism 4, 8, 83, 118, 144, 147, 160
municipal councils 97
municipalities 70, 72, 75, 77, 79, 104, 150
Muslims 4, 8, 15, 45
  Israel 72, 78, 81, 83–4
  participation 154, 157
Mussolini, B. 114, 122, 128

Naryn 40
nationalists 5, 17, 25, 27
  democracy 146, 157
  Iraq 94, 107
  Israel 63–4, 82–3, 87
  Italy 116, 129–30, 132
  Kyrgyzstan 41, 46, 48, 51, 53, 55
nationalization 94
Native Americans 146
nativism 147, 157
Navarra 104
Nazareth 71
negative protection 124
neo-liberalism 73

Netetva River 16
Netherlands 107
Nineva 103
non-governmental organizations (NGOs)
  Bosnia 21
  democracy 144, 146, 155–6, 158–9, 161
  Israel 84, 86
  Kyrgyzstan 52
  role 3
norms 2–5, 7, 10, 18, 85, 118–20
North Africans 154
North America 68
North Carolina Tests in Writing, Mathematics and Social Studies 151
Northern Ireland 107

Occupied Territories 71, 82
Office of the High Representative (OHR) 16–19, 21
Office for Social and Housing Affairs 30
Oguz Turks 94
oil 93–4, 97–9, 101, 103, 106–8, 153
O'Leary, B. 108
Ombudsmen 28
Omuraliev, N. 49–50
Operational Calendar 123
opposition 143–63
opzioni 122, 128
O'Reilly, C.C. 116
OSCE 16, 21
Osh 3, 7, 9, 39–58
Osh Aimagy 46
Osh State University 54
Ottoman Empire 94
Outline Plan 81

Paccetto 123
Palestine 70, 72, 80–1
Palestinians 5–6, 9, 63, 69–74, 76–86
Papademetriou, D. 148
Paris 143, 154
Paris Agreement 122
participation 143–63
parting-regimes 120–1, 131–4
partition 105
party system 47–8
passports 26, 30
path dependence 5, 10
Patriotic Union of Kurdistan (PUK) 97, 103
patron-client relations 41–2, 51–6
patronage 3, 7, 53–4, 56, 67, 78, 80

peace-keeping forces 16
peasants 26, 31
pensions 32
People's Alliance 152
perestroika 44
Petersen, R.D. 116
petroleum commission 106
philanthropy 52, 54
Philippines 145
Phillips, D.L. 102
pilgrimages 44, 55
place-making 71, 79–80, 83–4
planners 70, 77
pogroms 41
Poland 159
polarization 5, 8–9, 99, 101, 154, 160
police 26, 28, 76, 97, 125, 154, 159
politesse 3
political science 2, 41, 68
politics
  contentious 66–8, 80, 85
  informal 51–6
  local 1–11
  place-making 79–80
  symbolic 81–3
pooling-regimes 120
Portugal 154
Posen, B. 105
positive protection 124
post-colonialism 20, 41, 56
post-industrialization 133
post-modernism 156
post-Saddam Iraq 93–9, 101–2
poverty 73, 150–1
power language policies 118–21, 124–5, 128, 131, 133–5
power-sharing 6, 18, 94, 104, 107–9, 148
primordialism 115, 128, 132–3
printing houses 51
privatization 29
profit 23–4
property development 70, 77
Property Law Implementation Plan (PLIP) 21, 23, 27
property rights 9, 21, 25, 29, 96–7
proportional representation 75, 124
proportionality principle 125
proporzionale etnica 125
protest movements 27–31, 78, 82
provincial councils 97
Provincial Government 124, 132

Provincial Parliament 124, 129, 131
provision 20–7
public opinion 152–3, 158
Purcell, M. 65

race 116, 144, 151–2, 161
Radnitz, S. 53–4
RAI 3 125, 131
Raleigh 145, 150
Ramla 71
raseljeni 26, 29
rational choice theory 5
recession 153
reciprocity 30, 126
reconstruction 22–4, 26–8, 30–1, 55
recreation 17
referenda 93, 98, 101–9, 133, 152
refugees 5, 20–7, 29–31, 154
regeneration 76
Reilly, B. 118
reinforcement 5
relational citizenship 87
relational language policies 118–21, 124–35
religion 1–2, 4, 6, 8
  democracy 157
  Iraq 95, 99
  Israel 77–8, 82–5
  Kyrgyzstan 45, 48, 52
repossession 21, 23, 27, 29
representation 47–8, 50
Republika Srpska (RS) 15, 24–5
research 7, 10–11, 54
Research Triangle Park 145, 151
resettlement 9, 24
resistance 4, 57, 68–9, 77, 84
resource-sharing 106, 109
returnees 20–6, 29, 31, 96
reversed cities 6, 8, 10
rhetoric 29, 52, 104, 153, 157
riots 5, 9, 39, 41, 46, 48, 154–6, 162
Roma 40, 146, 159
Romania 4–6, 9, 145, 159
Romanians 5–6, 9
Romano, D. 7, 9, 93–110
Rome 121–3
Rubio-Marín, R. 127
rural areas 24–7, 31, 70, 103, 133
Russia 51
Russian language 43, 47
Russians 40
Russification 43

Sabirov, A. 48, 51–2, 55
Sabirov, D. 51–2, 54–5
Sabirova, H. 52
Sacco, E. 97
Saddam Hussein *see* Hussein
Al-Sadr, M. 99
St Germain, Treaty of 121
Sambanis, N. 105
sanctions 1, 4
Sarajevo 16
Sarkozy, N. 143
Sasse, G. 44, 56
scale 65–71, 85, 87
Scharpf, F. 18–19
Scholastic Aptitude Tests 151
schools 8–9, 52, 56, 77, 81, 84, 118–19,
    121, 125–6, 128, 131, 134, 144, 147
  democracy 144, 147, 161
  Italy 118–19, 121, 125–6, 128, 131, 134
  US 150–2
Scott, J.C. 25, 42
secession 8, 43, 48–9, 94
  Iraq 98, 101, 103, 106
  Italy 117
second languages 126, 131, 133
Second World War 9, 80, 122, 145–7, 156
sectarianism 93, 95–7, 99, 101, 105–9
securitization 120, 134, 136
security forces 82
segregation 72–3, 81, 126
  democracy 152, 155, 161
  Italy 129, 131, 133
self-fulfilling prophecy 4
Senegal 145, 159
Senegalese 3
separatism 55, 85, 104, 114, 123, 127,
    129, 134
Serb Republic 104
Serbs 15–16, 23–4, 28, 30
service delivery 17, 20, 54, 70, 78–9, 159
sexuality 65
Sharma, A. 20
Shiites 94, 96–9, 101, 103–4, 106
Silicon Valley 151
Silverman, M. 153
Skutnabb-Kangas, T. 134
slavery 145
Slavs 48
slogans 29–31
Slovakia 5–6
Slovaks 6

snowballing 43
social contract 153
social division matrix 20–7
social integration 148–60
social movements 66–7, 85
Socialist Federal Republic of
    Yugoslavia 16
Society of Uzbeks 51
sociology 2, 5, 68
solidarity 15–18, 21, 144
SOS Racisme 146
South Tyrol 9, 107, 113–15, 121–7
Soviet Union 39–47, 53, 55–6
Soysal, Y. 146, 148
Spain 104, 145, 154
Spanish 145
Spanish language 116
special city status 103–4, 109
Special European Representative 17
sports 17
state-building 18–20, 25, 42–3
statistics 7, 25–7, 43, 126
statists 148–9
Statute of Autonomy 8, 114, 122–9, 133
stay-put policy 95–6
stereotypes 31, 146, 153
Stolac 23
Strochein, S. 1–11
Students Together With Educators and
    Parents (STEP) 151–2
sub-Saharan Africa 145
Südtiroler Volkspartei (SVP) 123, 127,
    129–30, 132
Suleimaniya 102–3
Sunnis 97–9, 101, 103–4, 106
Sunnistan 101, 106
Suzak 54
Switzerland 23
Syria 101, 103

Ta'amim 94, 97–8, 102–3, 106, 108–9
Tajikistan 43, 45
Tajiks 40
Talas 40
tamo-vamo grad 16
Târgu Mureş 5–6
Tarrow, S. 67
Tashkent 44, 55
Tel Aviv-Jaffa 5, 9, 63–87
territorial marking 10
textbooks 51, 56

Todesmarsch 123, 133
Tolomei, E. 121, 127
top-down processes 20
topography 72, 125
toponymies 121
Torres, G. 116
Toulouse 4, 9, 145, 154–6, 160–1
Tourcoing 143
tourism 76, 133, 145, 159
town meetings 150, 152
trade 45–6, 133
trade unions 66, 82, 156, 159
Transitional Administrative Law 98, 104
Trentino Alto-Adige 122
Trento 122–3
Tulip revolution 48, 55
Tunisia 145, 159
Turin 158
Turkey 93, 101, 103–7
Turkish language 107
Turkmen 7, 93–5, 97–9, 101–9
Turkmen Front 98
Turkomen *see* Turkmen
Turks 94
Turner, B. 30, 146
Turon 49
Tuscany 158

Ukraine 5–6
Ukrainians 6
Umbria 158
UNDP 16
UNHCR 16, 21–2
Unitalia 130
United Nations 114, 123
United Nations Charter 123
United States 97, 108, 143–63
United States Council on Foreign Relations 102
United States Military 95, 97
urban areas 24–6, 29, 31–2, 65–71
urban planning 70–1, 76–7, 81
USSR 39, 44
utility companies 17
Uzbek language 43, 46–7, 51, 56
Uzbek National-Cultural Centre (UNCC) 49, 51–3
Uzbekistan 40, 44–6, 48, 51–3, 55
Uzbeks 3, 7, 9, 39–40, 42–6, 48–56
Uzgen 39, 46

Varshney, A. 4, 41
Vatican 157
Verdi-Grüne-Verc 129–30
Vertovec, S. 148
veto rights 124
Vetters, L. 3, 5, 7–8, 15–35
Vice Mayor for Arab Affairs 81
victimization 146
Vienna 122
Villepin, D. de 143
violence 3–4, 16, 39–43, 46
    democracy 143–4, 153–4, 156, 160, 162
    Iraq 97, 99, 101, 103, 105, 109
    Israel 84
    Italy 114
    Kyrgyzstan 55–6

Wadi Nisnas 82–4
Wales 116
Walzer, M. 147
Warsaw Pact Organization 43
Washington Agreement 17
waste disposal 17, 79
water 17, 46, 96
Weber, M. 3
websites 129
Weller, M. 43
Welsh language 116
West Bank 71
Western Balkans 19
whites 8, 116, 149, 151–2
Wolff, S. 43
women 54, 66, 80
workshops 52
World War I *see* First World War
World War II *see* Second World War

xenophobia 144, 146–7, 156–8

Yaffa 73
Yiftachel, O. 86
Young, C. 117
Young, I.M. 147
youth organizations 78, 80
Ysyk-kol 40
Yugoslav People's Army (JNA) 16, 28
Yugoslavia 16, 25, 29

Zagros mountains 94
zero-sum games 99, 101, 107, 117, 119–20, 128, 132, 134
Zionists 72, 77